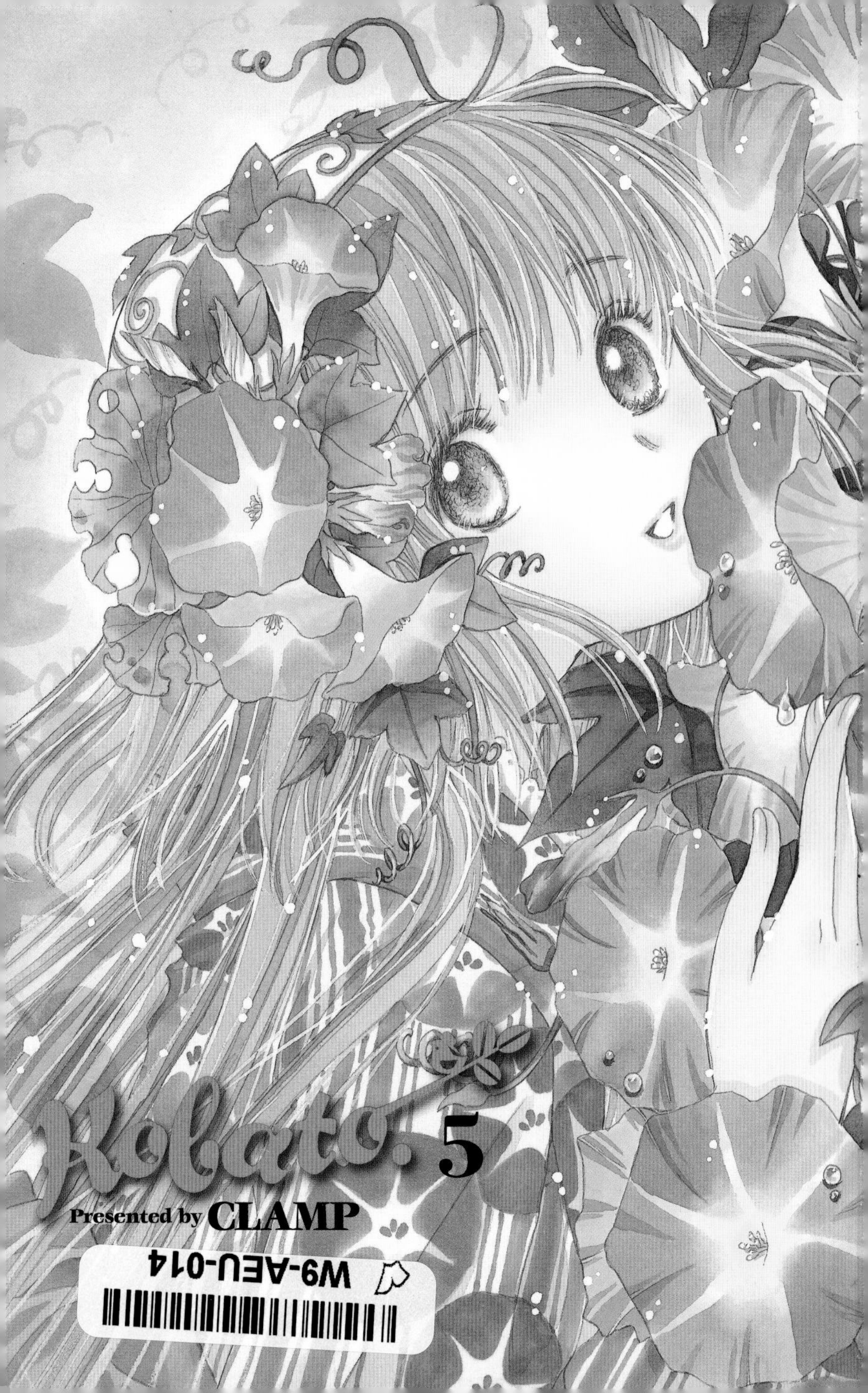
Kobato. 5
Presented by CLAMP

KOBATO.

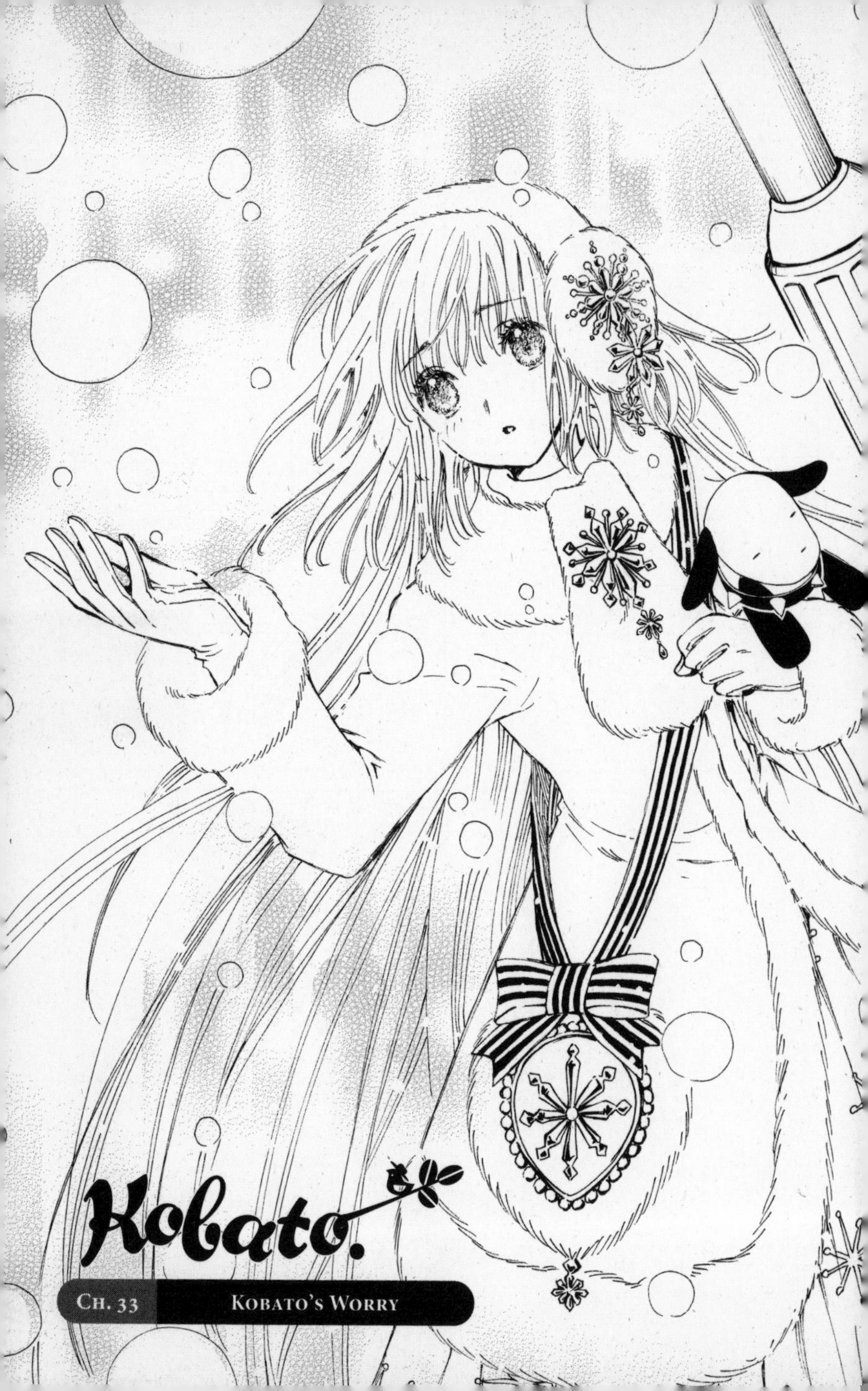
Kobato.
Ch. 33
Kobato's Worry

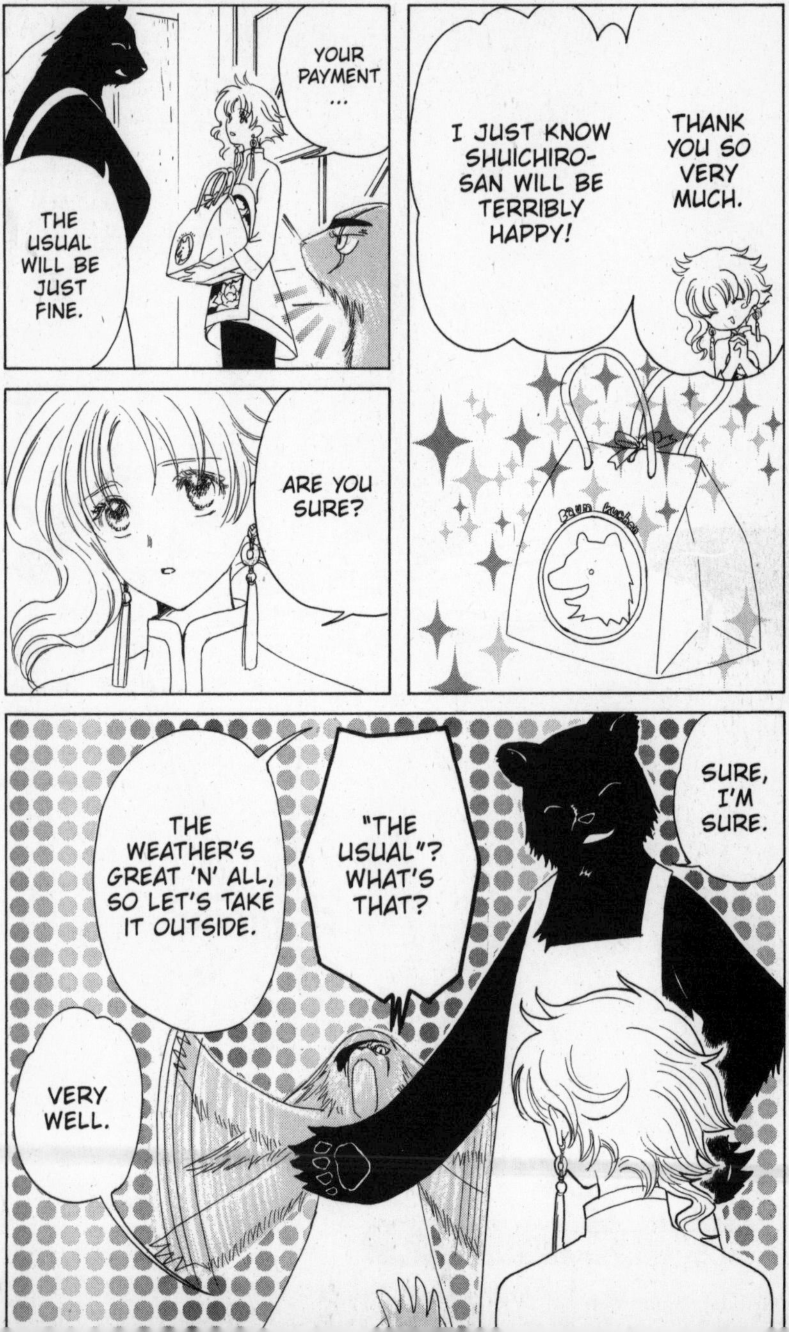
THANK YOU SO VERY MUCH.
I JUST KNOW SHUICHIRO-SAN WILL BE TERRIBLY HAPPY!
YOUR PAYMENT ...
THE USUAL WILL BE JUST FINE.
ARE YOU SURE?
SURE, I'M SURE.
"THE USUAL"? WHAT'S THAT?
THE WEATHER'S GREAT 'N' ALL, SO LET'S TAKE IT OUTSIDE.
VERY WELL.

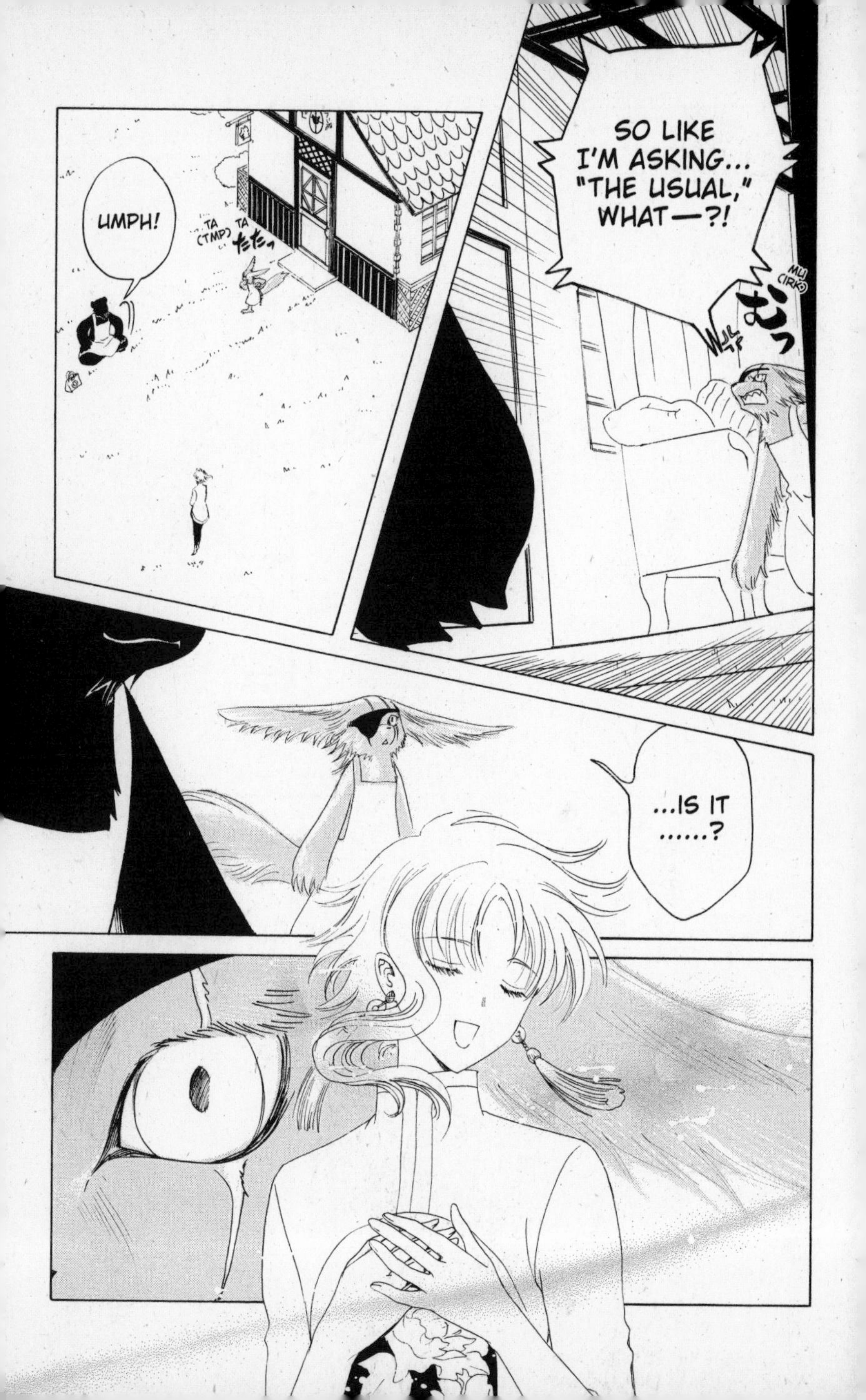
SO LIKE I'M ASKING... "THE USUAL," WHAT—?!
MU (IRK)
UMPH!
TA TA (TMP)
...IS IT ......?

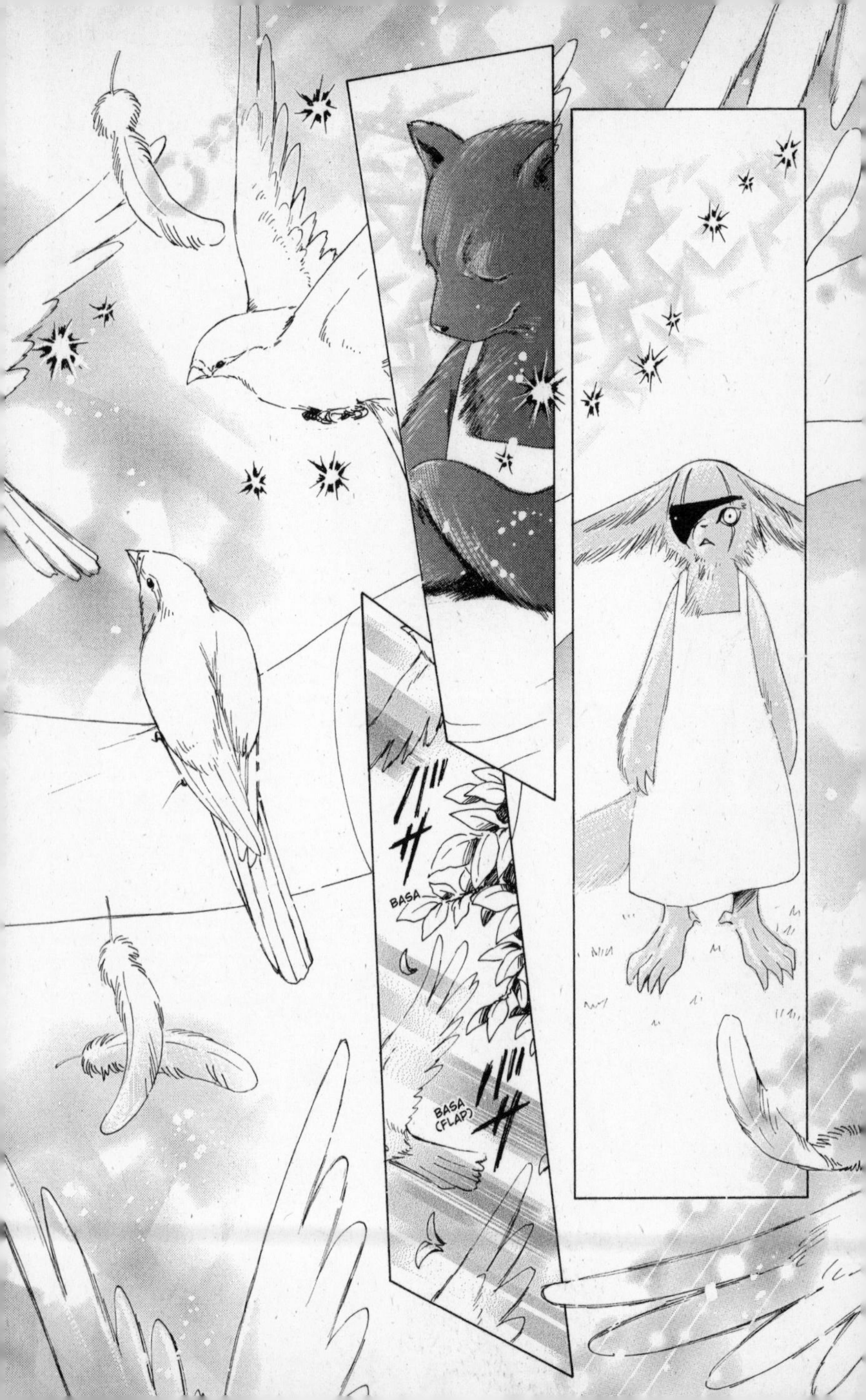
BASA
BASA (FLAP)

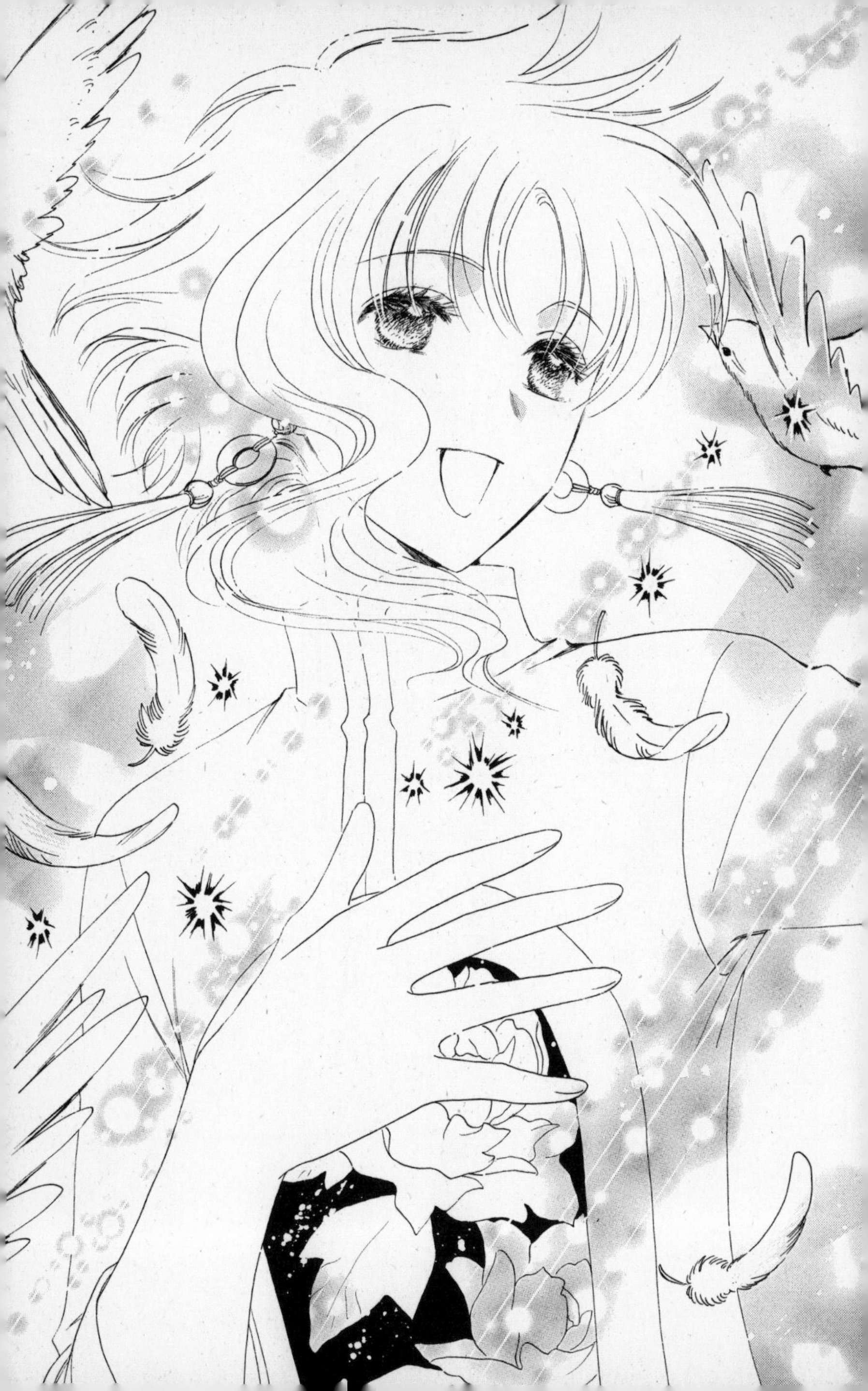

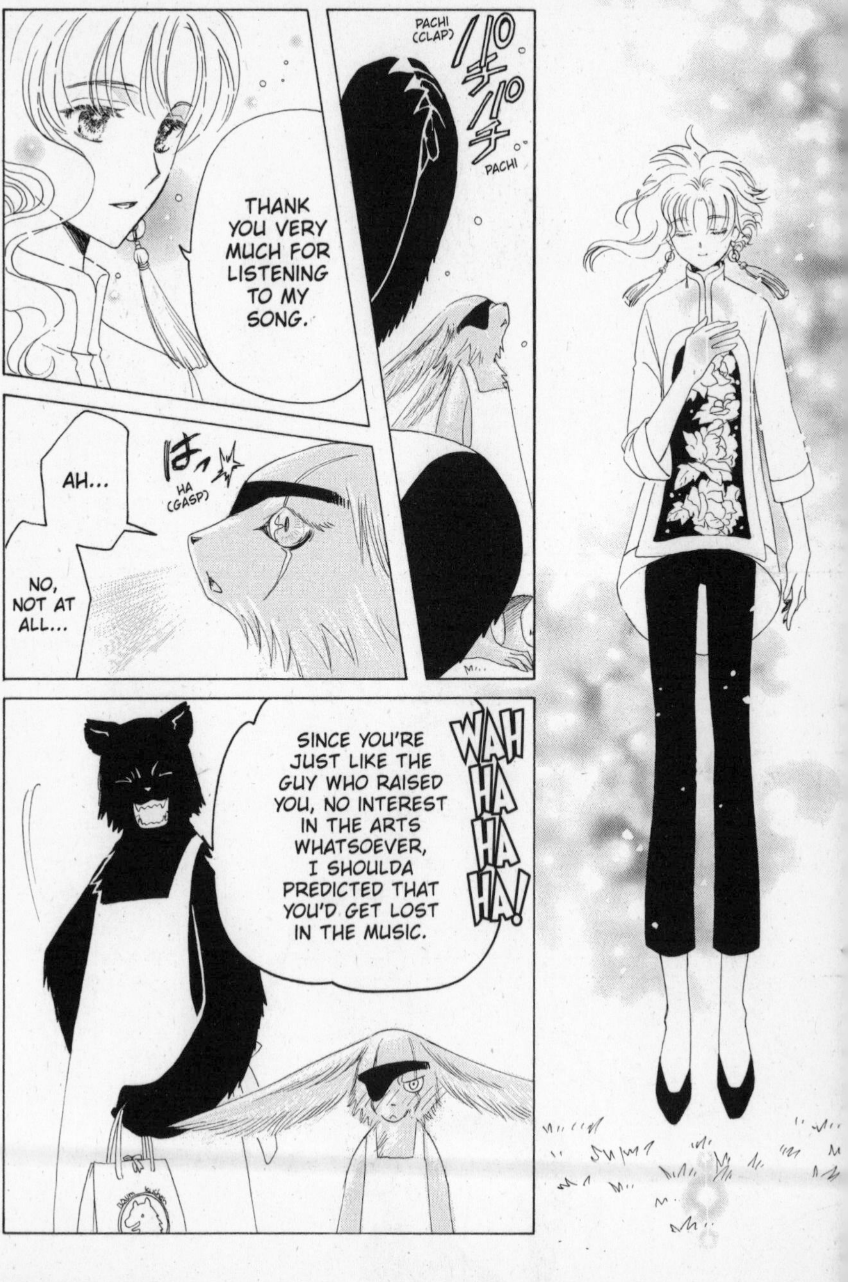

パチパチ
PACHI (CLAP)
PACHI
THANK YOU VERY MUCH FOR LISTENING TO MY SONG.
はっ
HA (GASP)
AH...
NO, NOT AT ALL...
M...
WAH HA HA HA HA!
SINCE YOU'RE JUST LIKE THE GUY WHO RAISED YOU, NO INTEREST IN THE ARTS WHATSOEVER, I SHOULDA PREDICTED THAT YOU'D GET LOST IN THE MUSIC.

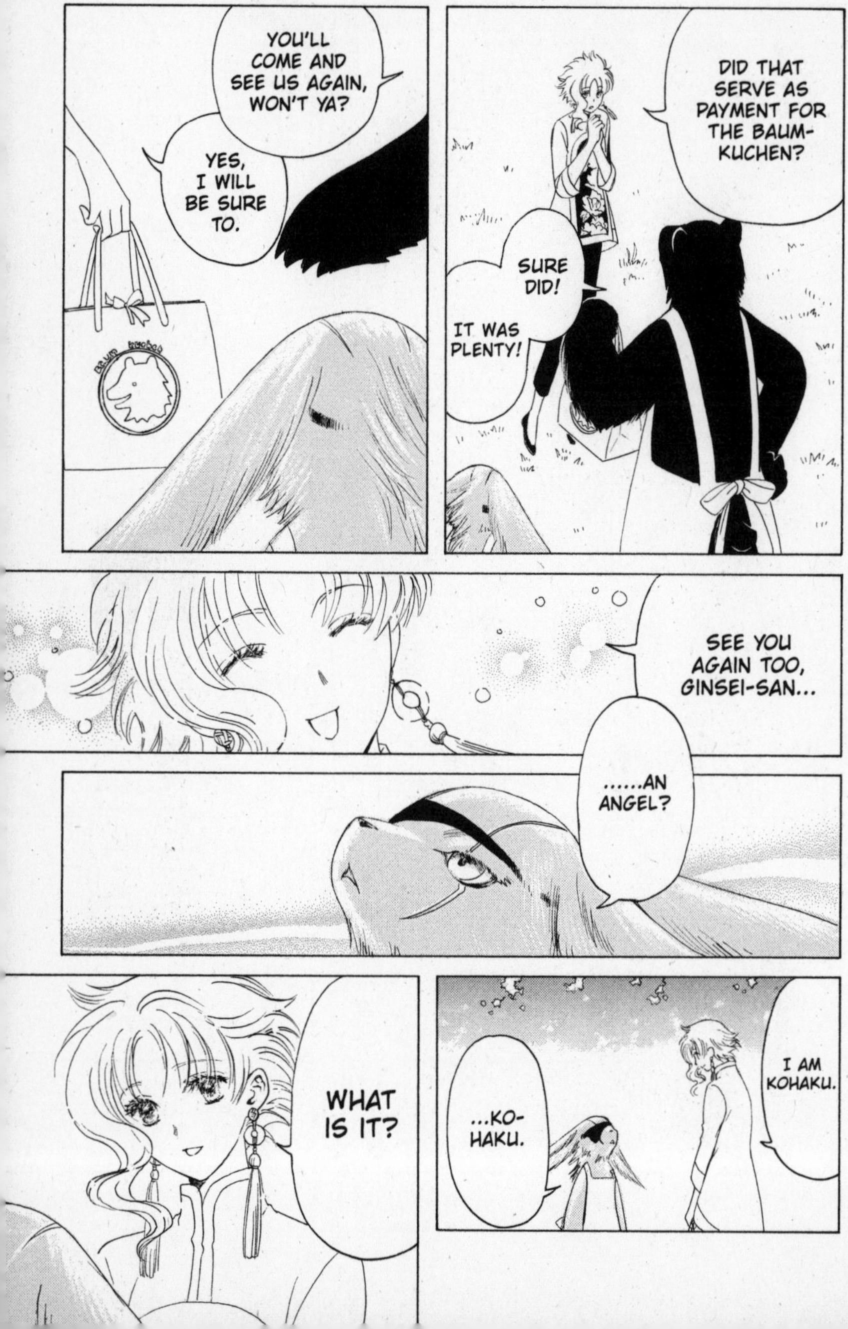
DID THAT SERVE AS PAYMENT FOR THE BAUMKUCHEN?
SURE DID!
IT WAS PLENTY!
YOU'LL COME AND SEE US AGAIN, WON'T YA?
YES, I WILL BE SURE TO.
SEE YOU AGAIN TOO, GINSEI-SAN...
......AN ANGEL?
I AM KOHAKU.
...KOHAKU.
WHAT IS IT?

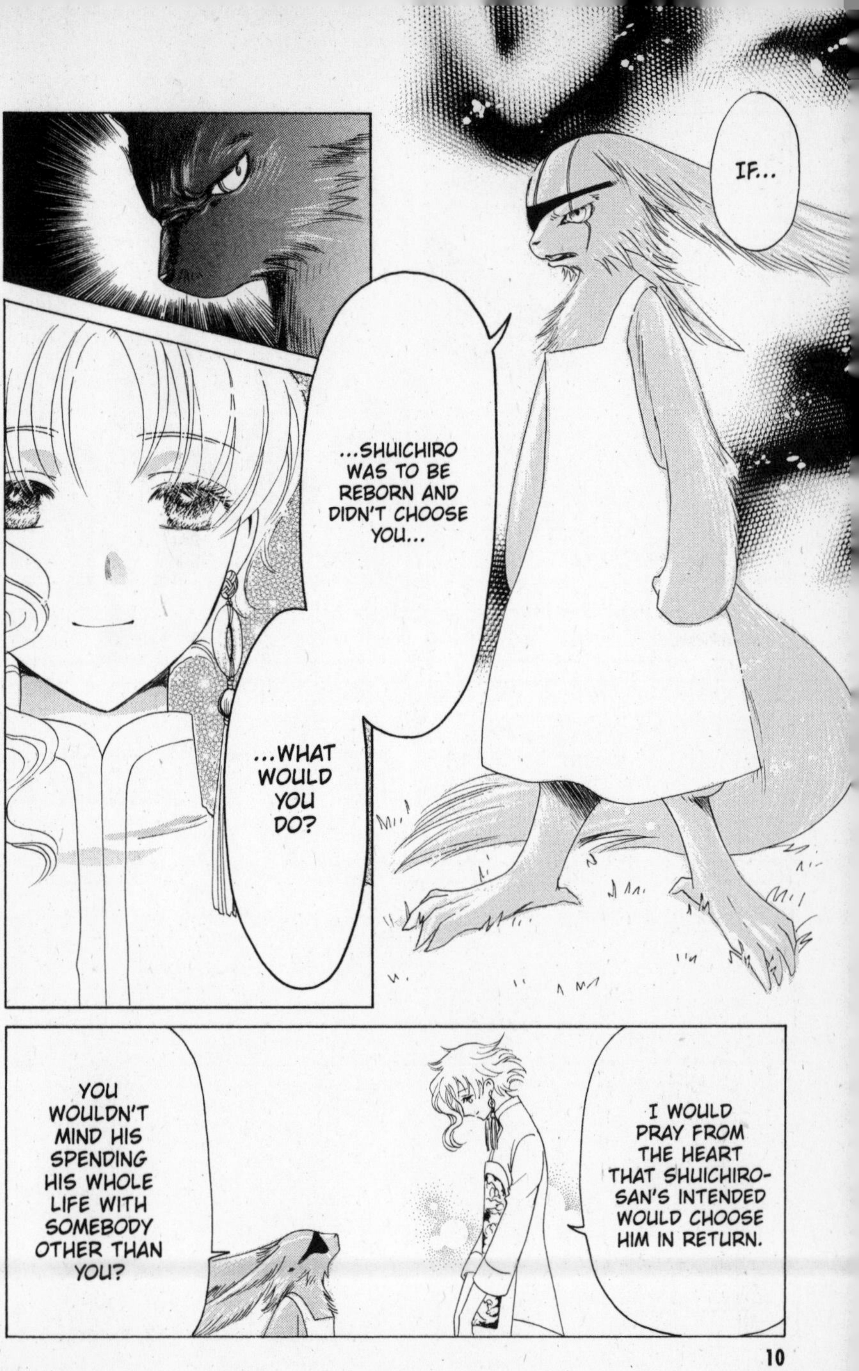
IF...
...SHUICHIRO WAS TO BE REBORN AND DIDN'T CHOOSE YOU...
...WHAT WOULD YOU DO?
I WOULD PRAY FROM THE HEART THAT SHUICHIRO-SAN'S INTENDED WOULD CHOOSE HIM IN RETURN.
YOU WOULDN'T MIND HIS SPENDING HIS WHOLE LIFE WITH SOMEBODY OTHER THAN YOU?

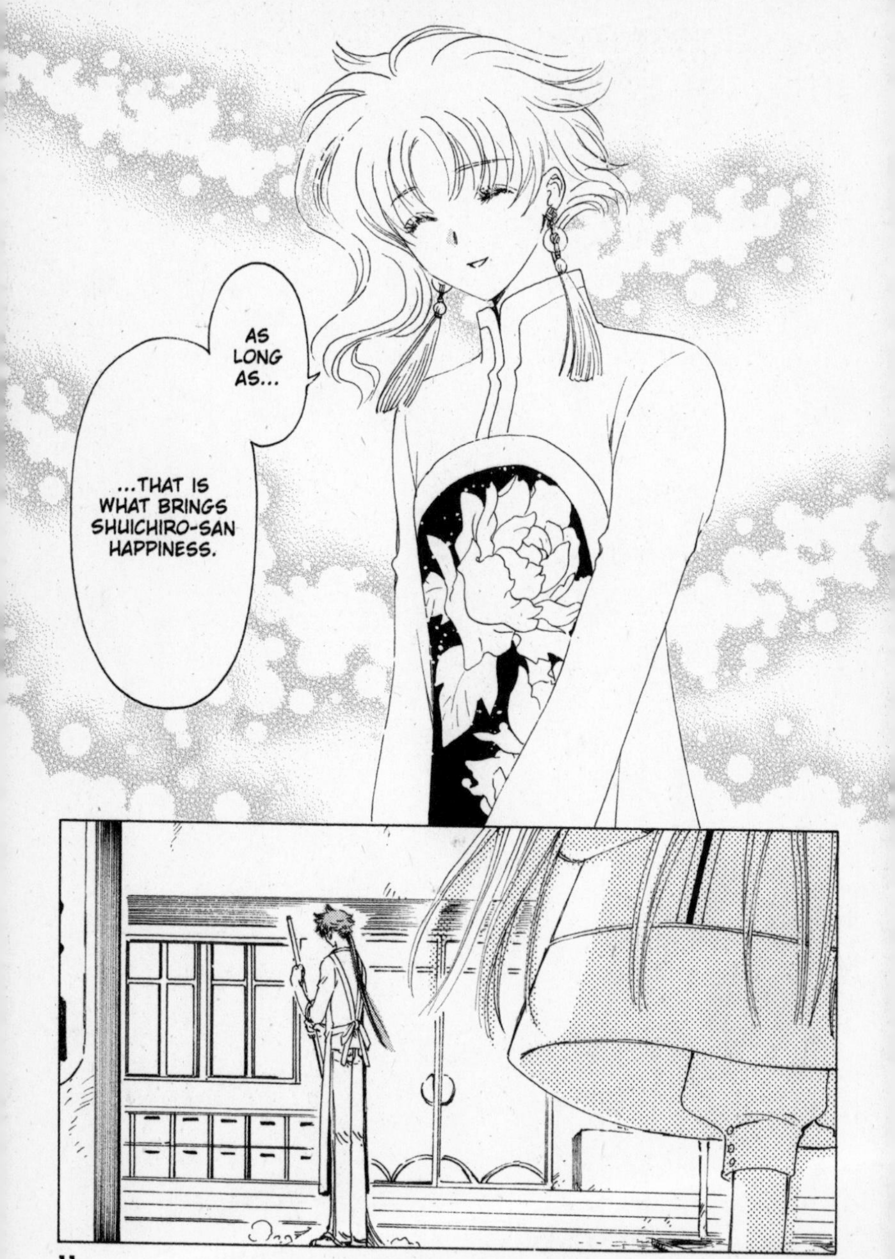
AS LONG AS...
...THAT IS WHAT BRINGS SHUICHIRO-SAN HAPPINESS.

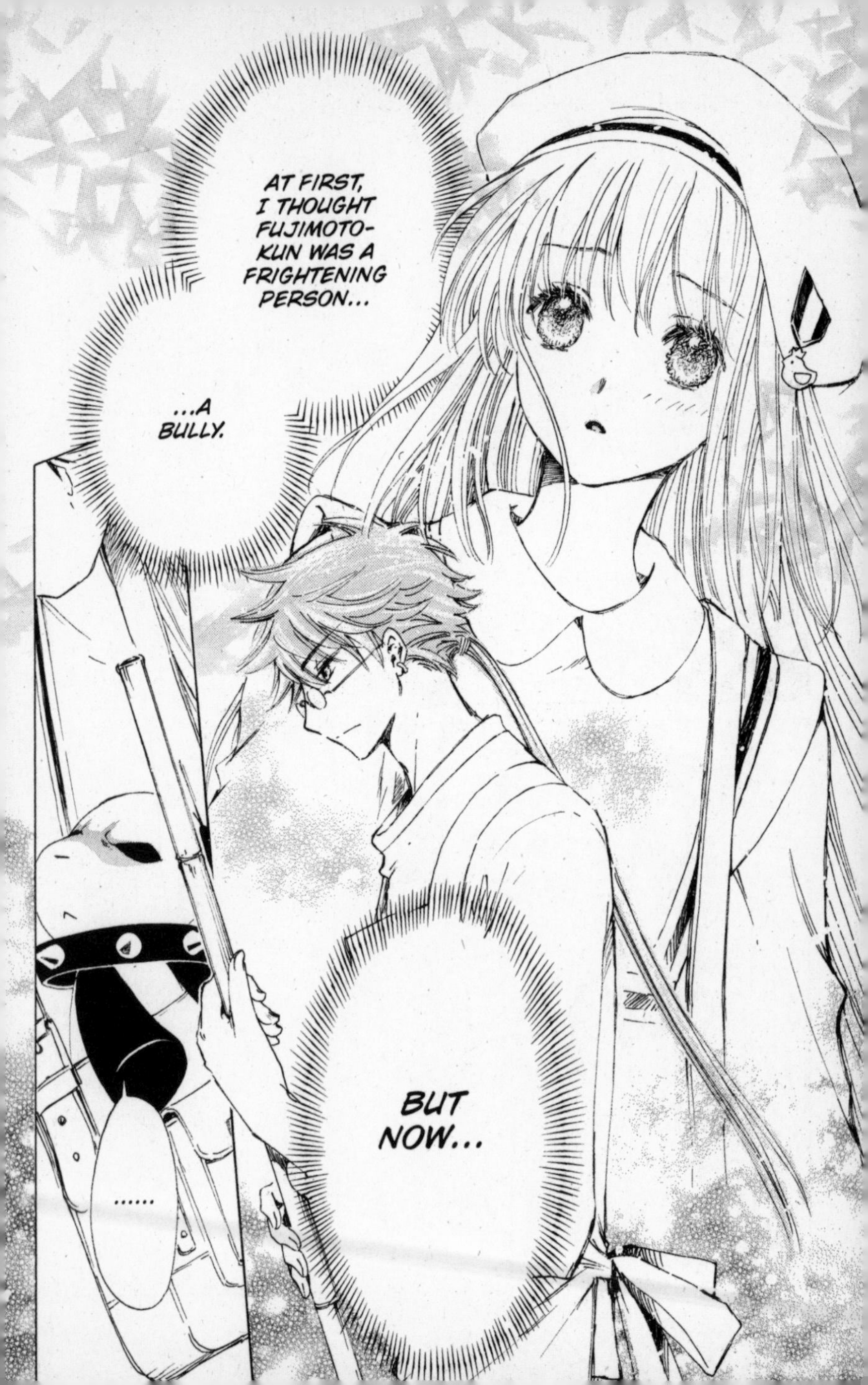
AT FIRST, I THOUGHT FUJIMOTO-KUN WAS A FRIGHTENING PERSON...
...A BULLY.
BUT NOW...
......

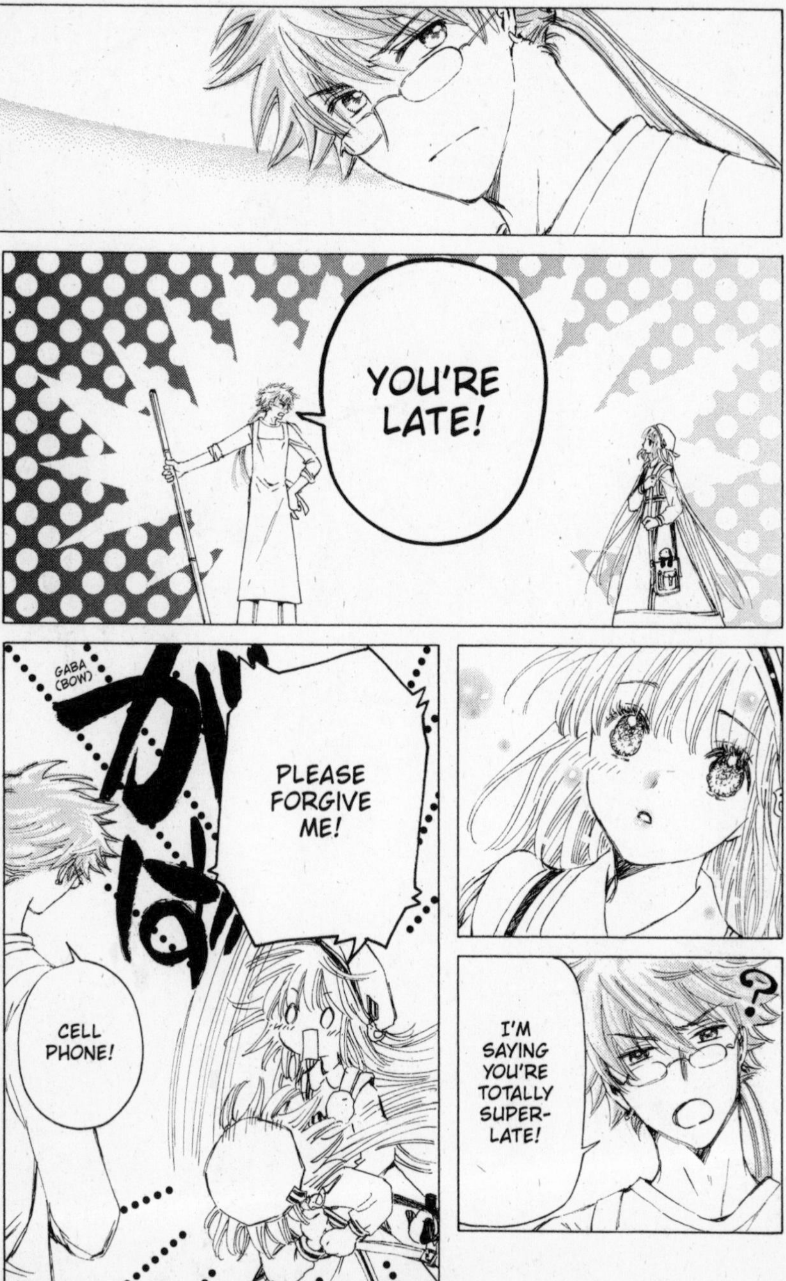
YOU'RE LATE!
?
I'M SAYING YOU'RE TOTALLY SUPER-LATE!
PLEASE FORGIVE ME!
GABA (BOW)
CELL PHONE!

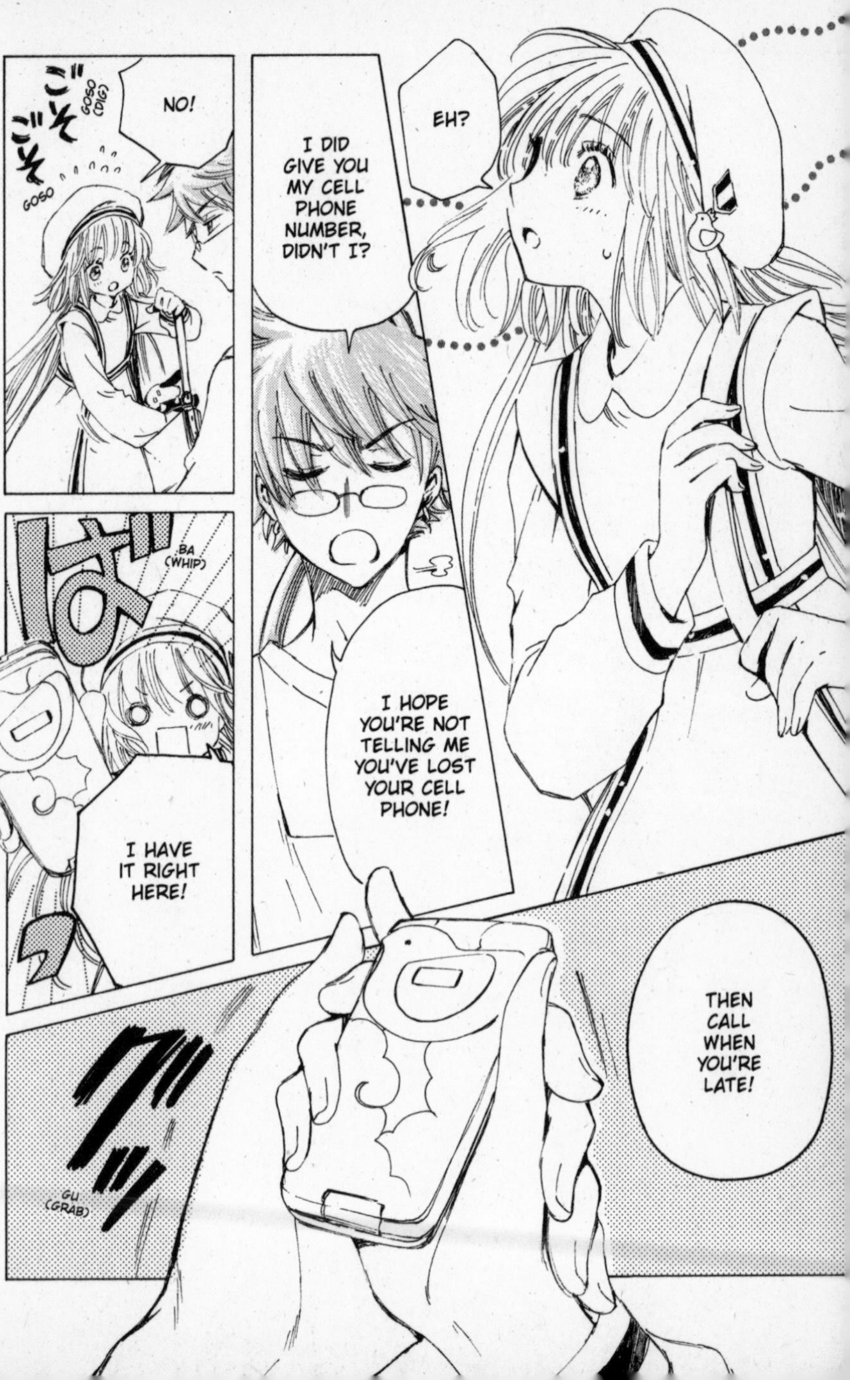
EH?
I DID GIVE YOU MY CELL PHONE NUMBER, DIDN'T I?
I HOPE YOU'RE NOT TELLING ME YOU'VE LOST YOUR CELL PHONE!
NO!
GOSO (DIG)
GOSO
BA (WHIP)
I HAVE IT RIGHT HERE!
THEN CALL WHEN YOU'RE LATE!
GU (GRAB)

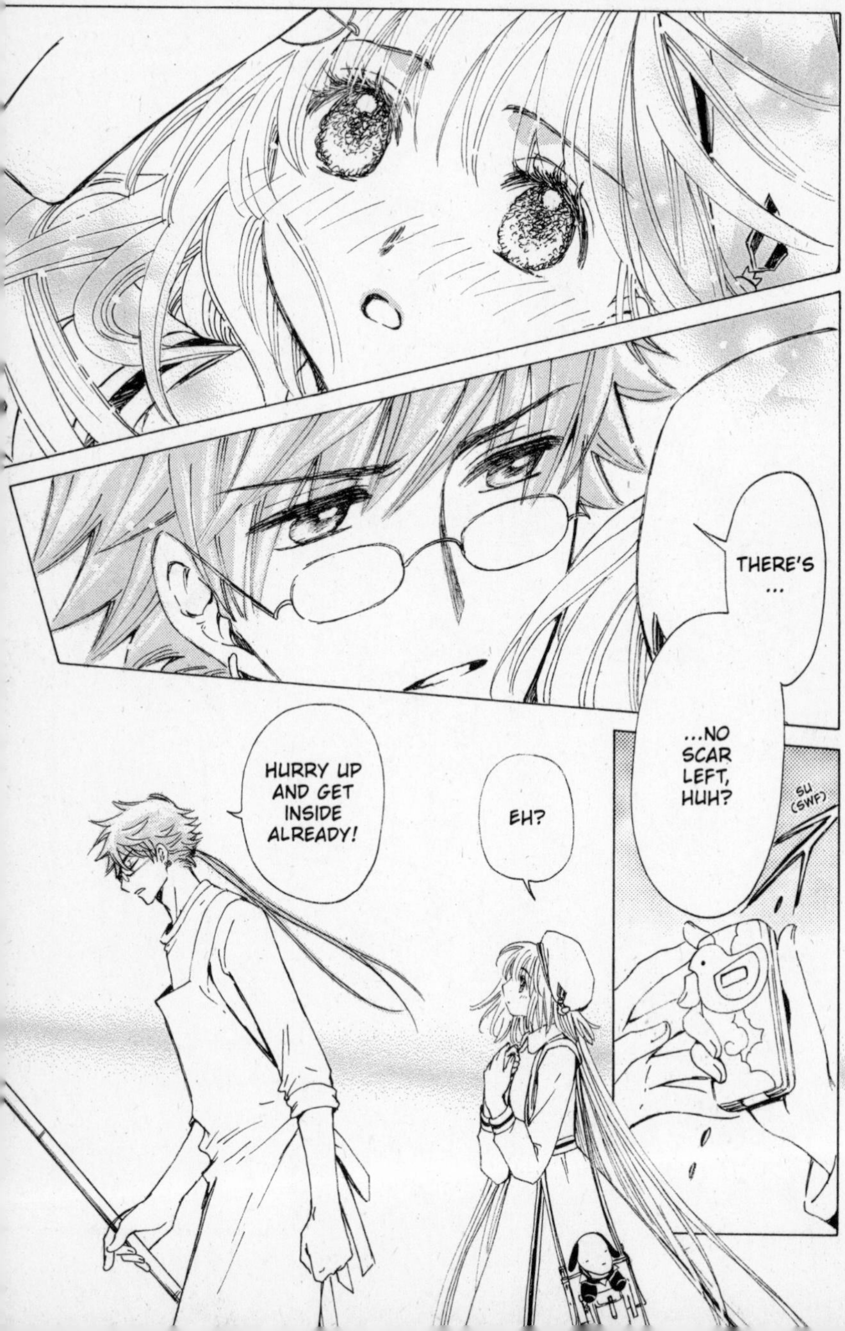
THERE'S ...
...NO SCAR LEFT, HUH?
SU (SWF)
EH?
HURRY UP AND GET INSIDE ALREADY!

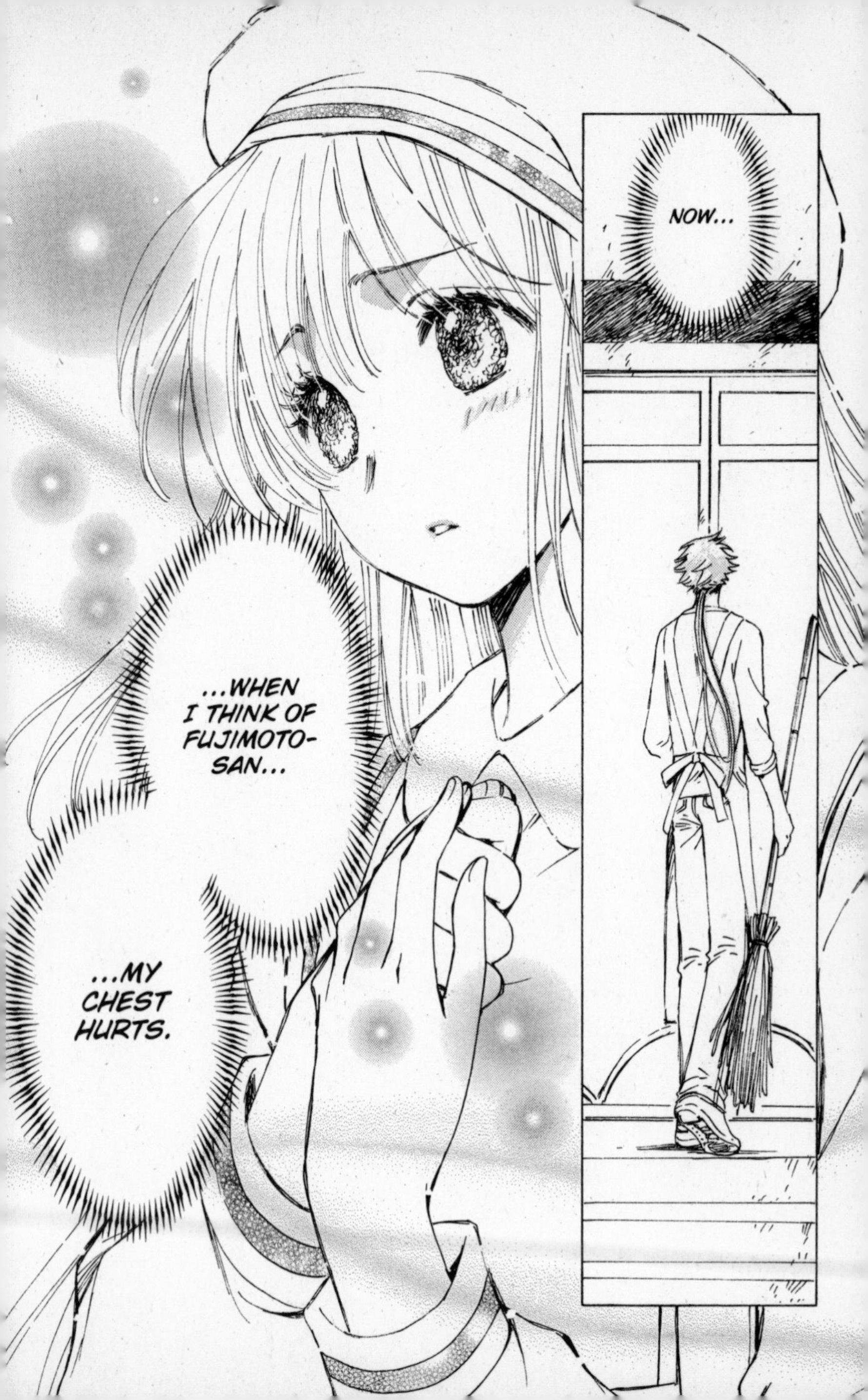
NOW...
...WHEN I THINK OF FUJIMOTO-SAN...
...MY CHEST HURTS.

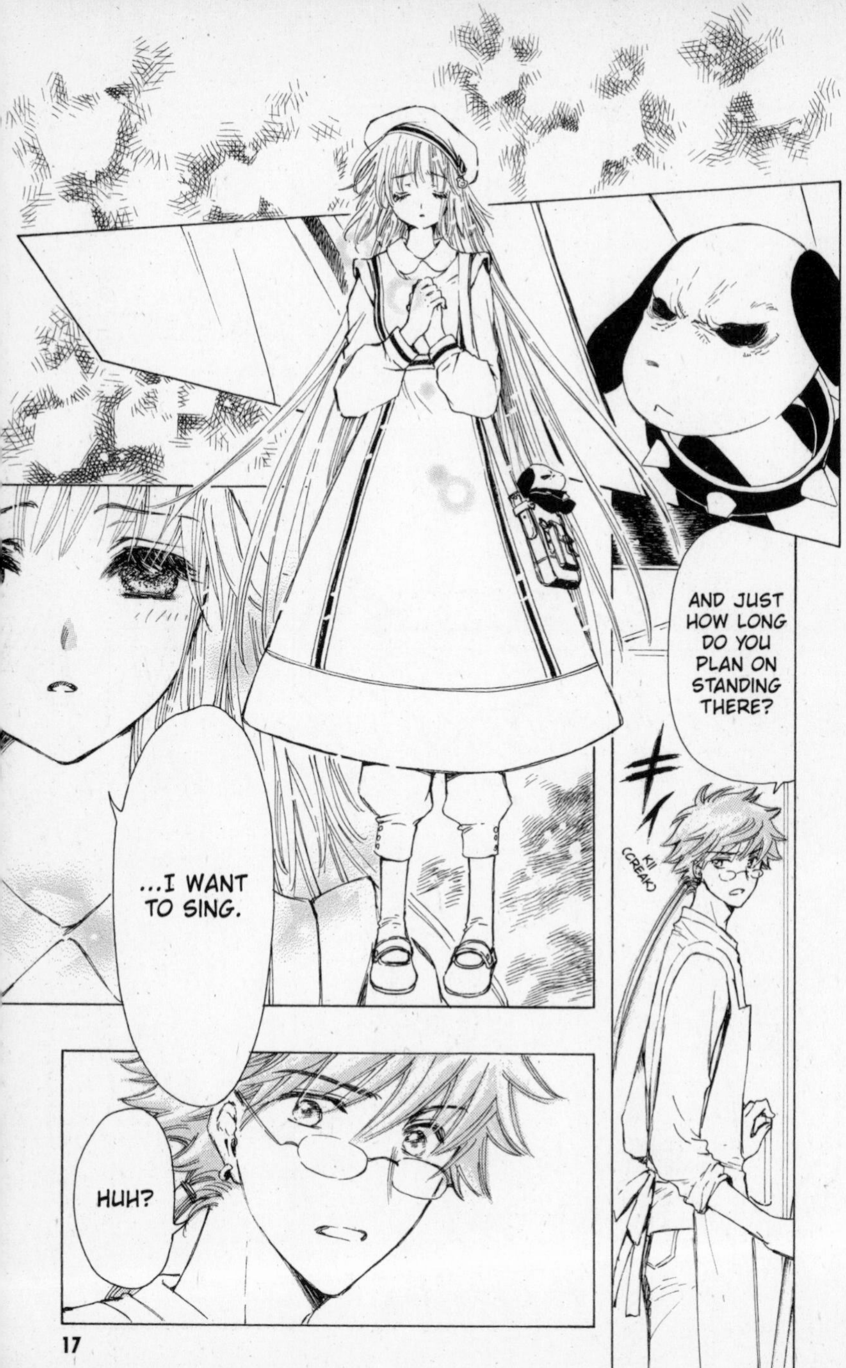
AND JUST HOW LONG DO YOU PLAN ON STANDING THERE?
KII
CREAK
...I WANT TO SING.
HUH?

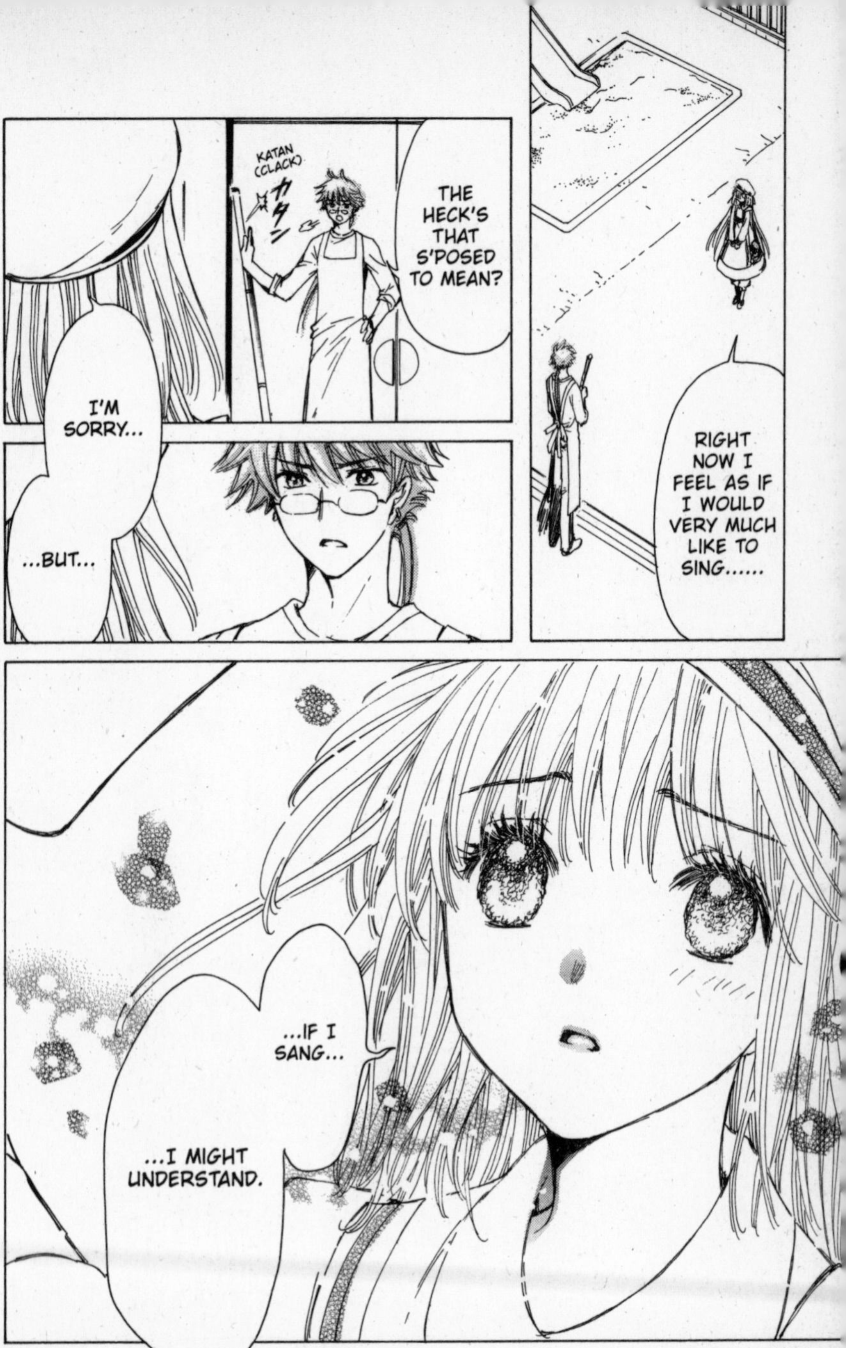
RIGHT NOW I FEEL AS IF I WOULD VERY MUCH LIKE TO SING......
THE HECK'S THAT S'POSED TO MEAN?
KATAN (CLACK)
カタン
I'M SORRY...
...BUT...
...IF I SANG...
...I MIGHT UNDERSTAND.

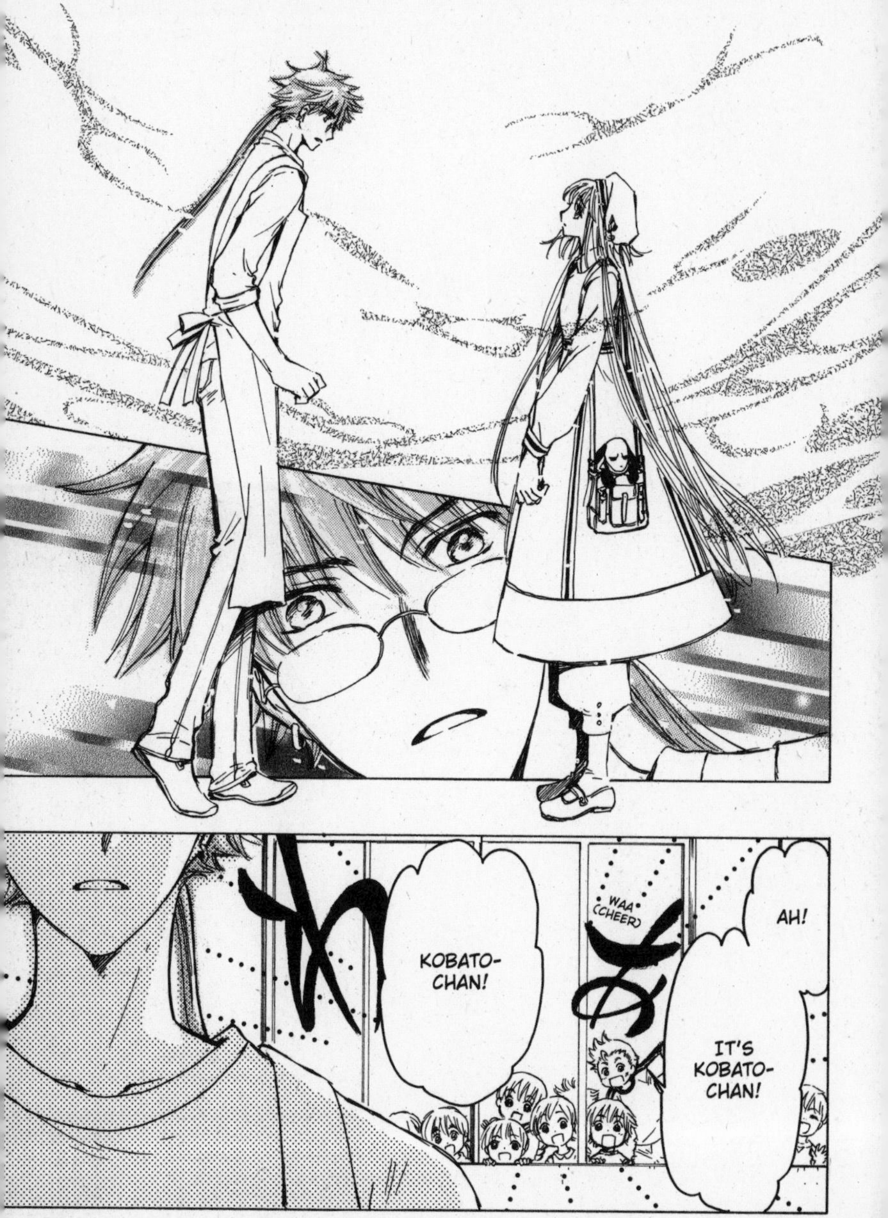
AH!
IT'S KOBATO-CHAN!
WAA (CHEER)
KOBATO-CHAN!

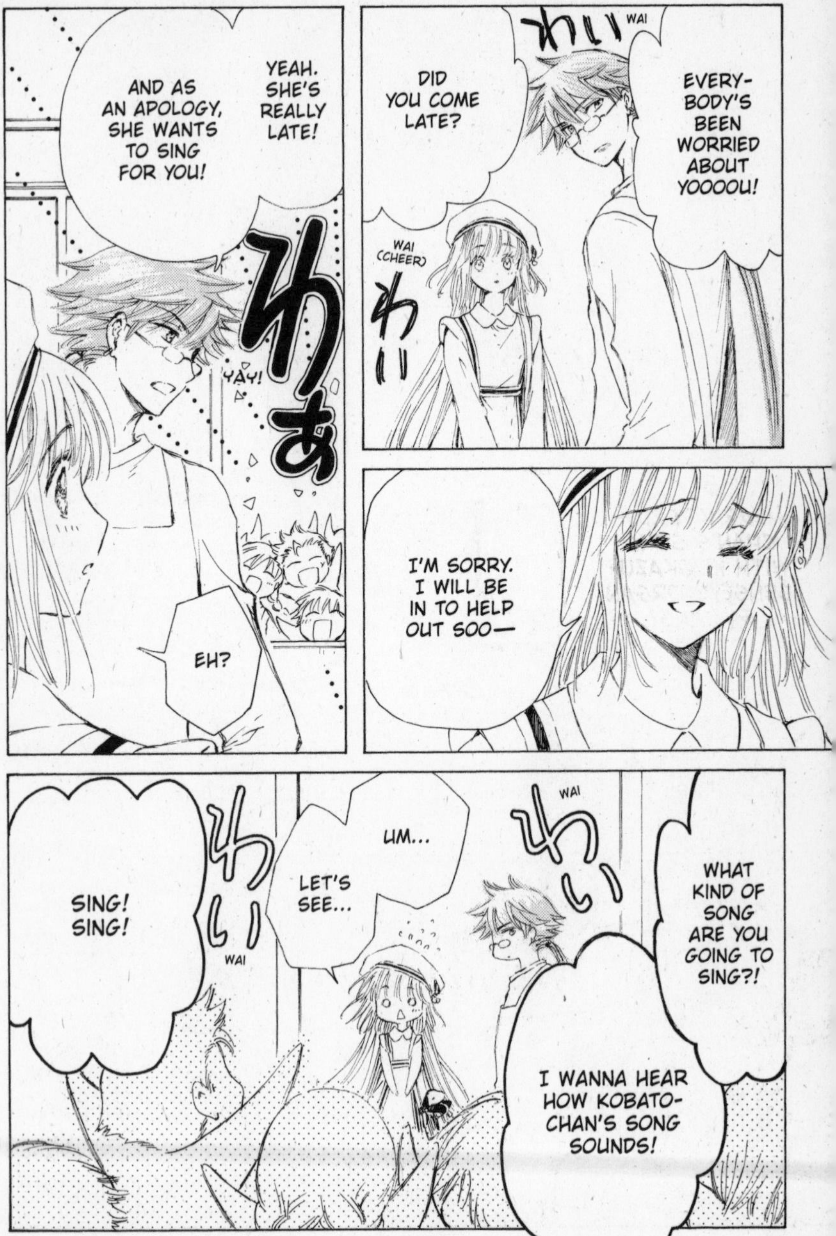
わい
WAI
EVERY-BODY'S BEEN WORRIED ABOUT YOOOOU!
DID YOU COME LATE?
WAI (CHEER)
わい
I'M SORRY. I WILL BE IN TO HELP OUT SOO—
YEAH. SHE'S REALLY LATE!
AND AS AN APOLOGY, SHE WANTS TO SING FOR YOU!
わあ
YAY!
EH?
わい
WAI
WHAT KIND OF SONG ARE YOU GOING TO SING?!
I WANNA HEAR HOW KOBATO-CHAN'S SONG SOUNDS!
UM...
LET'S SEE...
わい
WAI
SING! SING!

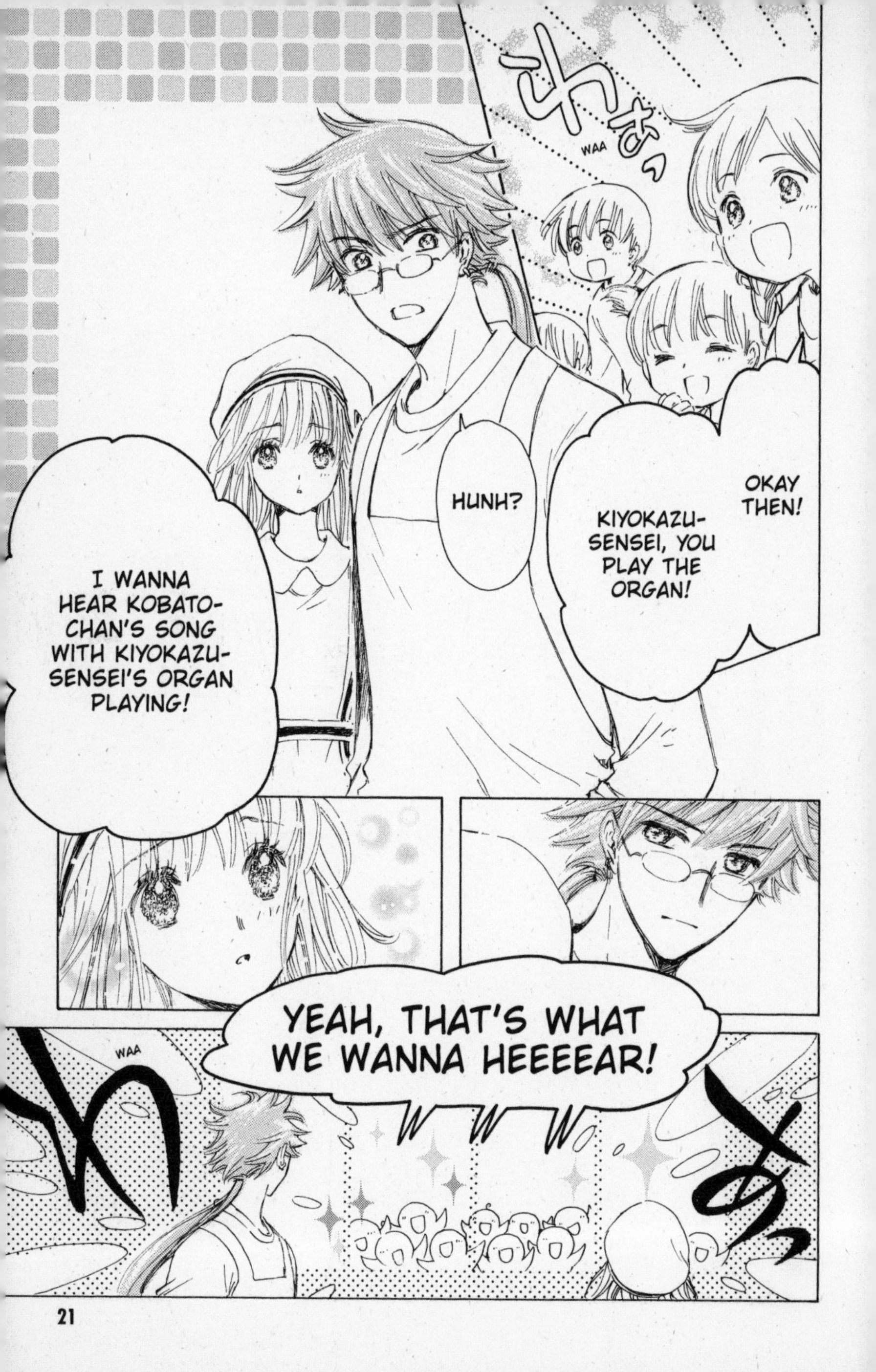
WAA
OKAY THEN!
KIYOKAZU-SENSEI, YOU PLAY THE ORGAN!
HUNH?
I WANNA HEAR KOBATO-CHAN'S SONG WITH KIYOKAZU-SENSEI'S ORGAN PLAYING!
YEAH, THAT'S WHAT WE WANNA HEEEEAR!
WAA

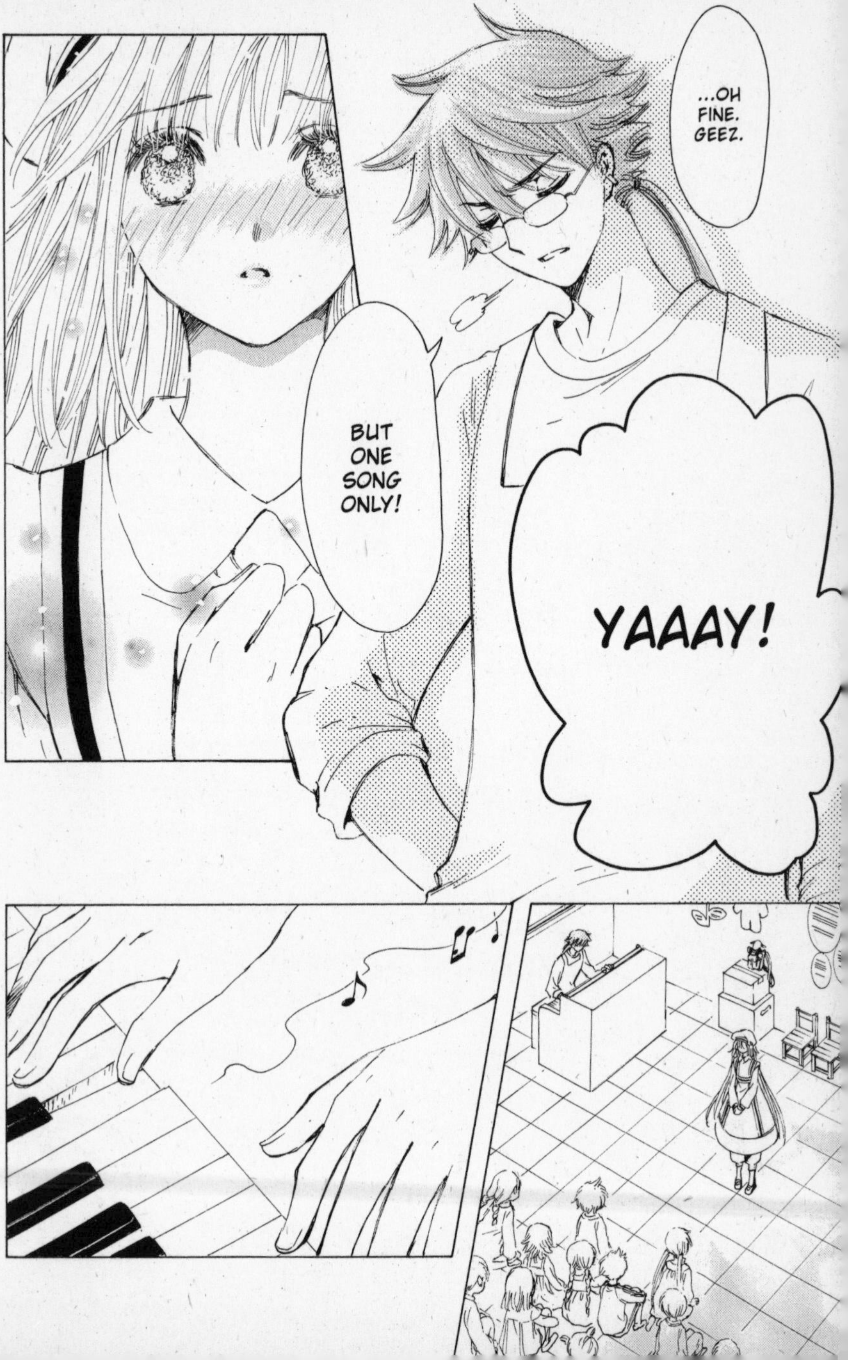
...OH FINE. GEEZ.
BUT ONE SONG ONLY!
YAAAY!

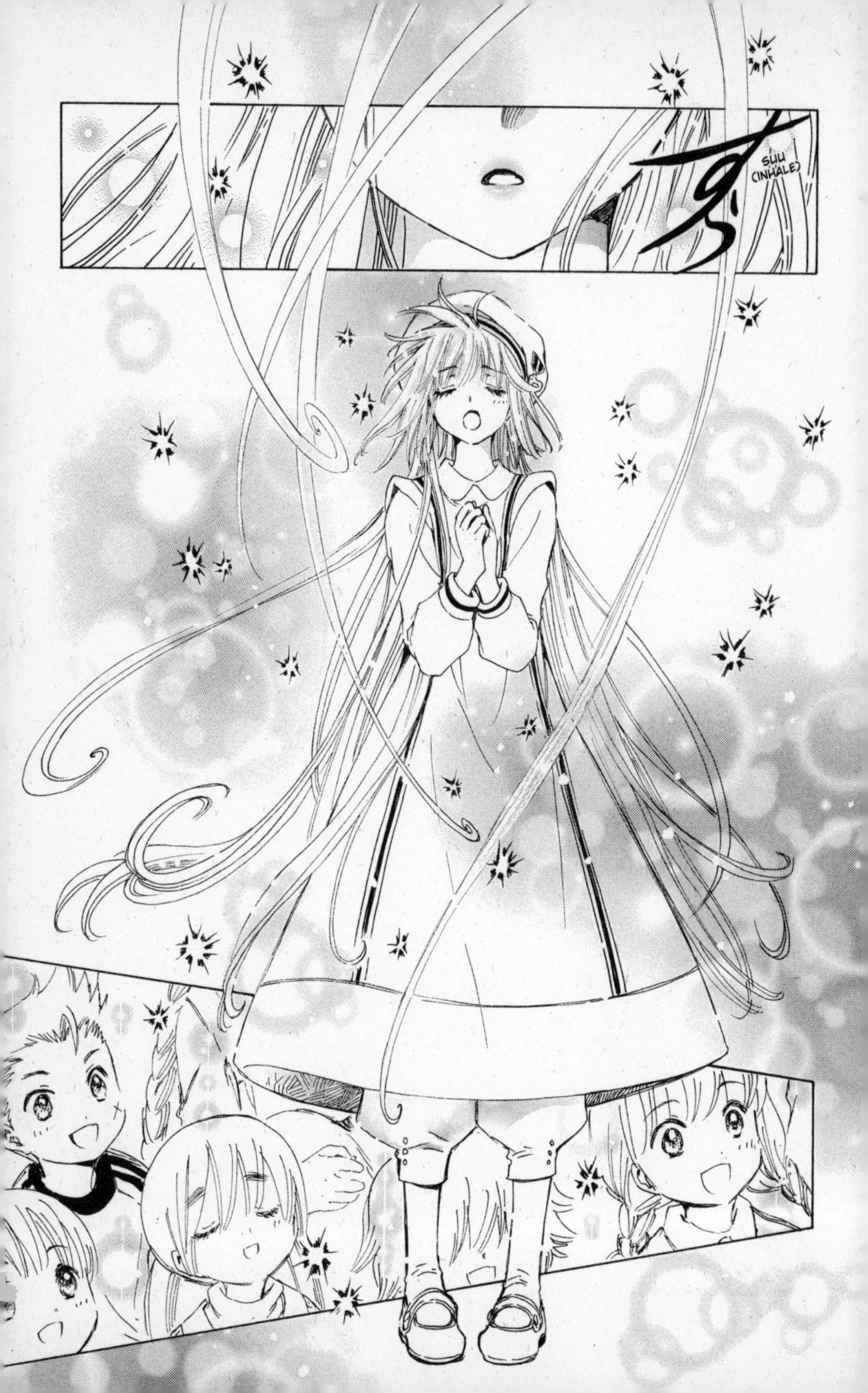
すぅ
SUU (INHALE)

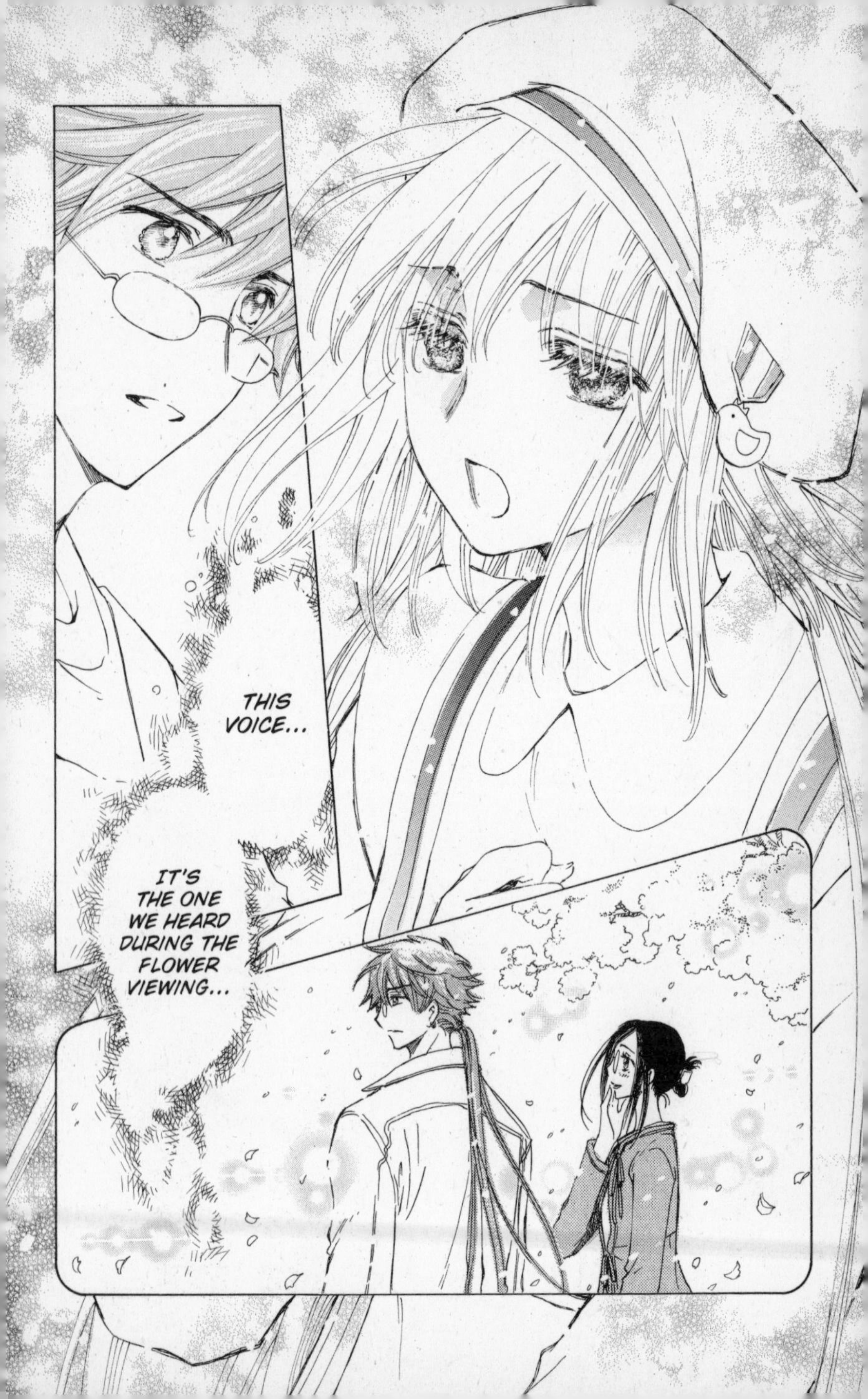
THIS VOICE...
IT'S THE ONE WE HEARD DURING THE FLOWER VIEWING...

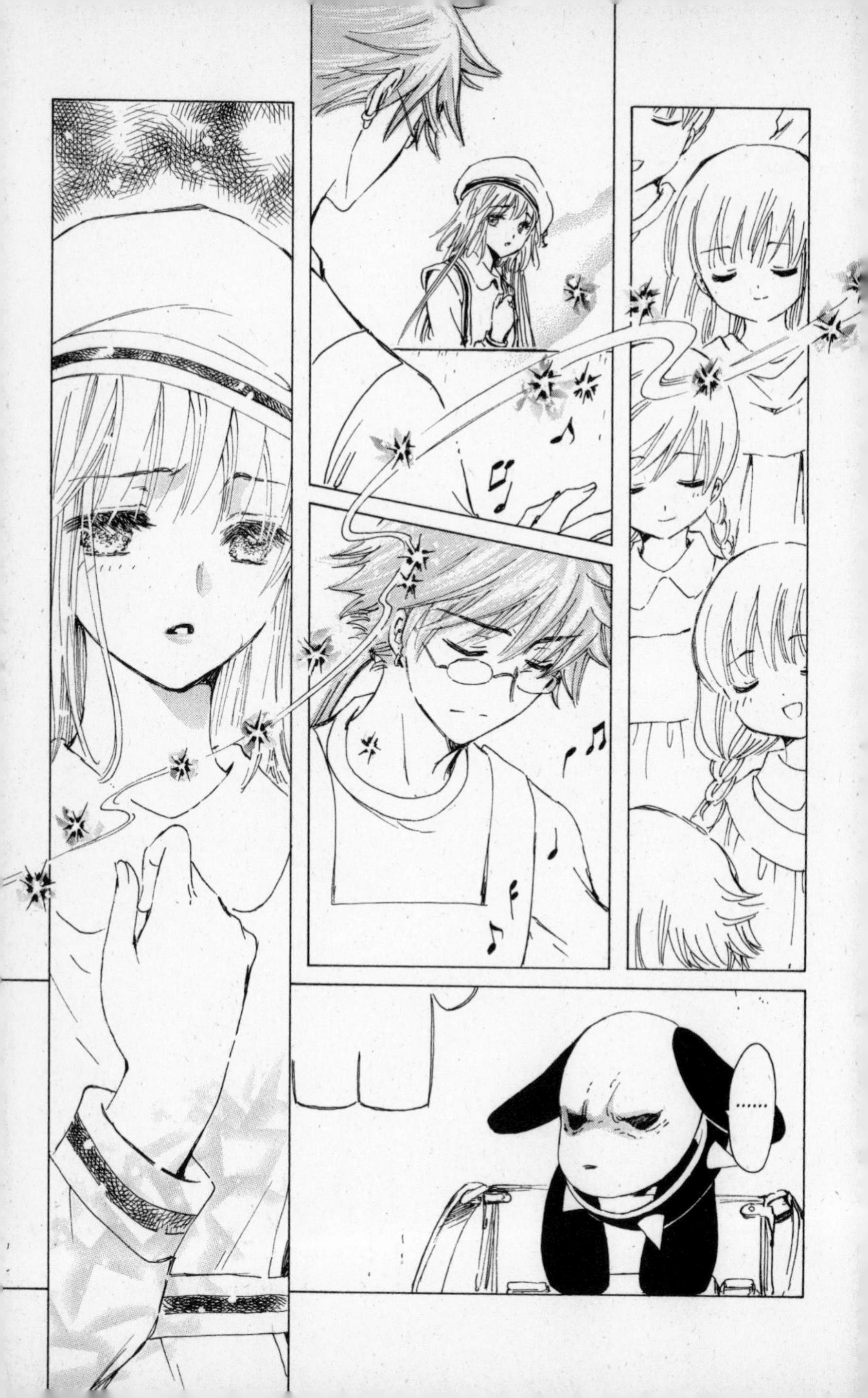
……

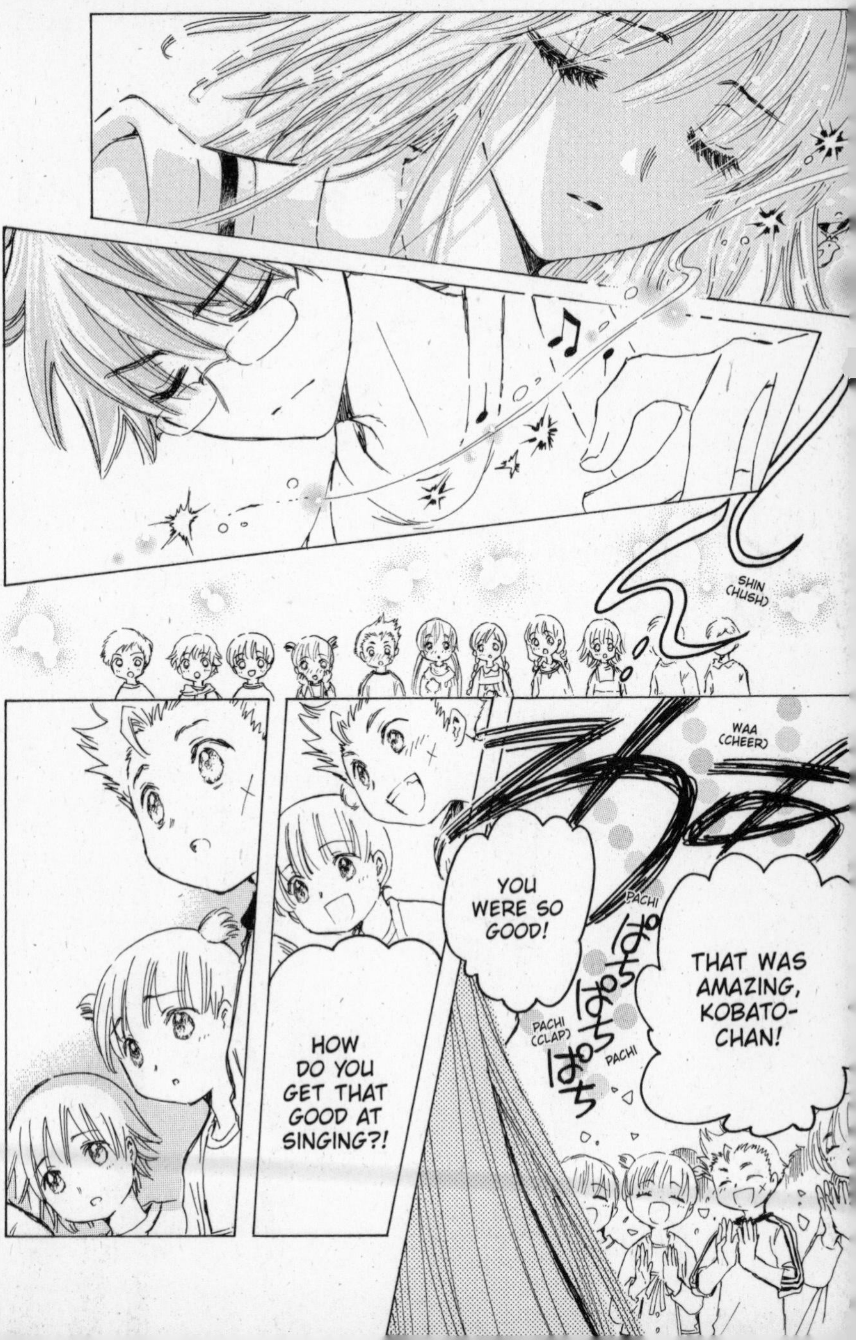
SHIN (HUSH)
WAA (CHEER)
THAT WAS AMAZING, KOBATO-CHAN!
PACHI
YOU WERE SO GOOD!
PACHI (CLAP)
PACHI
HOW DO YOU GET THAT GOOD AT SINGING?!

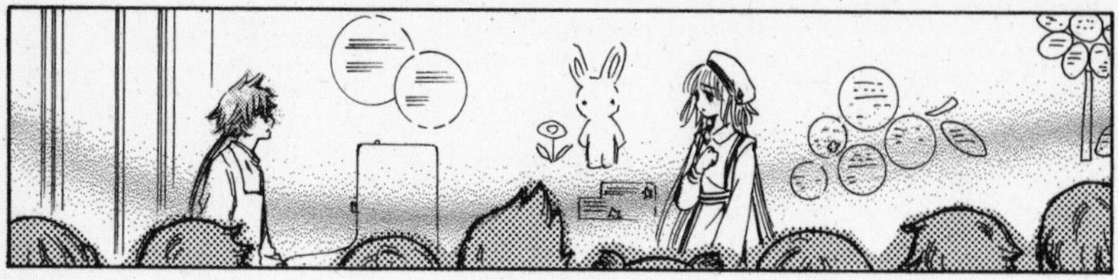

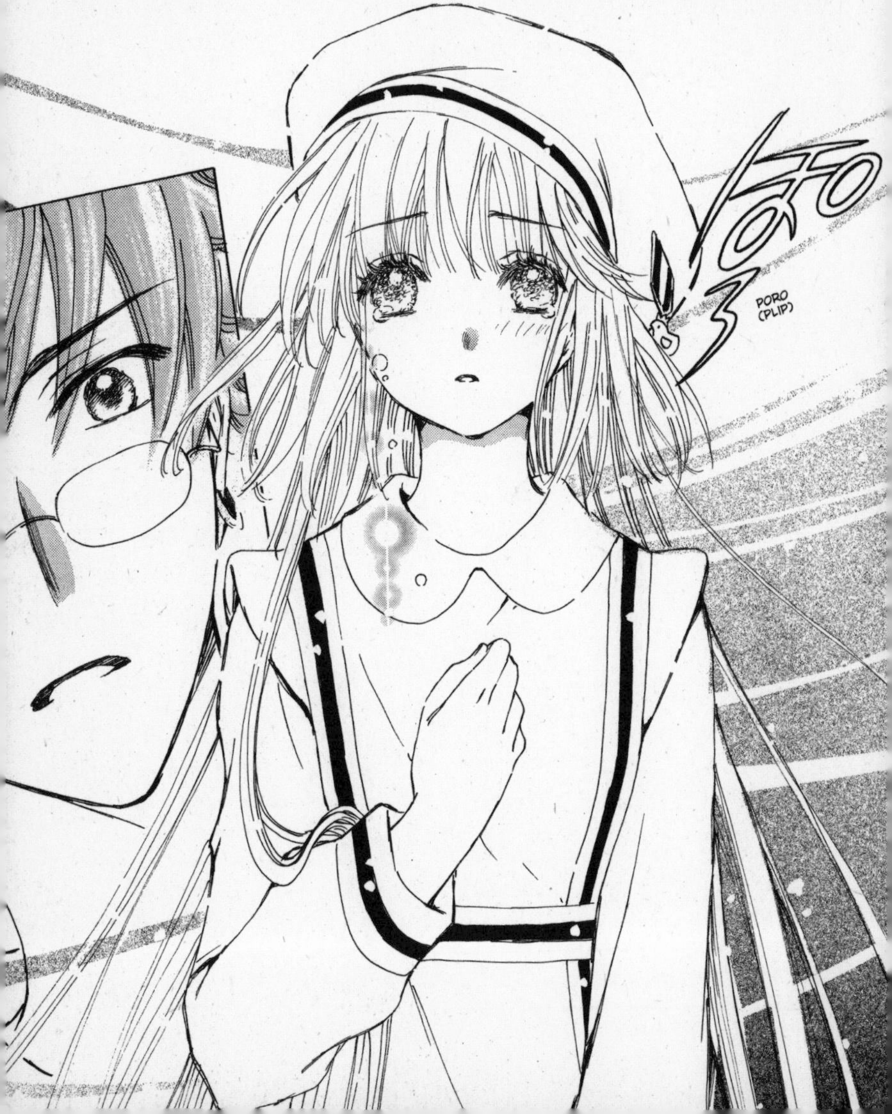
PORO
(PLIP)

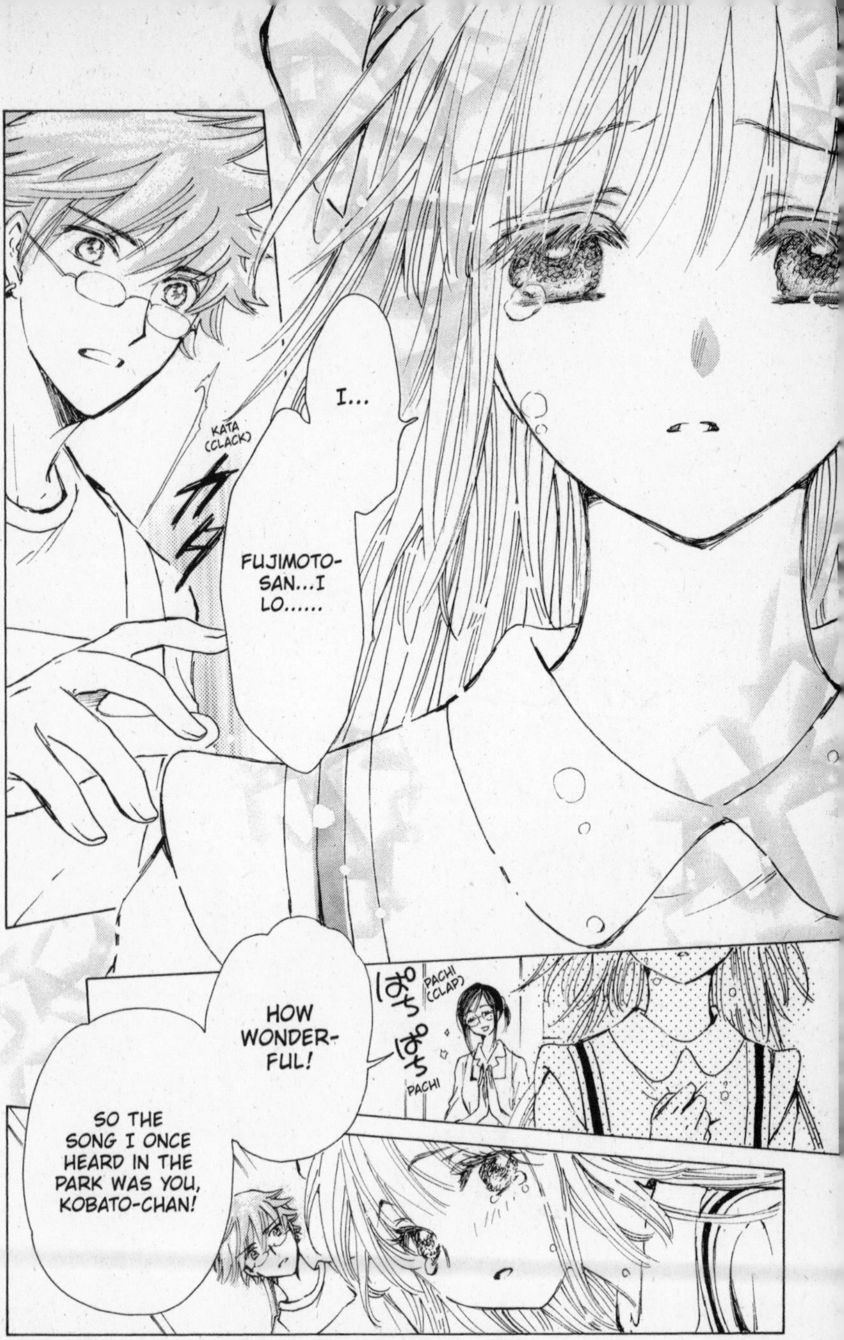
I...
FUJIMOTO-SAN...I LO......
KATA (CLACK)
カタ
HOW WONDERFUL!
ぱち ぱち
PACHI (CLAP)
PACHI
SO THE SONG I ONCE HEARD IN THE PARK WAS YOU, KOBATO-CHAN!

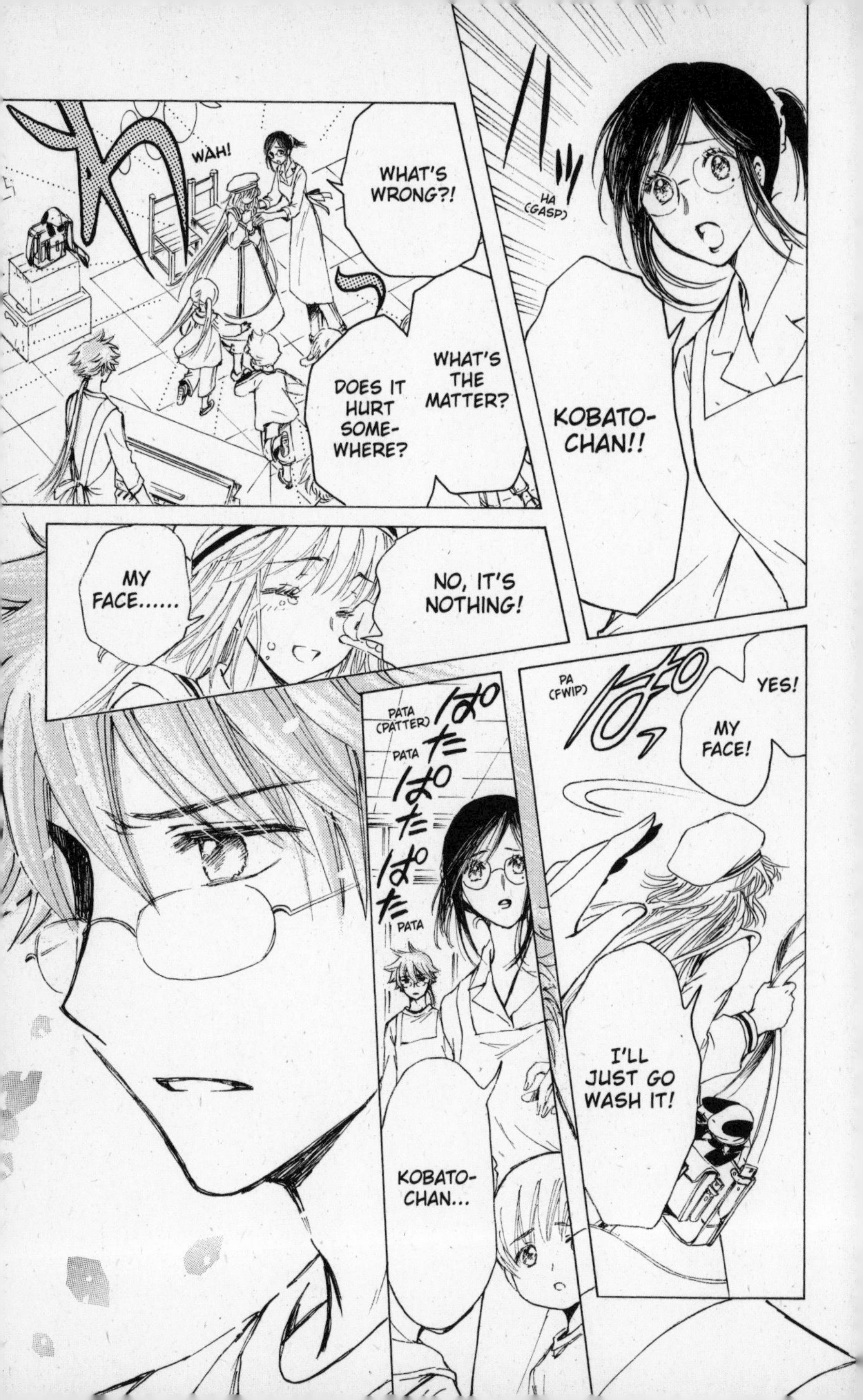
HA (GASP)
KOBATO-CHAN!!
WAH!
WHAT'S WRONG?!
WHAT'S THE MATTER?
DOES IT HURT SOMEWHERE?
NO, IT'S NOTHING!
MY FACE......
ぱっ
PA (FWIP)
YES!
MY FACE!
I'LL JUST GO WASH IT!
ぱたぱたぱた
PATA (PATTER)
PATA
PATA
KOBATO-CHAN...

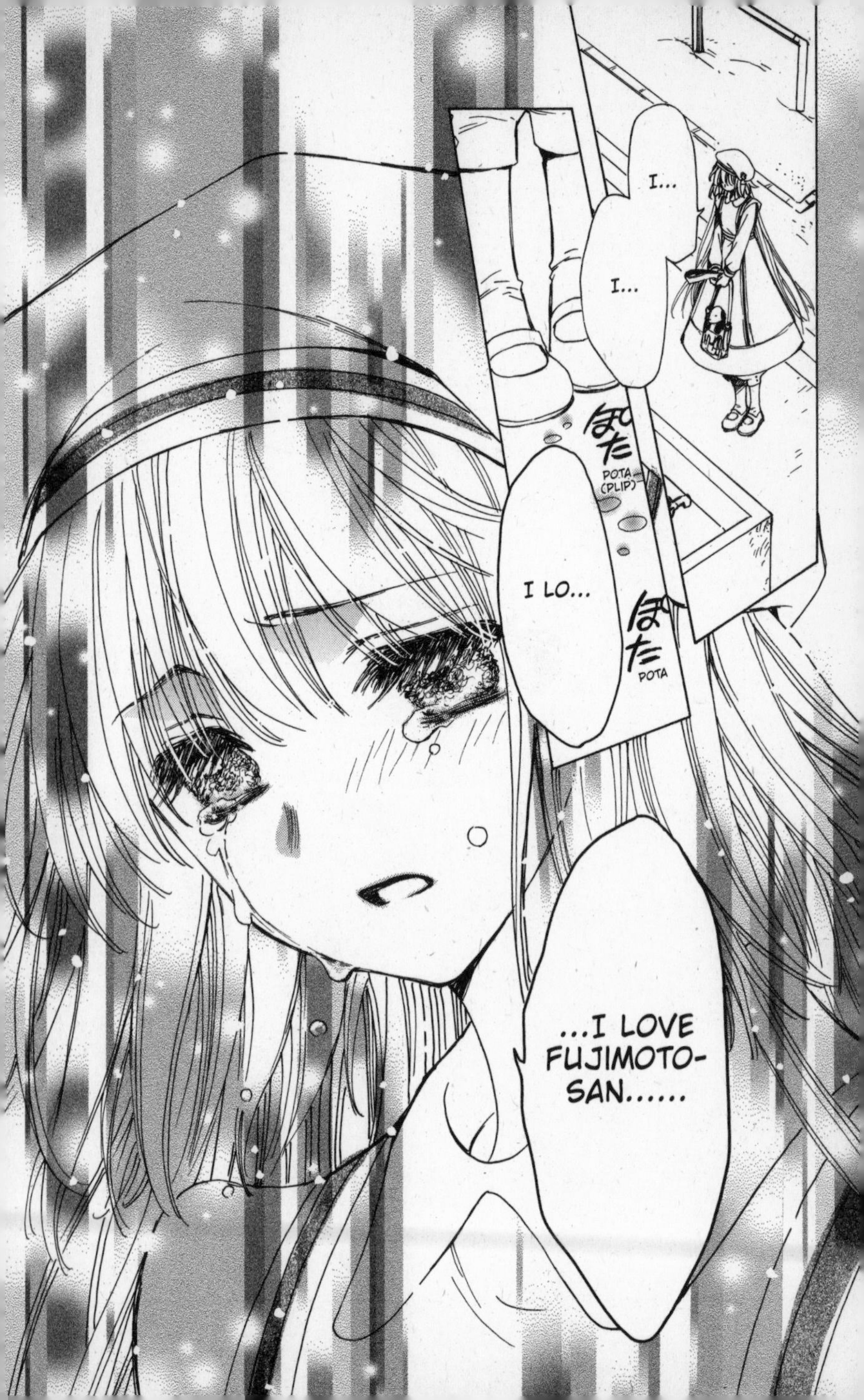
I...
I...
ぽた
POTA (PLIP)
I LO...
ぽた
POTA
...I LOVE FUJIMOTO-SAN......

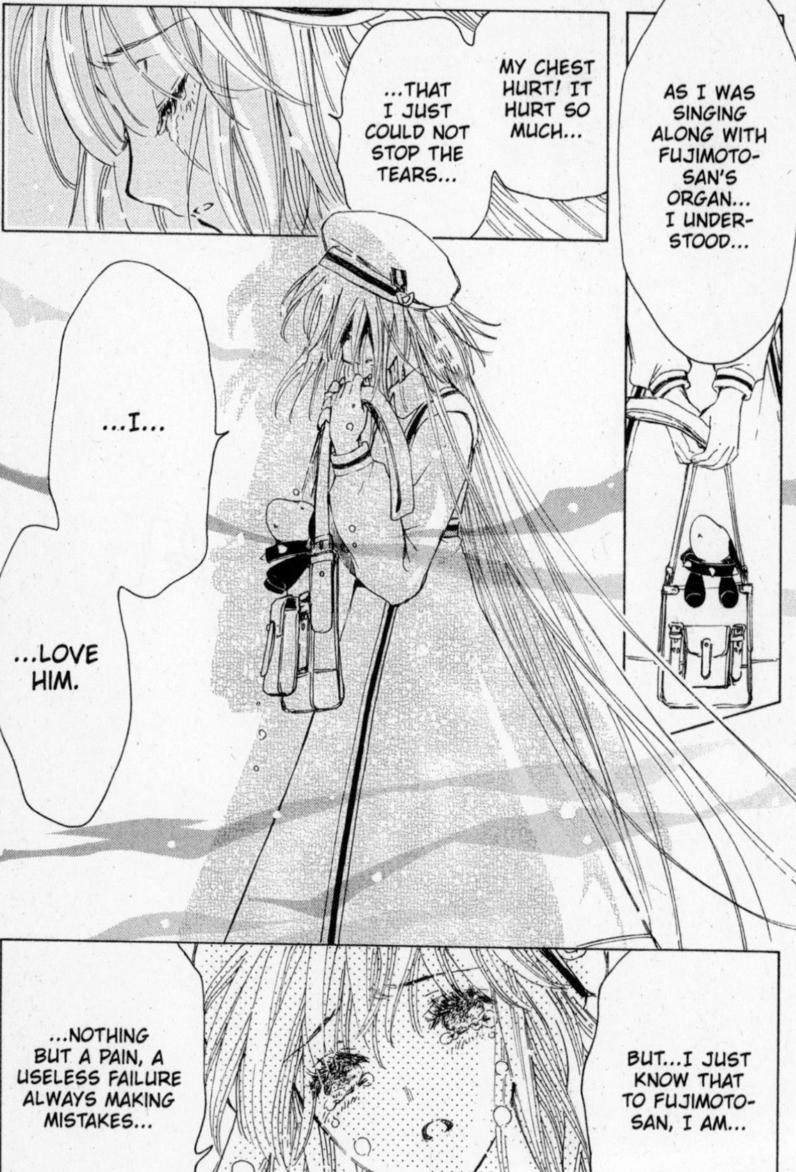
AS I WAS SINGING ALONG WITH FUJIMOTO-SAN'S ORGAN... I UNDERSTOOD...
MY CHEST HURT! IT HURT SO MUCH...
...THAT I JUST COULD NOT STOP THE TEARS...
...I...
...LOVE HIM.
BUT...I JUST KNOW THAT TO FUJIMOTO-SAN, I AM...
...NOTHING BUT A PAIN, A USELESS FAILURE ALWAYS MAKING MISTAKES...

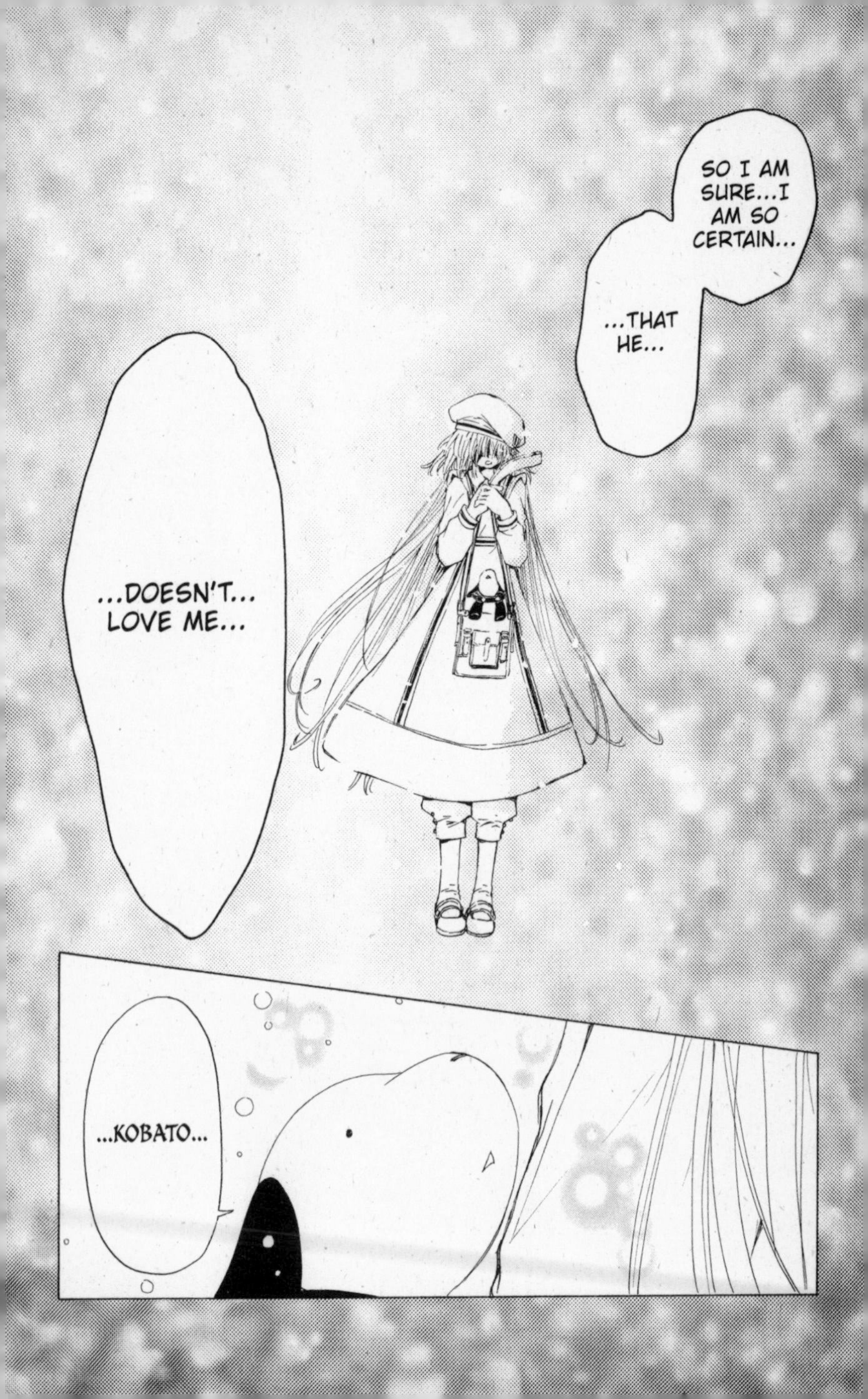
SO I AM SURE...I AM SO CERTAIN...
...THAT HE...
...DOESN'T... LOVE ME...
...KOBATO...

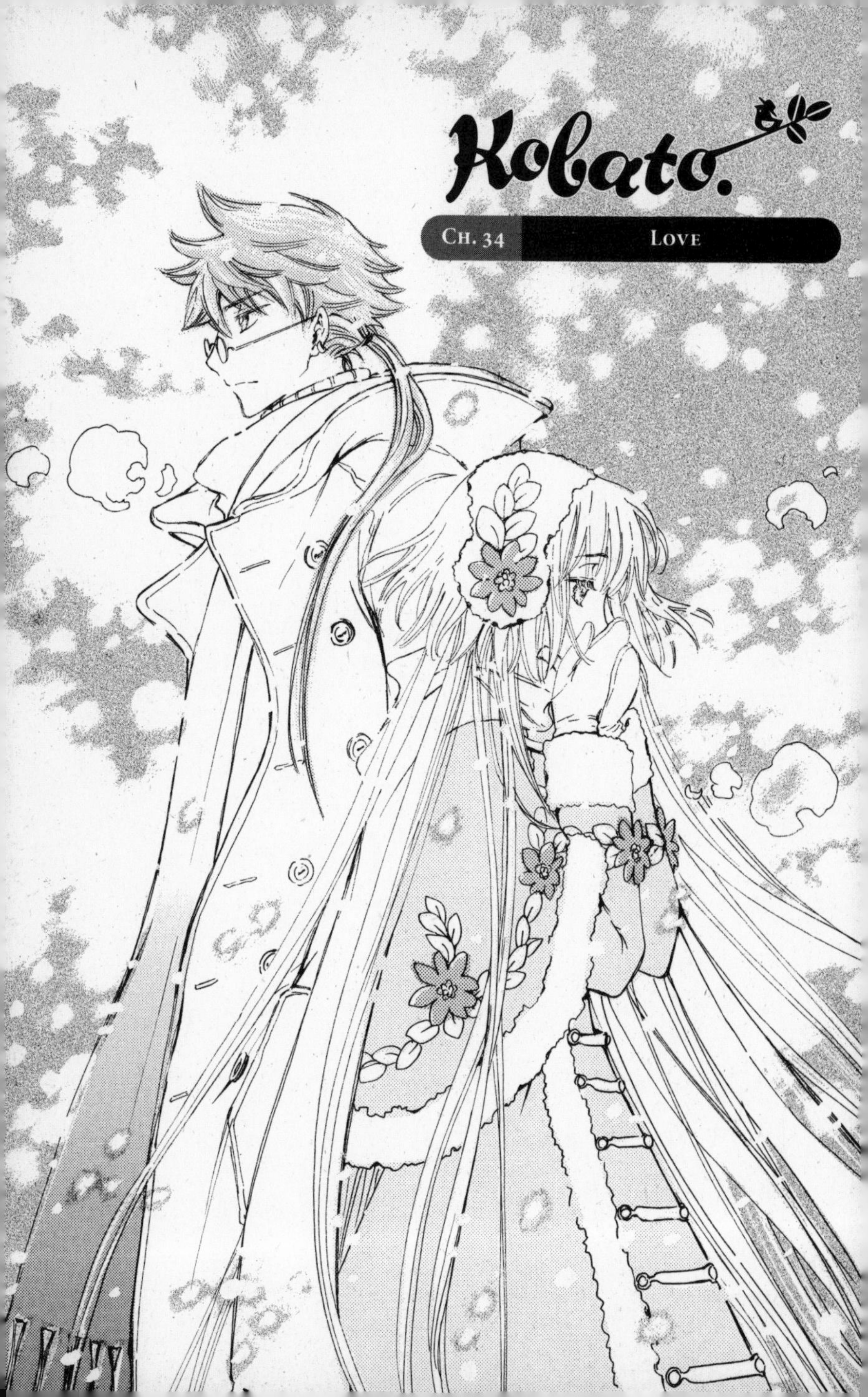
Kobato.
Ch. 34
Love

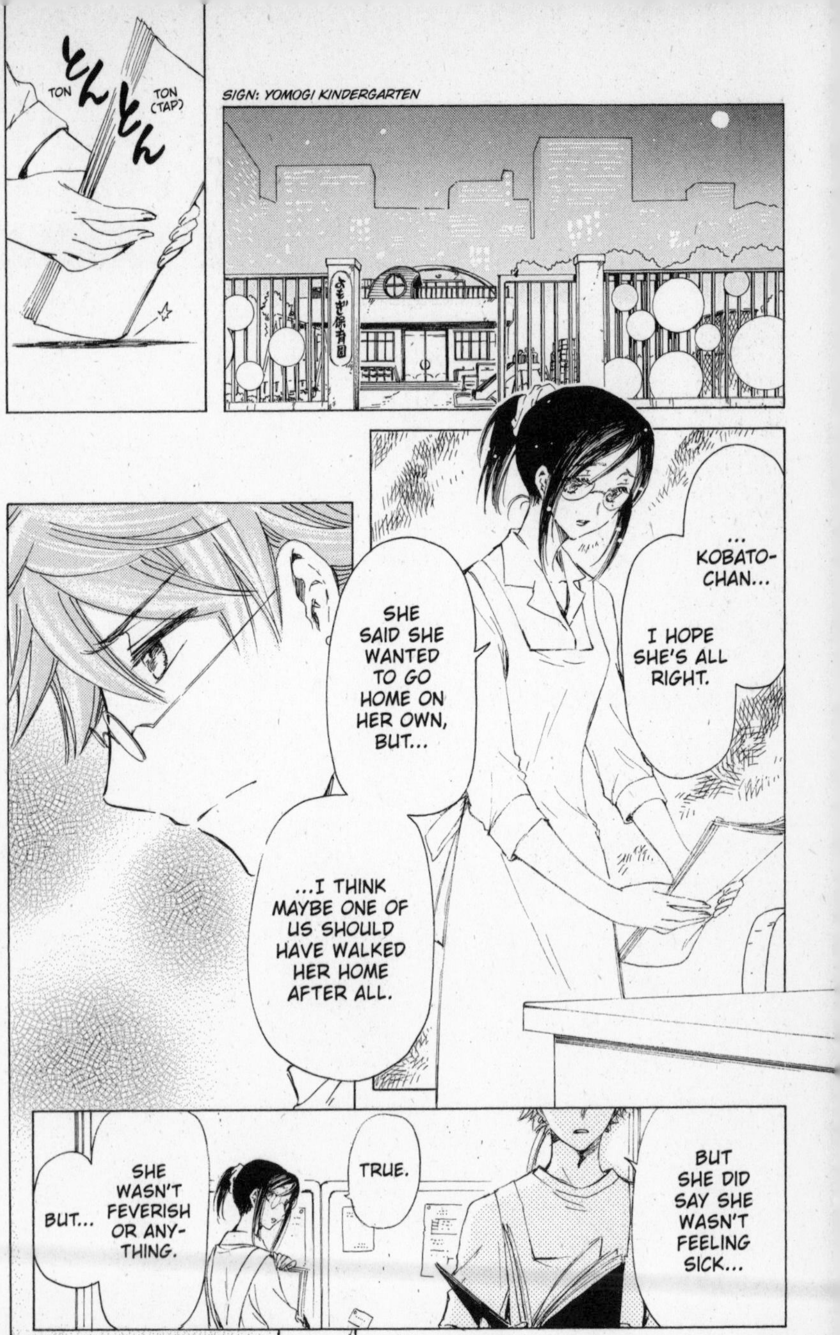
SIGN: YOMOGI KINDERGARTEN
とんとん
TON TON (TAP)
... KOBATO-CHAN...
I HOPE SHE'S ALL RIGHT.
SHE SAID SHE WANTED TO GO HOME ON HER OWN, BUT...
...I THINK MAYBE ONE OF US SHOULD HAVE WALKED HER HOME AFTER ALL.
BUT SHE DID SAY SHE WASN'T FEELING SICK...
TRUE.
SHE WASN'T FEVERISH OR ANY-THING.
BUT...

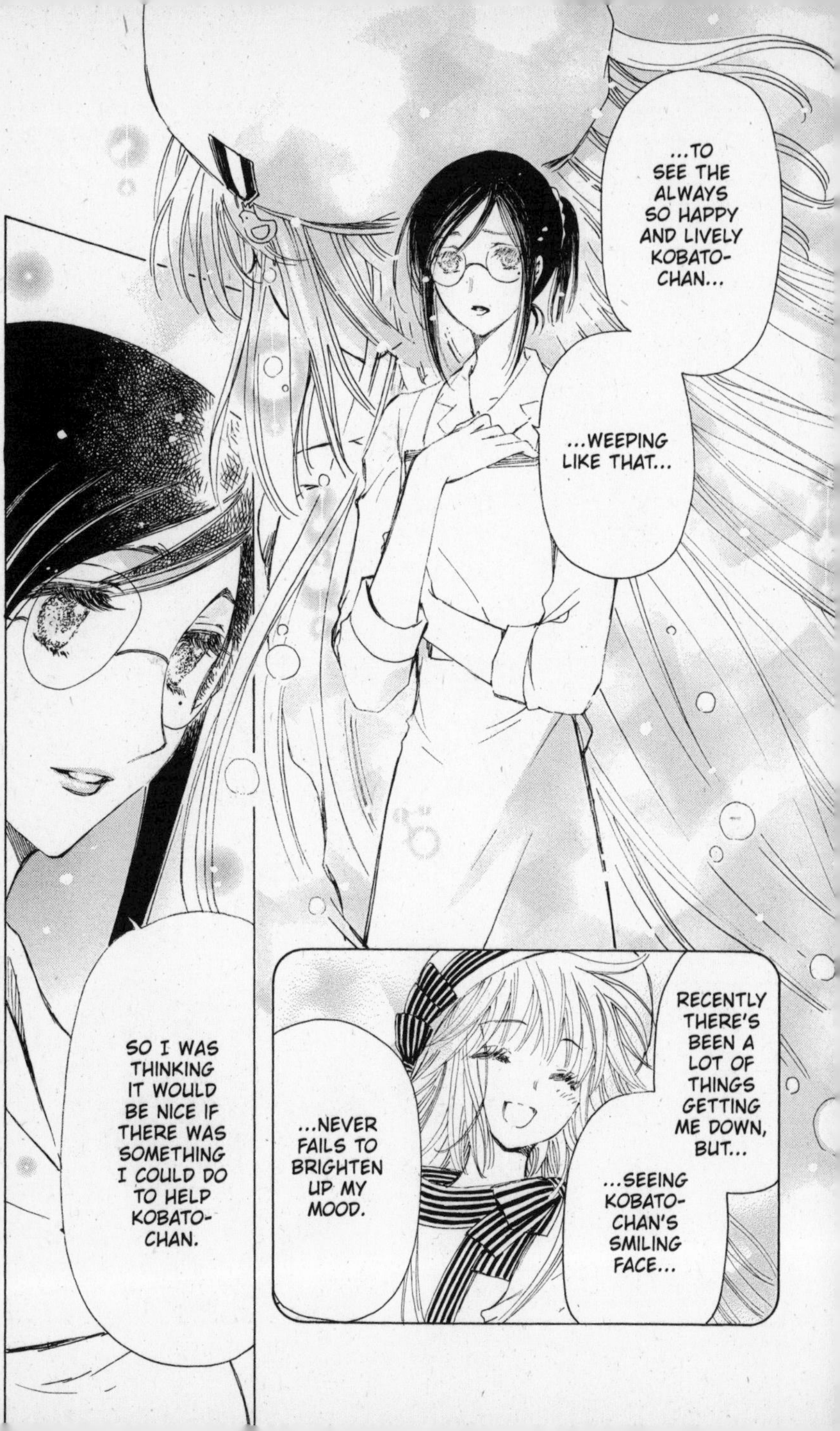
...TO SEE THE ALWAYS SO HAPPY AND LIVELY KOBATO-CHAN...
...WEEPING LIKE THAT...
RECENTLY THERE'S BEEN A LOT OF THINGS GETTING ME DOWN, BUT...
...SEEING KOBATO-CHAN'S SMILING FACE...
...NEVER FAILS TO BRIGHTEN UP MY MOOD.
SO I WAS THINKING IT WOULD BE NICE IF THERE WAS SOMETHING I COULD DO TO HELP KOBATO-CHAN.

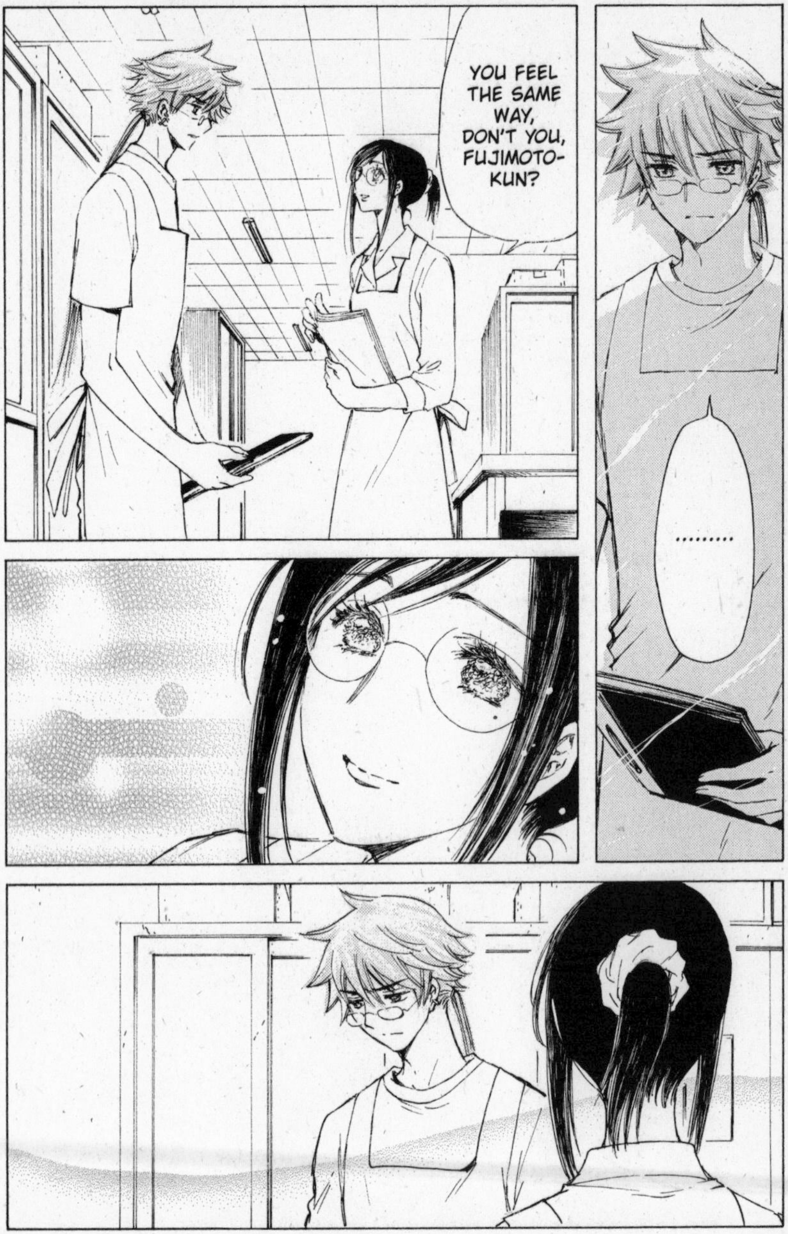
YOU FEEL THE SAME WAY, DON'T YOU, FUJIMOTO-KUN?
....

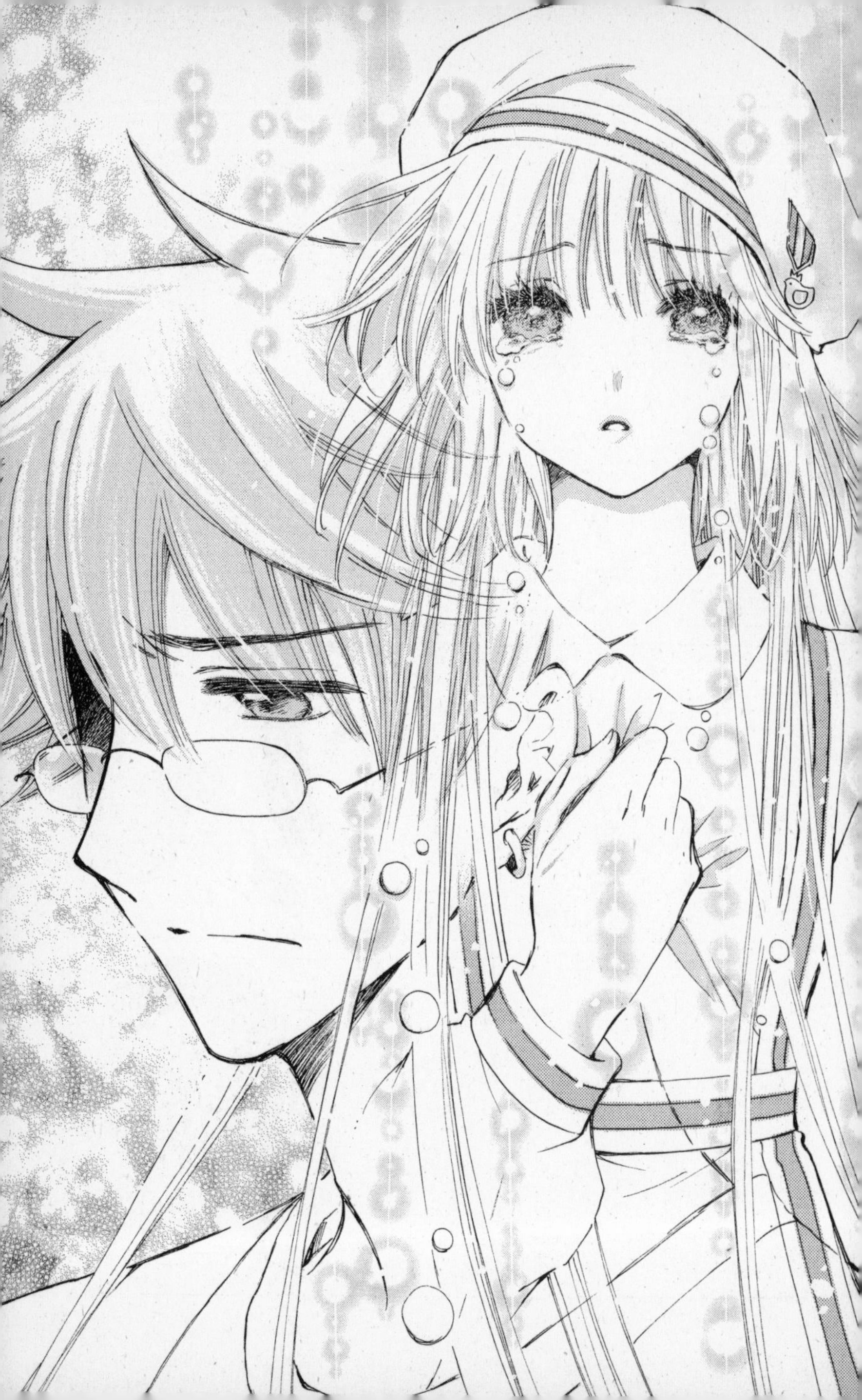

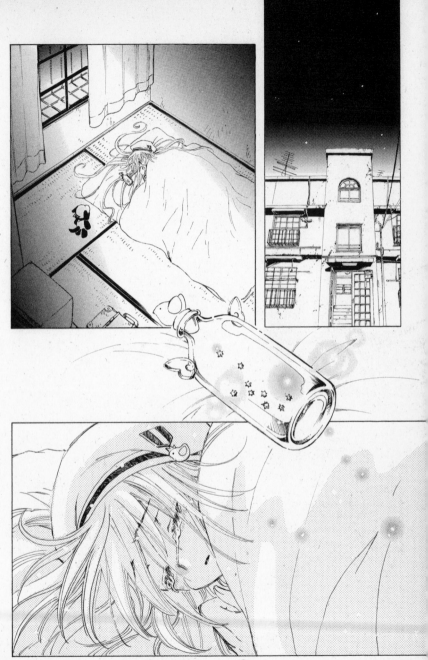

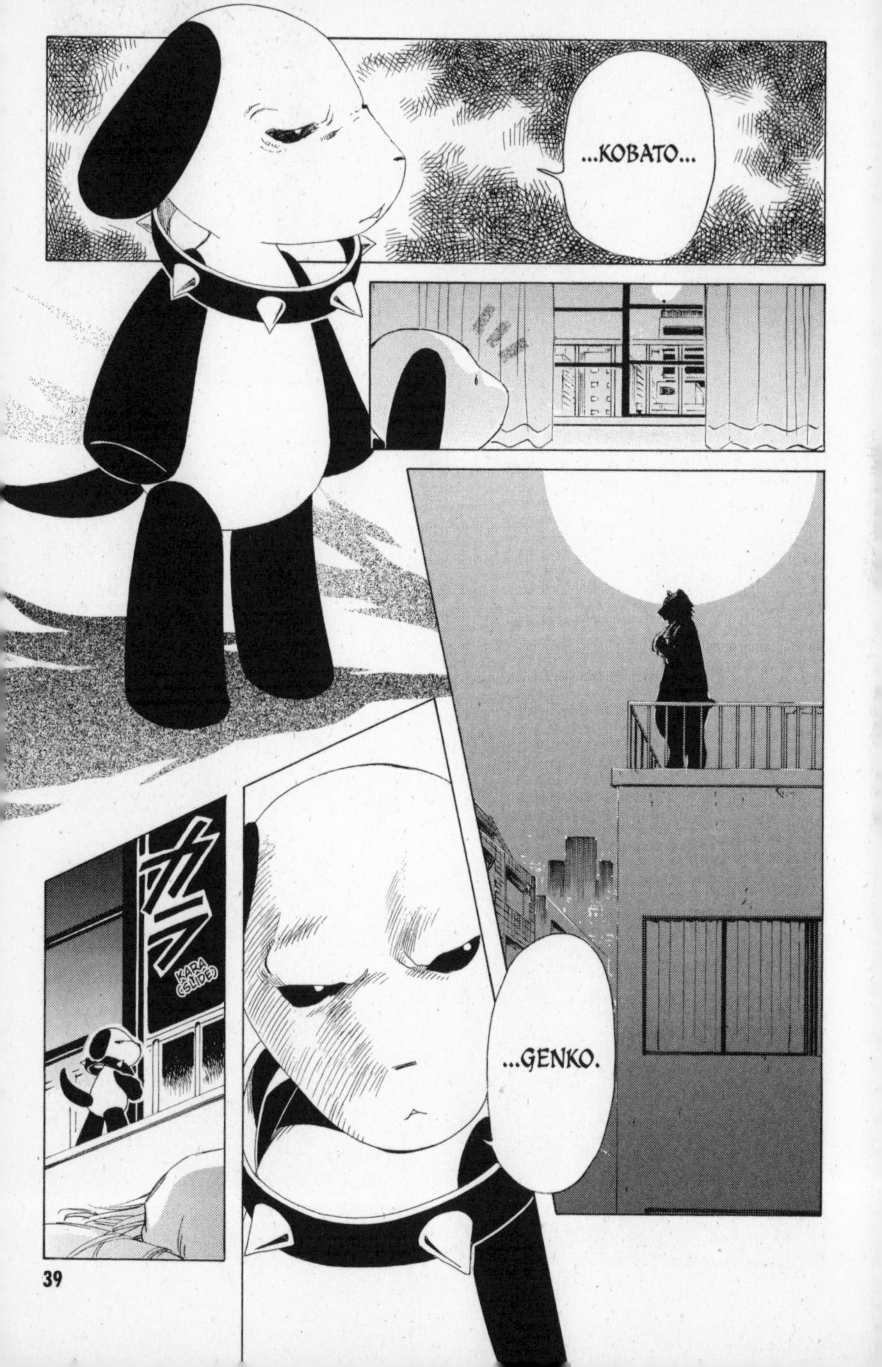
...KOBATO...
KARA (SLIDE)
...GENKO.

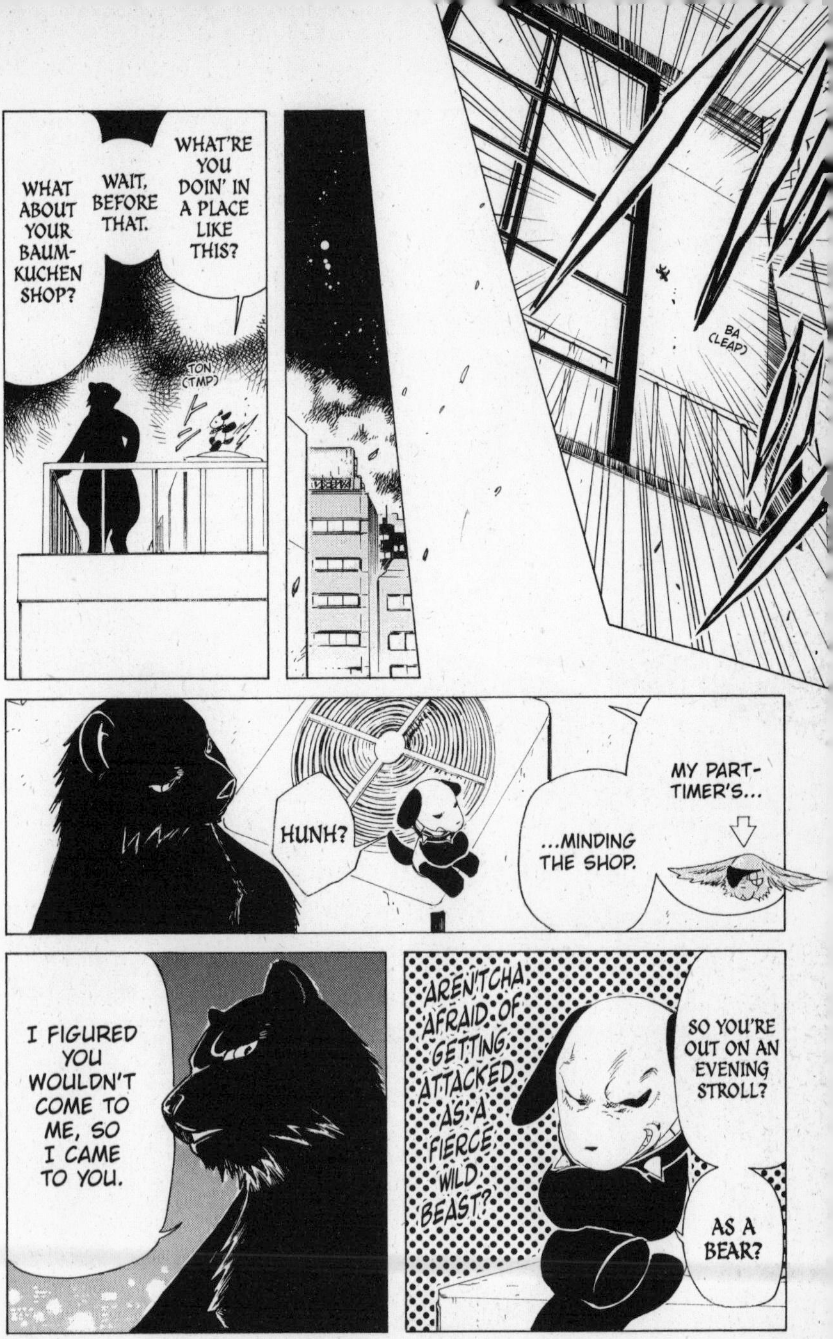
BA (LEAP)
WHAT'RE YOU DOIN' IN A PLACE LIKE THIS?
WAIT, BEFORE THAT.
WHAT ABOUT YOUR BAUM-KUCHEN SHOP?
TON (TMP)
MY PART-TIMER'S...
...MINDING THE SHOP.
HUNH?
SO YOU'RE OUT ON AN EVENING STROLL?
AREN'TCHA AFRAID OF GETTING ATTACKED AS A FIERCE WILD BEAST?
AS A BEAR?
I FIGURED YOU WOULDN'T COME TO ME, SO I CAME TO YOU.

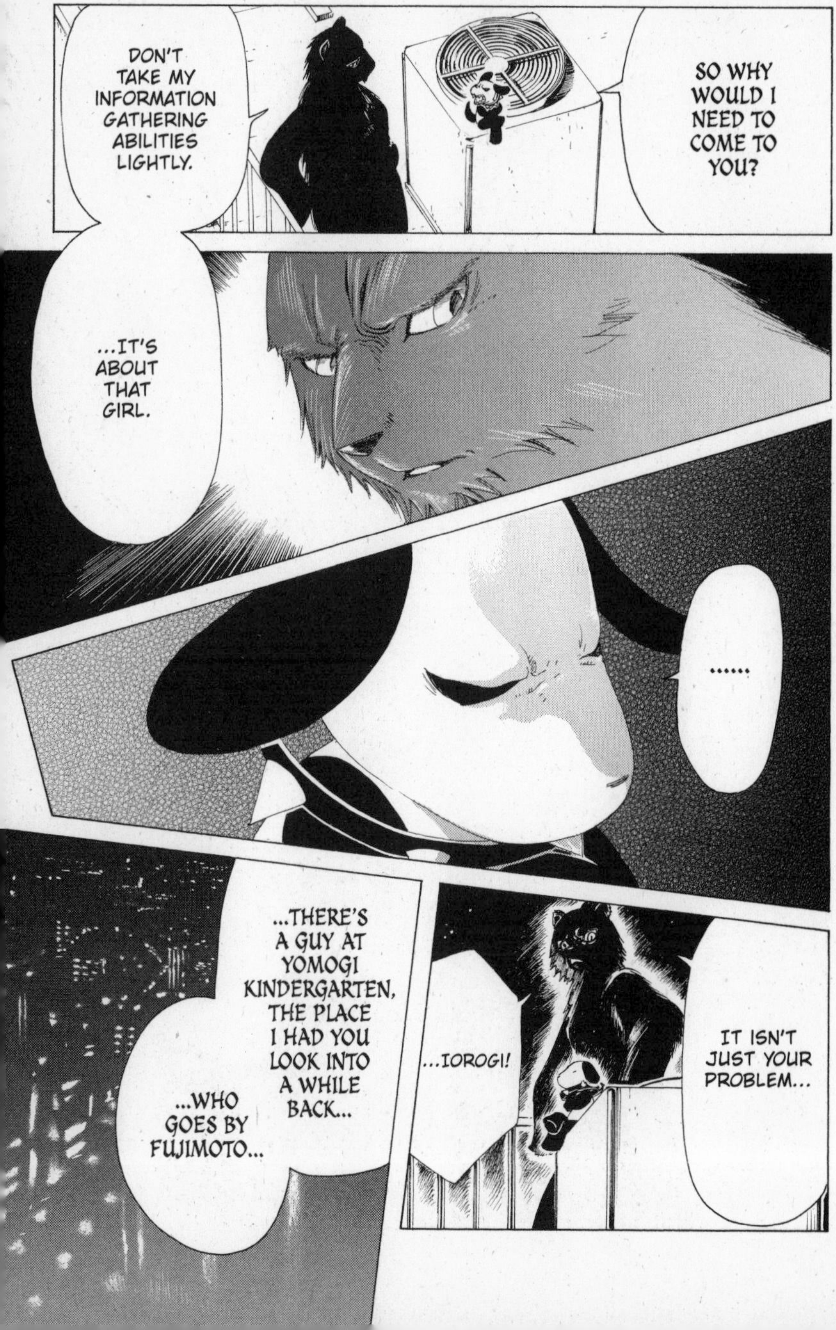
SO WHY WOULD I NEED TO COME TO YOU?
DON'T TAKE MY INFORMATION GATHERING ABILITIES LIGHTLY.
...IT'S ABOUT THAT GIRL.
......
IT ISN'T JUST YOUR PROBLEM...
...IOROGI!
...THERE'S A GUY AT YOMOGI KINDERGARTEN, THE PLACE I HAD YOU LOOK INTO A WHILE BACK...
...WHO GOES BY FUJIMOTO...

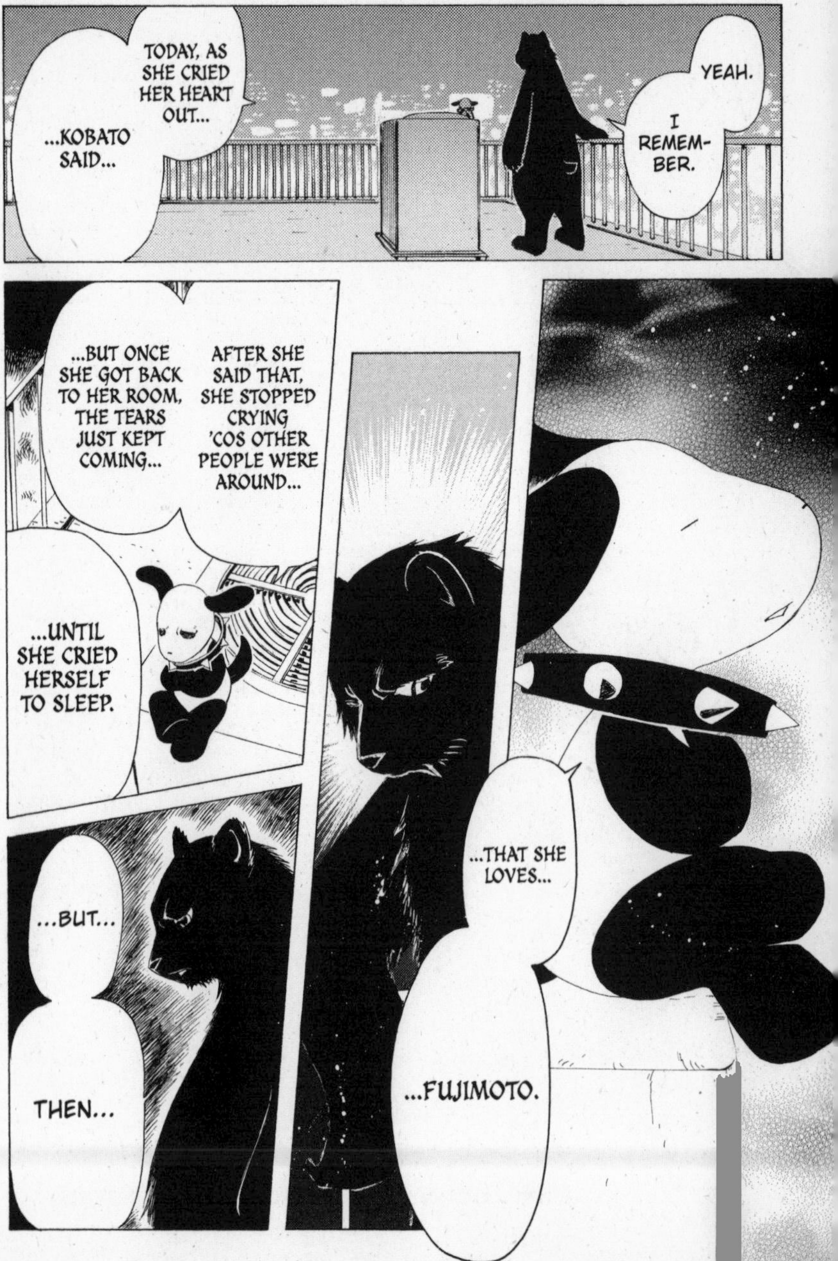
YEAH. I REMEMBER.
TODAY, AS SHE CRIED HER HEART OUT...
...KOBATO SAID...
...THAT SHE LOVES...
...FUJIMOTO.
AFTER SHE SAID THAT, SHE STOPPED CRYING 'COS OTHER PEOPLE WERE AROUND...
...BUT ONCE SHE GOT BACK TO HER ROOM, THE TEARS JUST KEPT COMING...
...UNTIL SHE CRIED HERSELF TO SLEEP.
...BUT...
THEN...

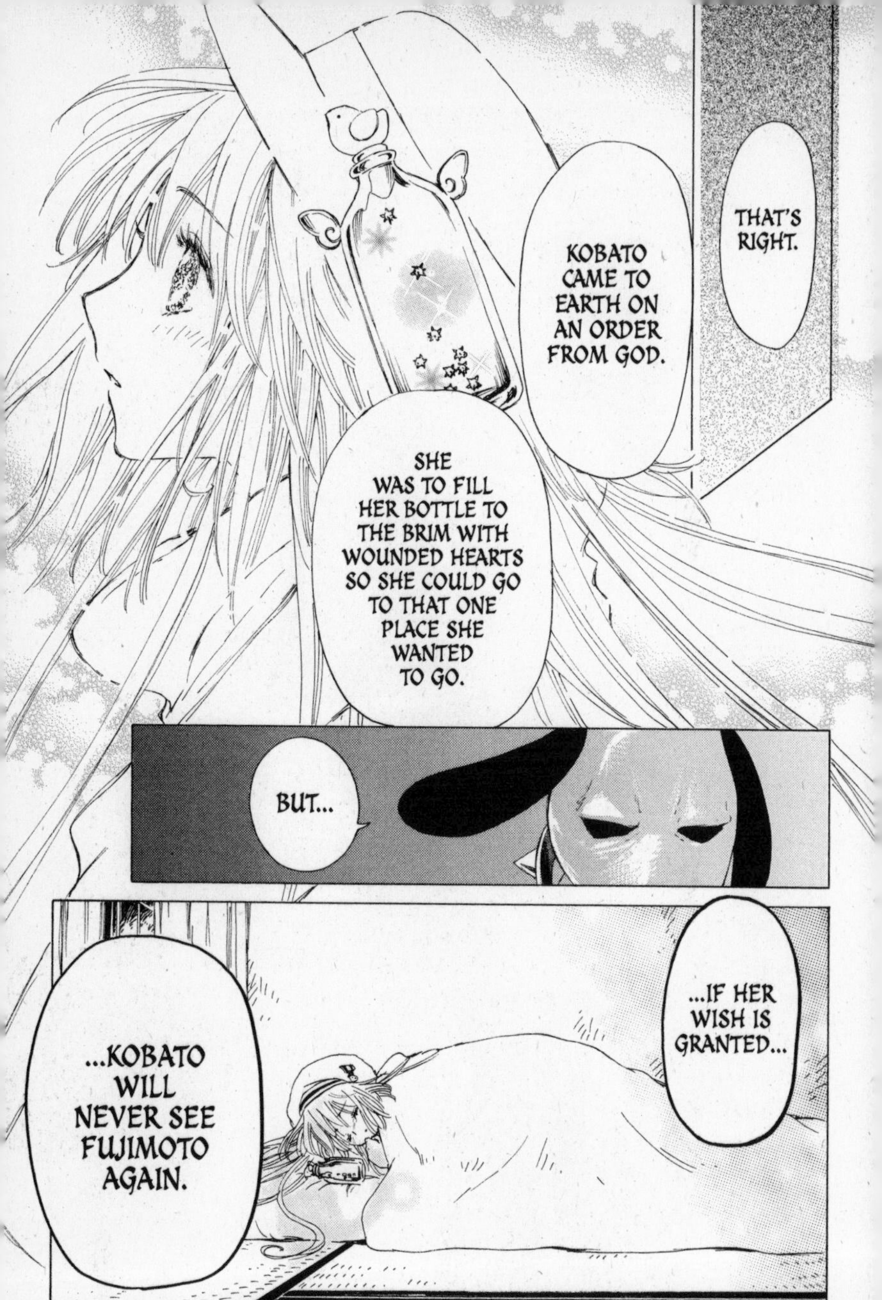
THAT'S RIGHT.
KOBATO CAME TO EARTH ON AN ORDER FROM GOD.
SHE WAS TO FILL HER BOTTLE TO THE BRIM WITH WOUNDED HEARTS SO SHE COULD GO TO THAT ONE PLACE SHE WANTED TO GO.
BUT...
...IF HER WISH IS GRANTED...
...KOBATO WILL NEVER SEE FUJIMOTO AGAIN.

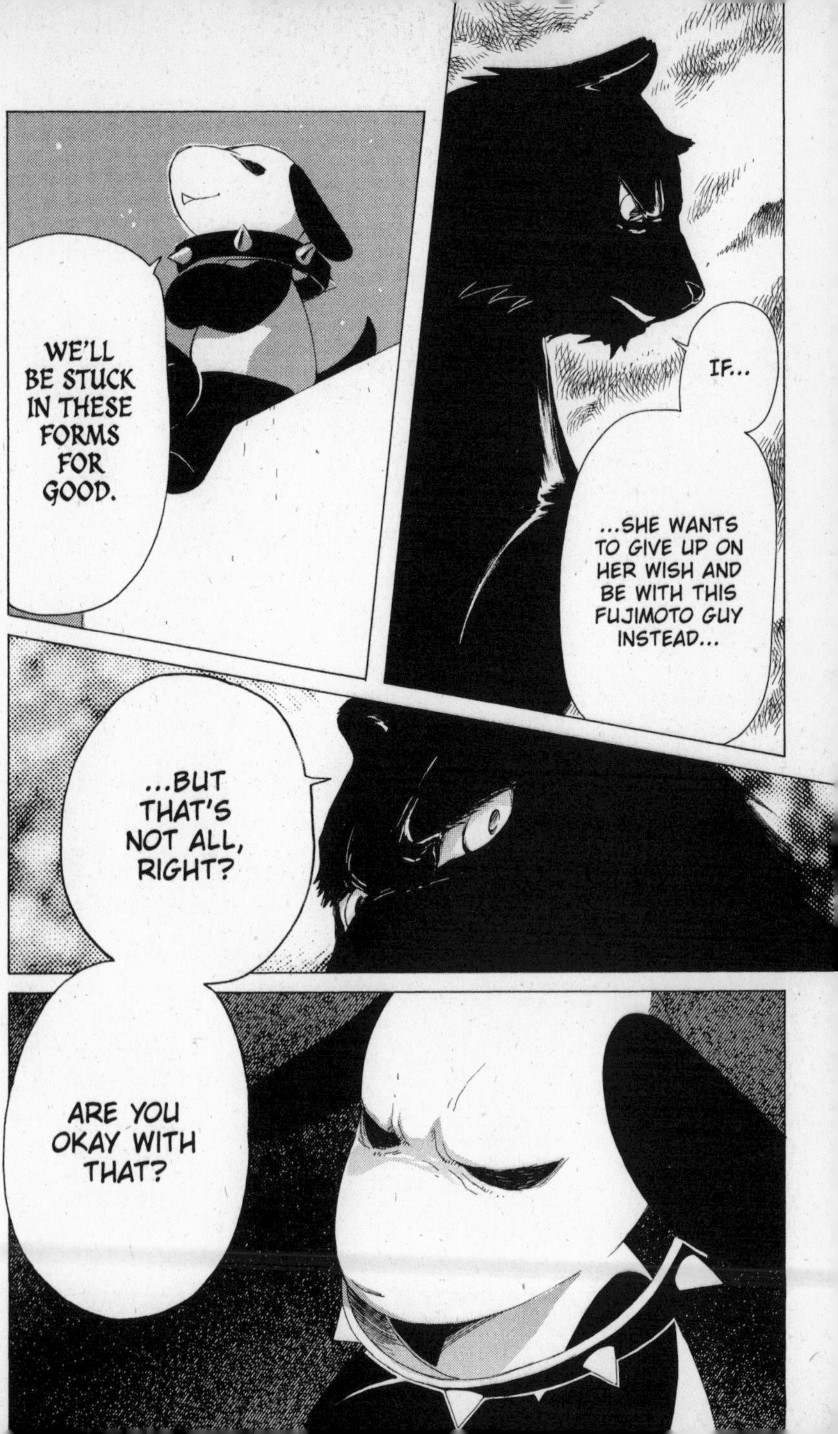
IF...
...SHE WANTS TO GIVE UP ON HER WISH AND BE WITH THIS FUJIMOTO GUY INSTEAD...
WE'LL BE STUCK IN THESE FORMS FOR GOOD.
...BUT THAT'S NOT ALL, RIGHT?
ARE YOU OKAY WITH THAT?

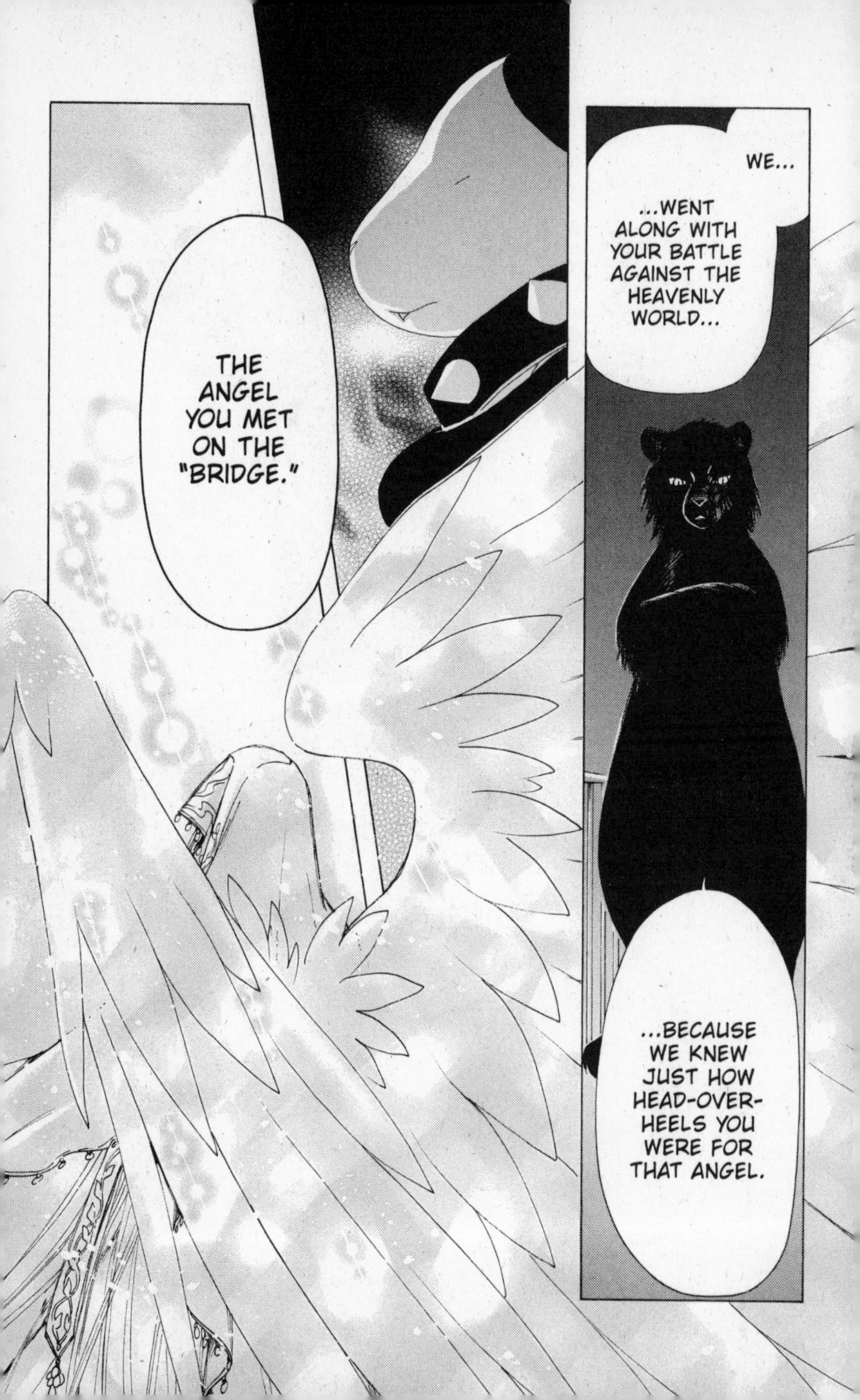
WE...
...WENT ALONG WITH YOUR BATTLE AGAINST THE HEAVENLY WORLD...
...BECAUSE WE KNEW JUST HOW HEAD-OVER-HEELS YOU WERE FOR THAT ANGEL.
THE ANGEL YOU MET ON THE "BRIDGE."

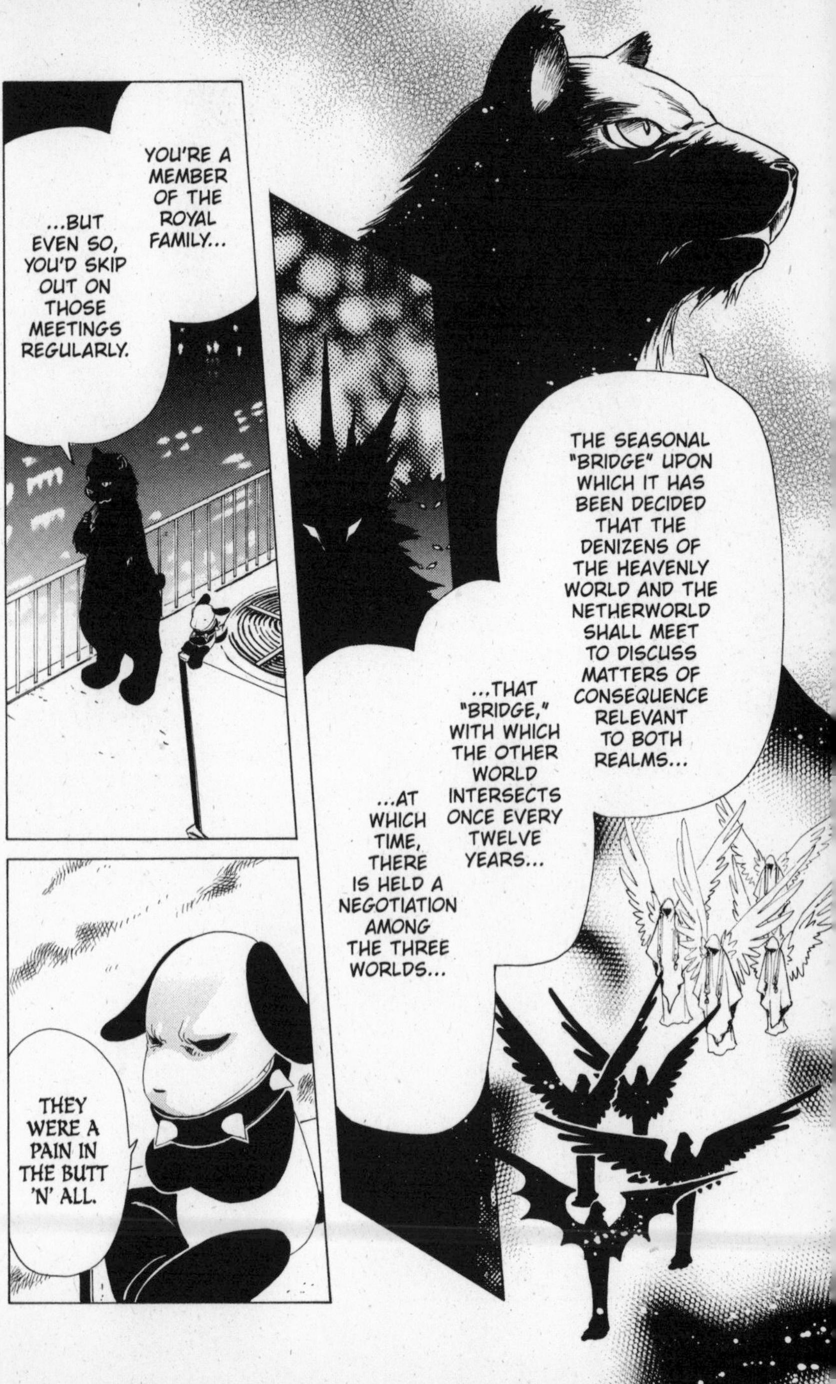
THE SEASONAL "BRIDGE" UPON WHICH IT HAS BEEN DECIDED THAT THE DENIZENS OF THE HEAVENLY WORLD AND THE NETHERWORLD SHALL MEET TO DISCUSS MATTERS OF CONSEQUENCE RELEVANT TO BOTH REALMS...
..."THAT "BRIDGE," WITH WHICH THE OTHER WORLD INTERSECTS ONCE EVERY TWELVE YEARS...
...AT WHICH TIME, THERE IS HELD A NEGOTIATION AMONG THE THREE WORLDS...
YOU'RE A MEMBER OF THE ROYAL FAMILY...
...BUT EVEN SO, YOU'D SKIP OUT ON THOSE MEETINGS REGULARLY.
THEY WERE A PAIN IN THE BUTT 'N' ALL.

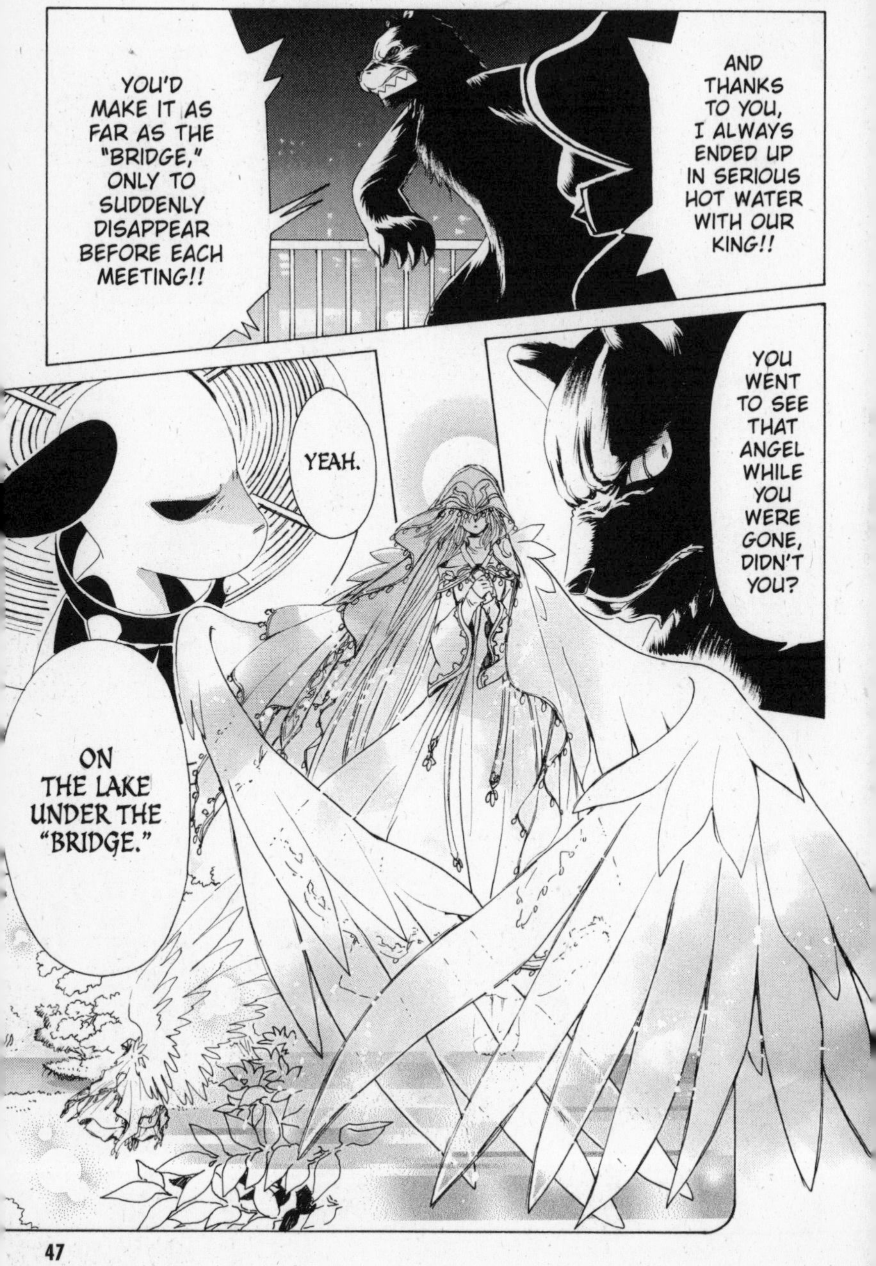
AND THANKS TO YOU, I ALWAYS ENDED UP IN SERIOUS HOT WATER WITH OUR KING!!
YOU'D MAKE IT AS FAR AS THE "BRIDGE," ONLY TO SUDDENLY DISAPPEAR BEFORE EACH MEETING!!
YOU WENT TO SEE THAT ANGEL WHILE YOU WERE GONE, DIDN'T YOU?
YEAH.
ON THE LAKE UNDER THE "BRIDGE."

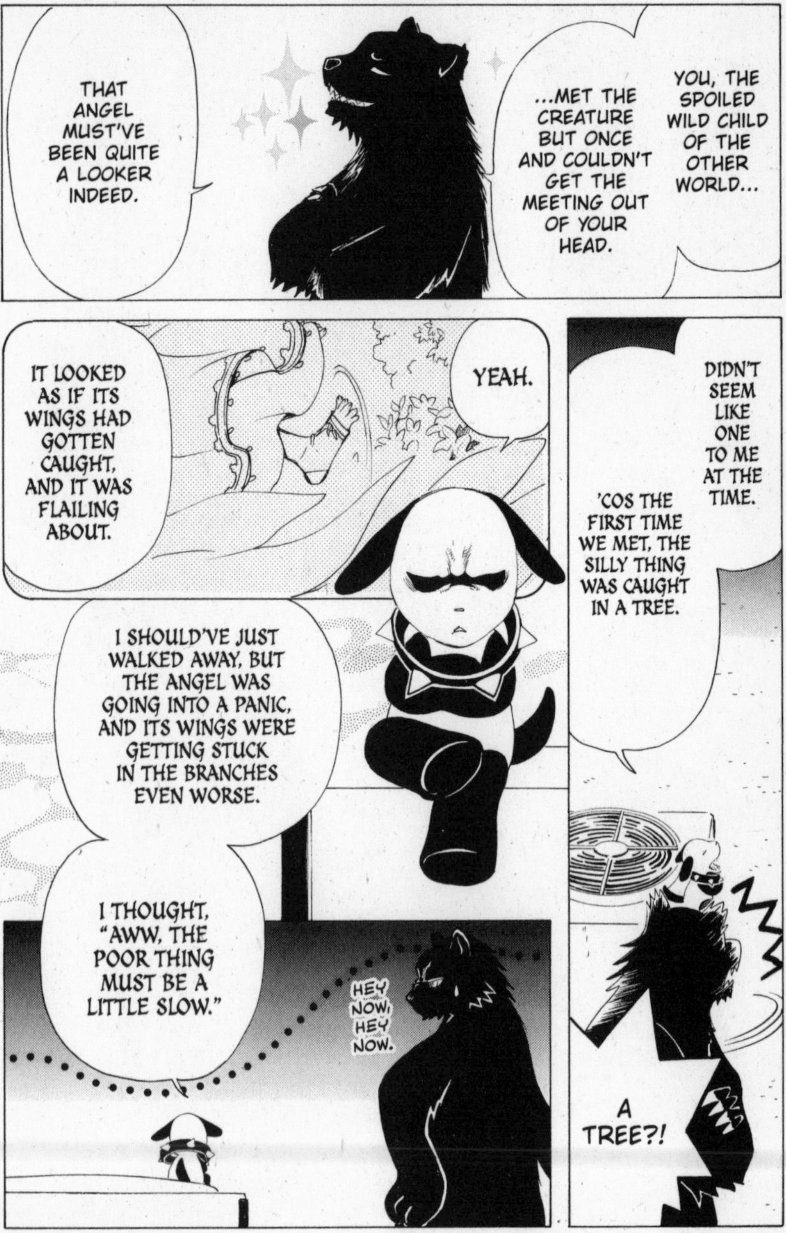
YOU, THE SPOILED WILD CHILD OF THE OTHER WORLD...
...MET THE CREATURE BUT ONCE AND COULDN'T GET THE MEETING OUT OF YOUR HEAD.
THAT ANGEL MUST'VE BEEN QUITE A LOOKER INDEED.
DIDN'T SEEM LIKE ONE TO ME AT THE TIME.
'COS THE FIRST TIME WE MET, THE SILLY THING WAS CAUGHT IN A TREE.
A TREE?!
YEAH.
IT LOOKED AS IF ITS WINGS HAD GOTTEN CAUGHT, AND IT WAS FLAILING ABOUT.
I SHOULD'VE JUST WALKED AWAY, BUT THE ANGEL WAS GOING INTO A PANIC, AND ITS WINGS WERE GETTING STUCK IN THE BRANCHES EVEN WORSE.
I THOUGHT, "AWW, THE POOR THING MUST BE A LITTLE SLOW."
HEY NOW, HEY NOW.

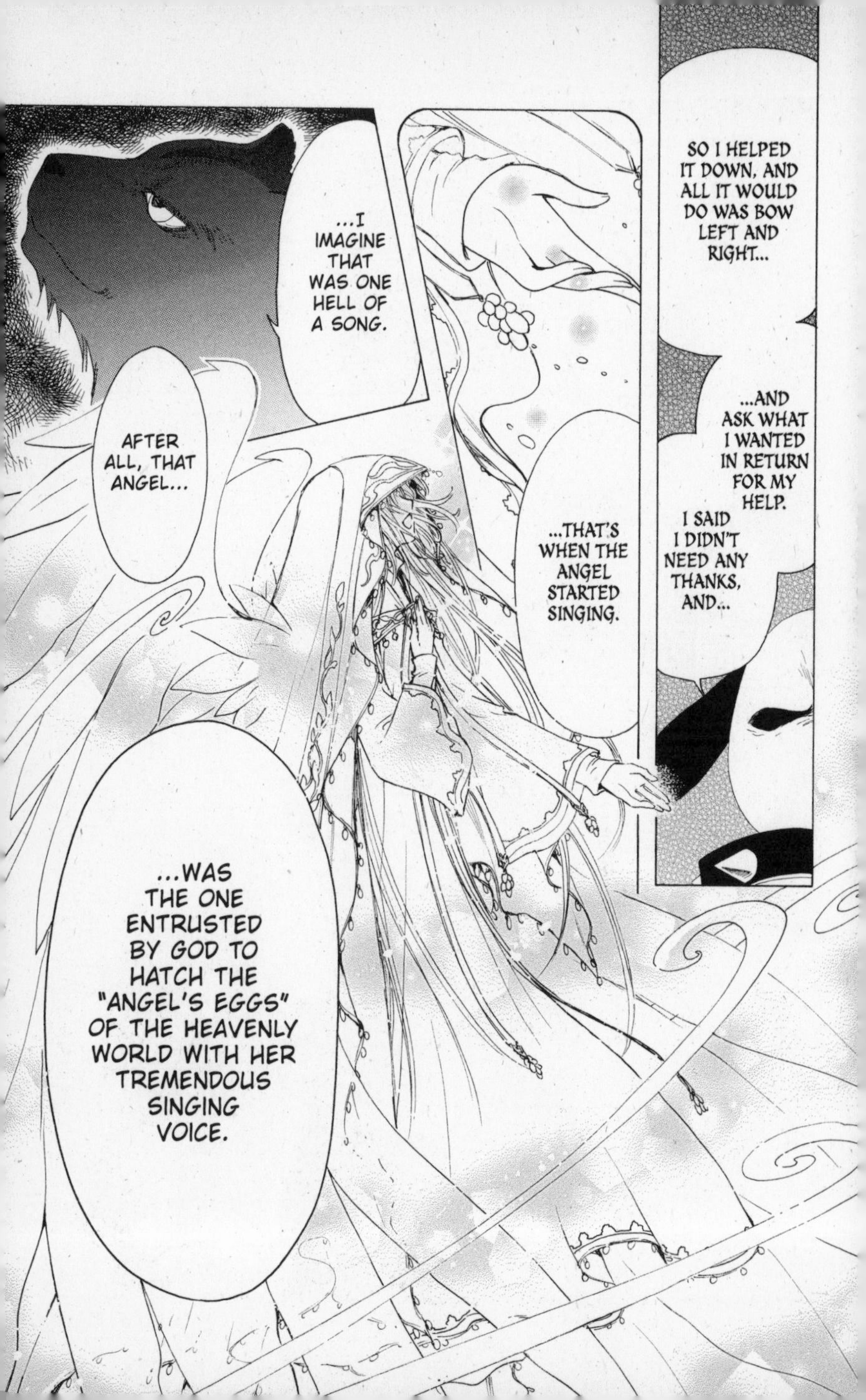
SO I HELPED IT DOWN, AND ALL IT WOULD DO WAS BOW LEFT AND RIGHT...
...AND ASK WHAT I WANTED IN RETURN FOR MY HELP.
I SAID I DIDN'T NEED ANY THANKS, AND...
...THAT'S WHEN THE ANGEL STARTED SINGING.
...I IMAGINE THAT WAS ONE HELL OF A SONG.
AFTER ALL, THAT ANGEL...
...WAS THE ONE ENTRUSTED BY GOD TO HATCH THE "ANGEL'S EGGS" OF THE HEAVENLY WORLD WITH HER TREMENDOUS SINGING VOICE.

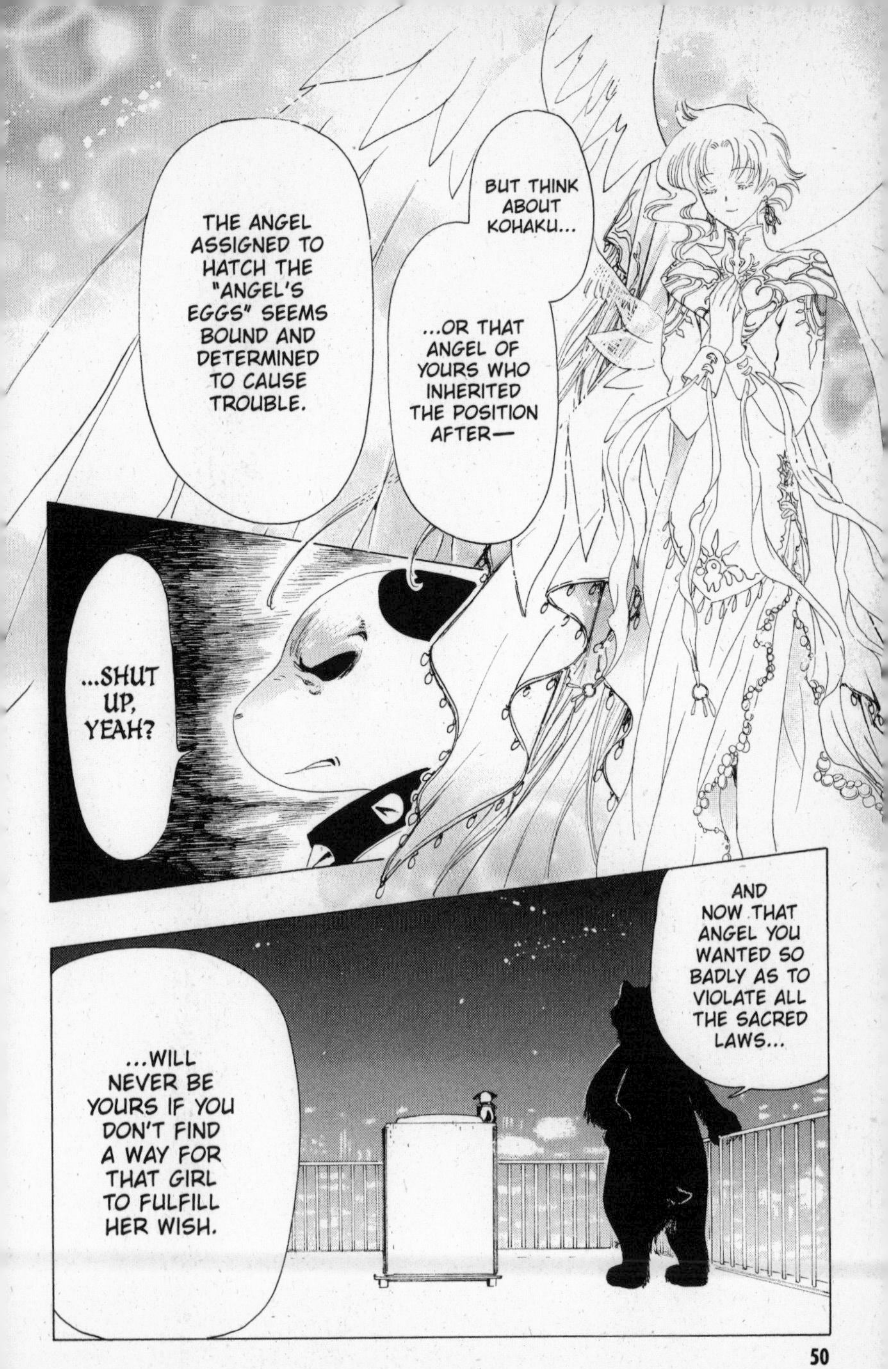
BUT THINK ABOUT KOHAKU...
...OR THAT ANGEL OF YOURS WHO INHERITED THE POSITION AFTER—
THE ANGEL ASSIGNED TO HATCH THE "ANGEL'S EGGS" SEEMS BOUND AND DETERMINED TO CAUSE TROUBLE.
...SHUT UP, YEAH?
AND NOW THAT ANGEL YOU WANTED SO BADLY AS TO VIOLATE ALL THE SACRED LAWS...
...WILL NEVER BE YOURS IF YOU DON'T FIND A WAY FOR THAT GIRL TO FULFILL HER WISH.

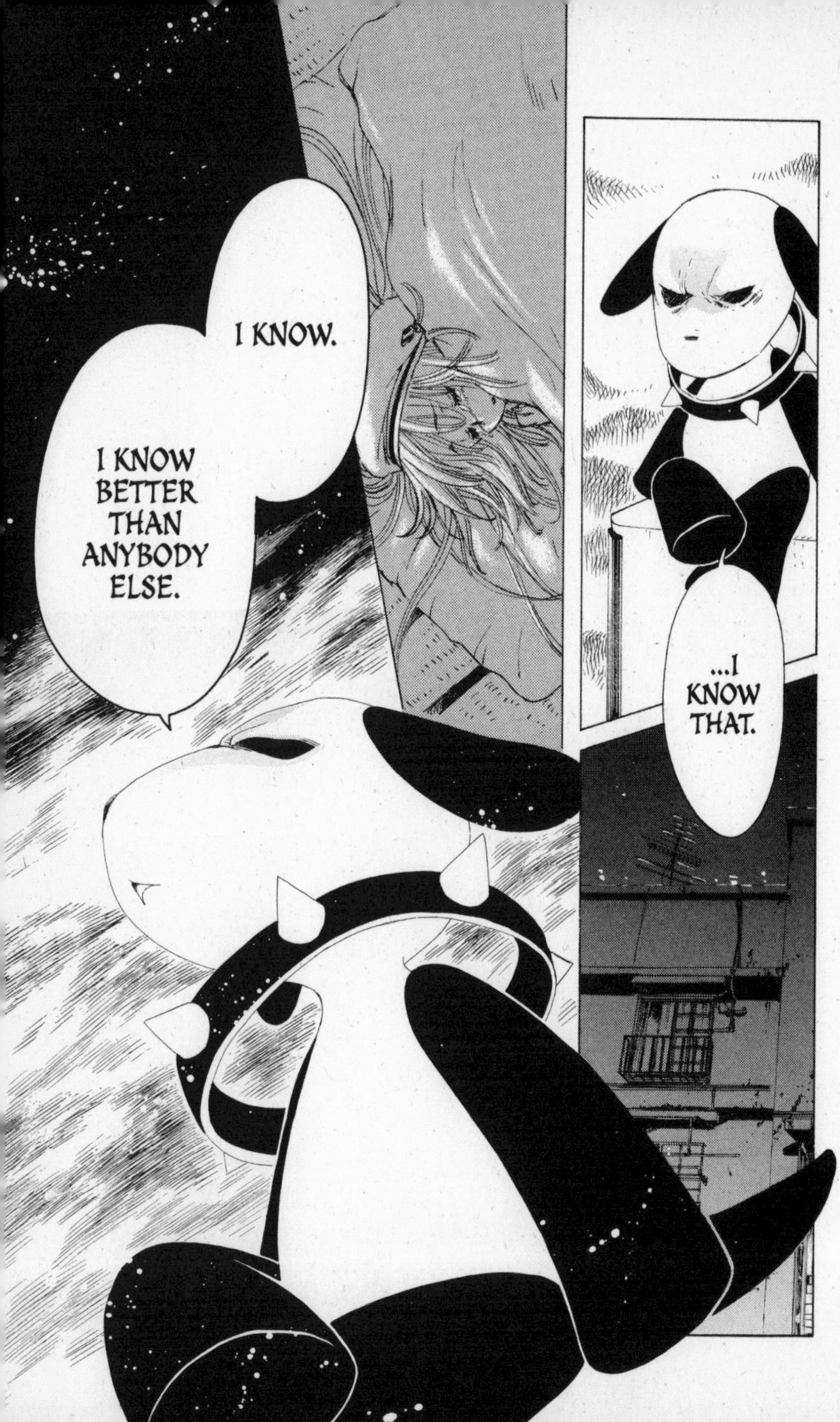
...I KNOW THAT.
I KNOW.
I KNOW BETTER THAN ANYBODY ELSE.

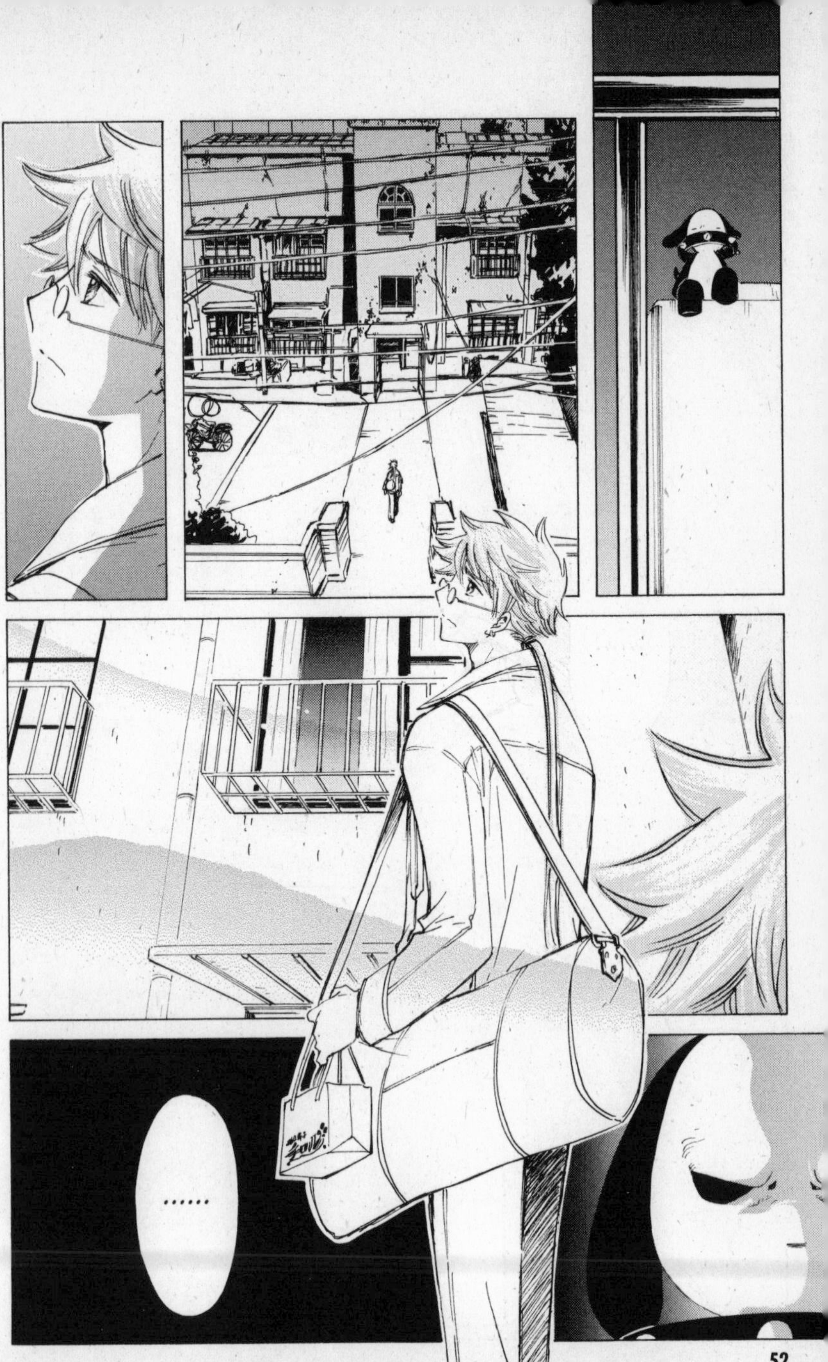
......

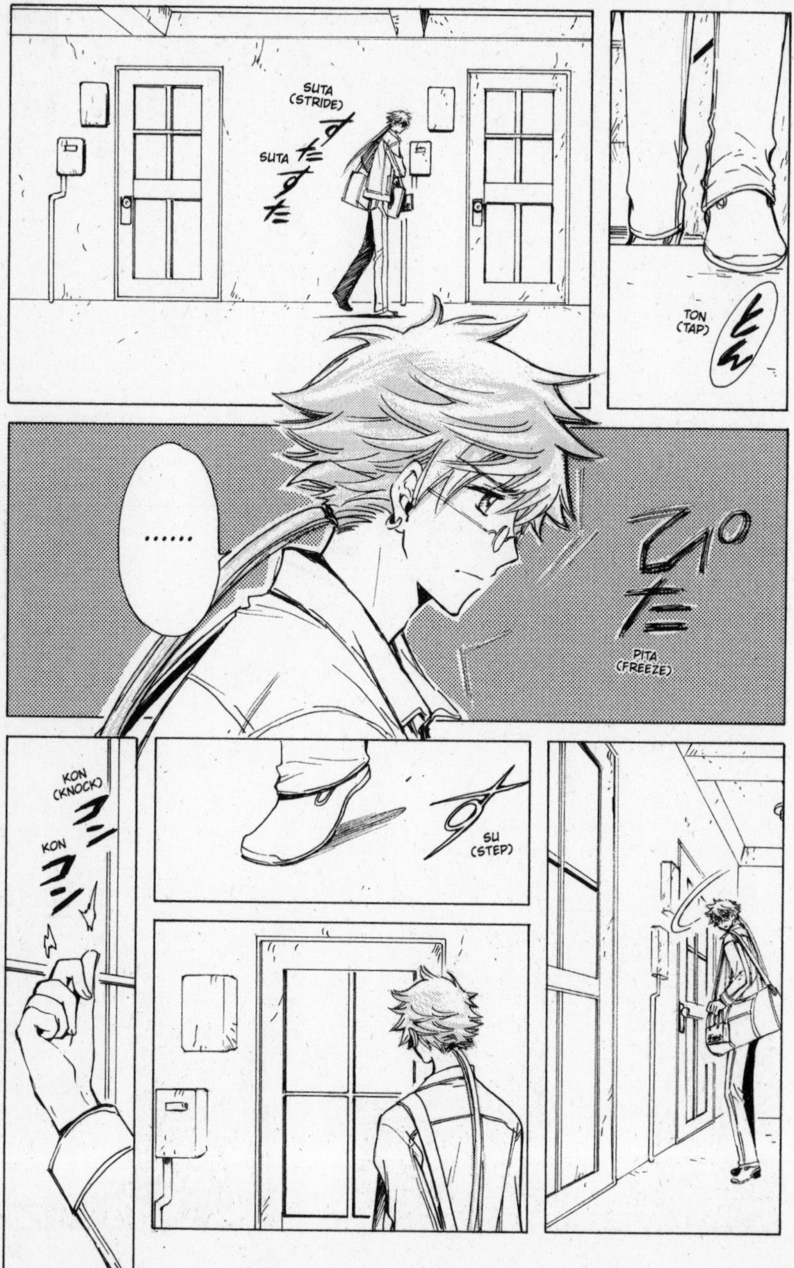
TON (TAP)
とん
SUTA (STRIDE)
すた
SUTA
すた
......
ぴた
PITA (FREEZE)
す
SU (STEP)
KON (KNOCK)
コン
KON
コン

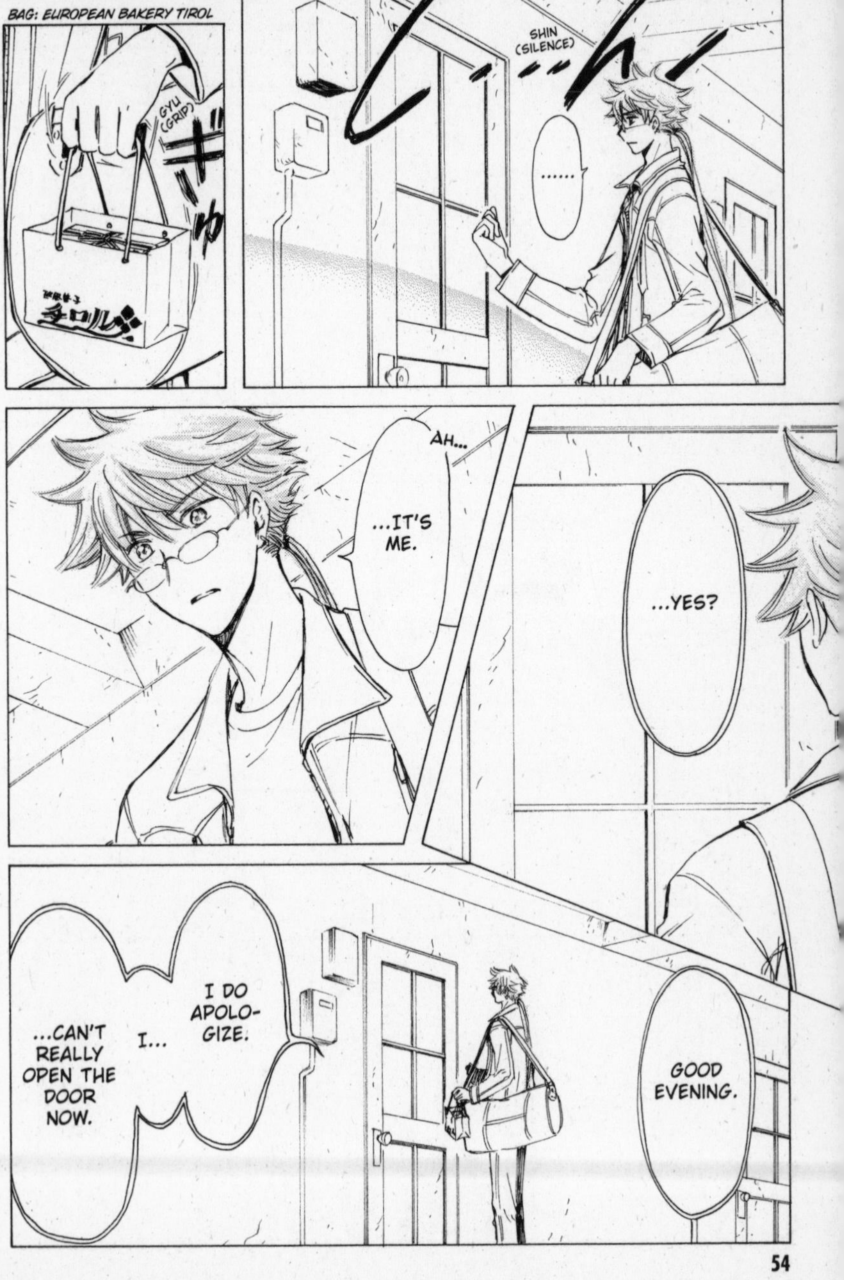
SHIN (SILENCE)
......
GYU (GRIP)
BAG: EUROPEAN BAKERY TIROL
...YES?
AH...
...IT'S ME.
GOOD EVENING.
I DO APOLOGIZE.
I...
...CAN'T REALLY OPEN THE DOOR NOW.

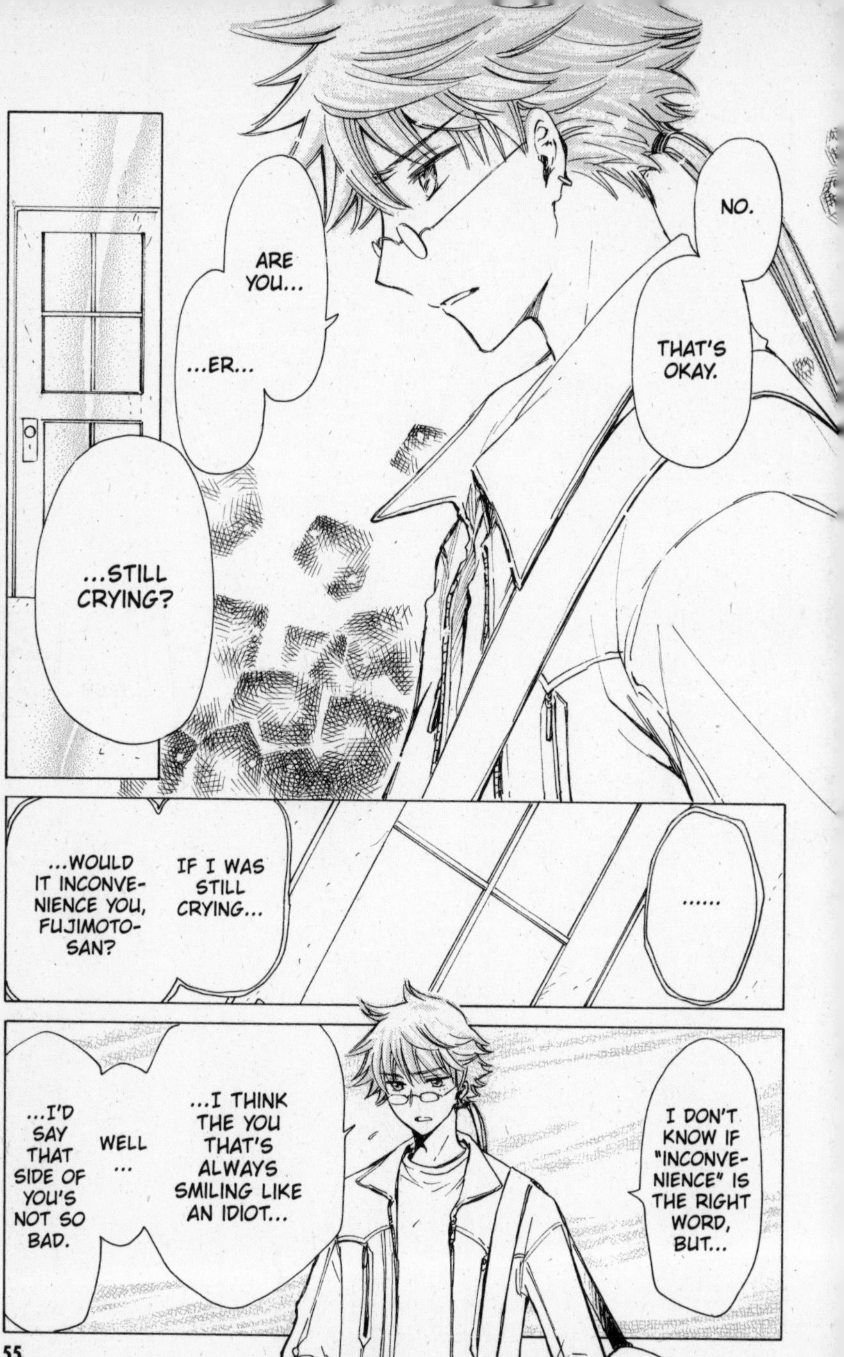
ARE YOU...
...ER...
...STILL CRYING?
NO.
THAT'S OKAY.
......
IF I WAS STILL CRYING...
...WOULD IT INCONVENIENCE YOU, FUJIMOTO-SAN?
I DON'T KNOW IF "INCONVENIENCE" IS THE RIGHT WORD, BUT...
...I THINK THE YOU THAT'S ALWAYS SMILING LIKE AN IDIOT...
WELL ...
...I'D SAY THAT SIDE OF YOU'S NOT SO BAD.

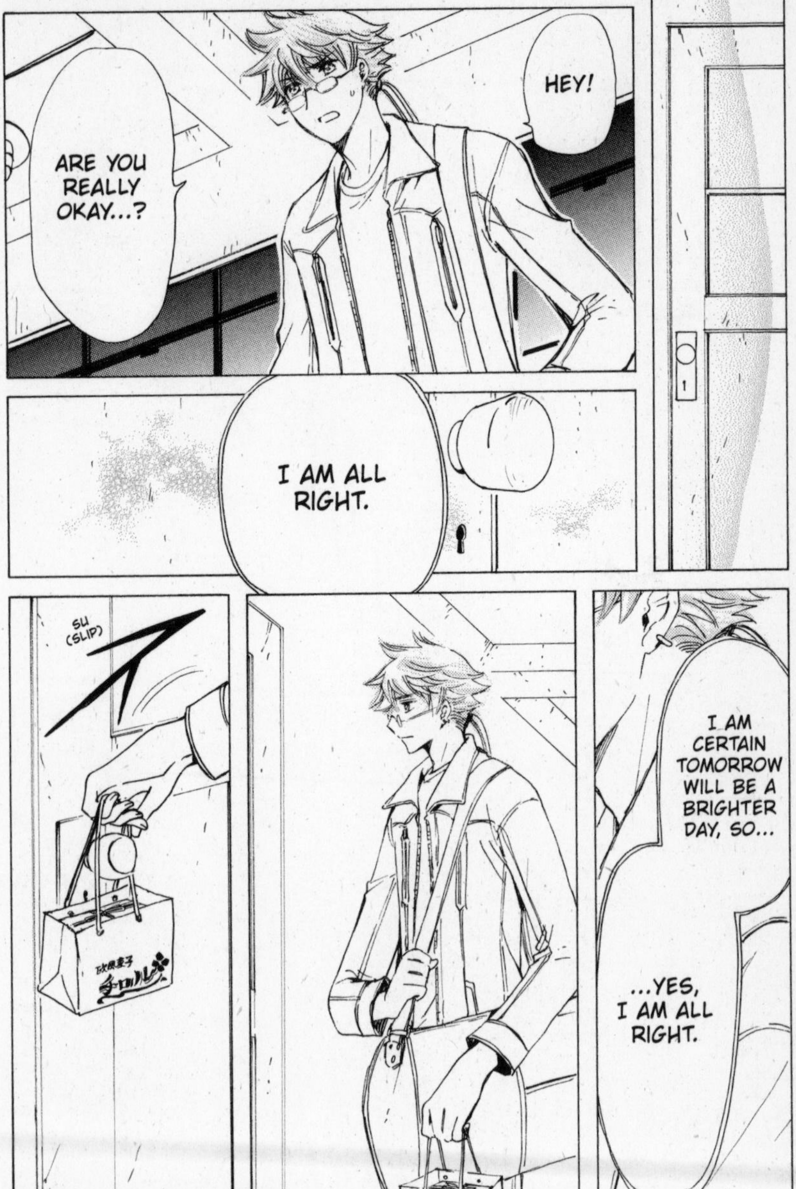
HEY!
ARE YOU REALLY OKAY...?
I AM ALL RIGHT.
I AM CERTAIN TOMORROW WILL BE A BRIGHTER DAY, SO...
...YES, I AM ALL RIGHT.
SU (SLIP)

BAG: EUROPEAN BAKERY TIROL

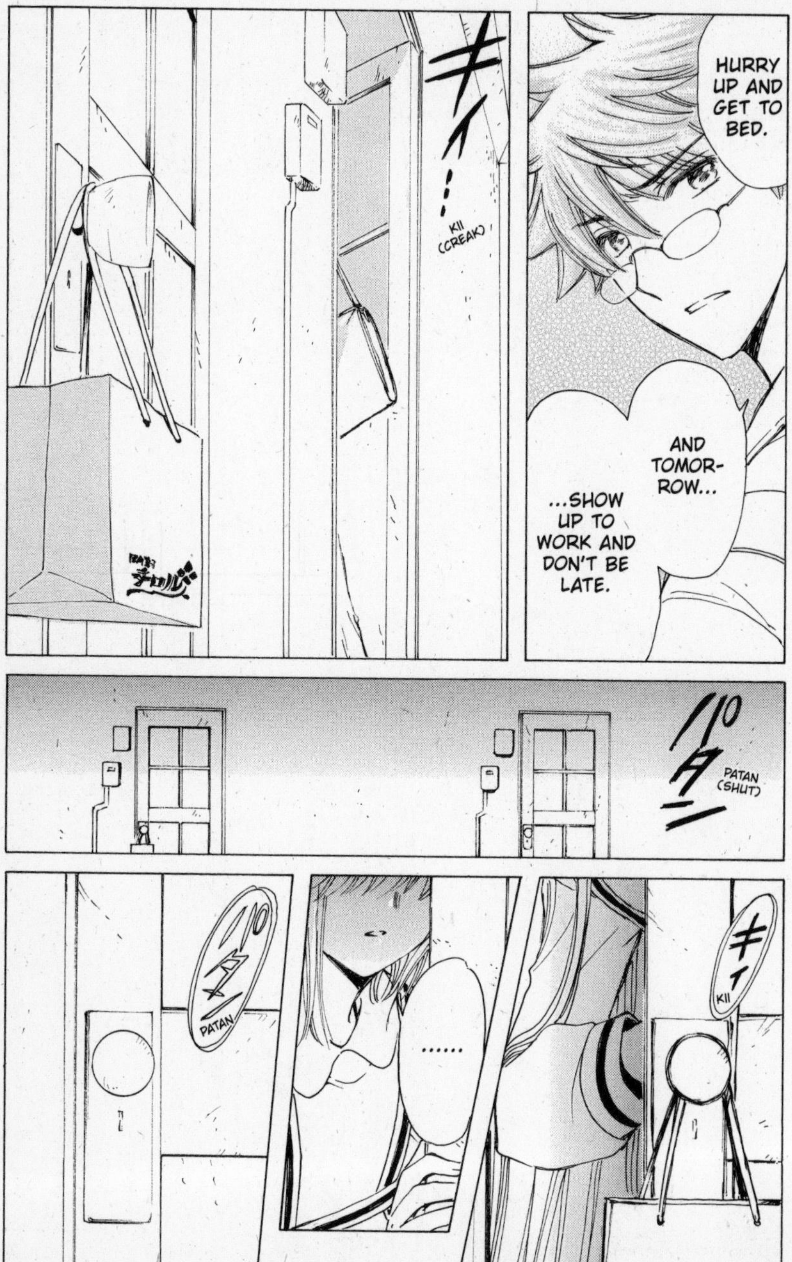
HURRY UP AND GET TO BED.
AND TOMOR-ROW...
...SHOW UP TO WORK AND DON'T BE LATE.
キイ!!
KII (CREAK)
パタン
PATAN (SHUT)
キイ
KII
......
パタン
PATAN

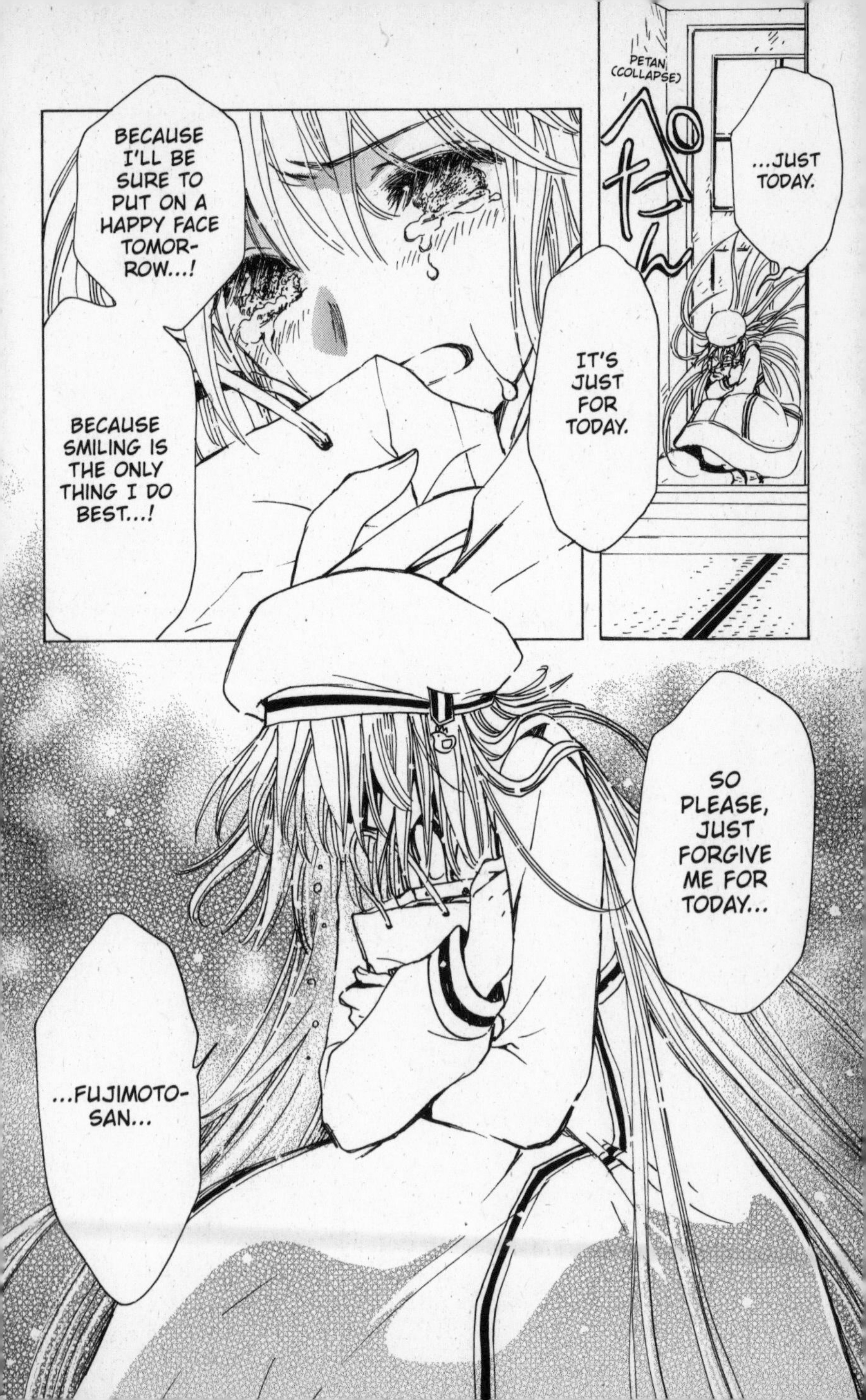
ぺたん
PETAN (COLLAPSE)
...JUST TODAY.
IT'S JUST FOR TODAY.
BECAUSE I'LL BE SURE TO PUT ON A HAPPY FACE TOMOR-ROW...!
BECAUSE SMILING IS THE ONLY THING I DO BEST...!
SO PLEASE, JUST FORGIVE ME FOR TODAY...
...FUJIMOTO-SAN...

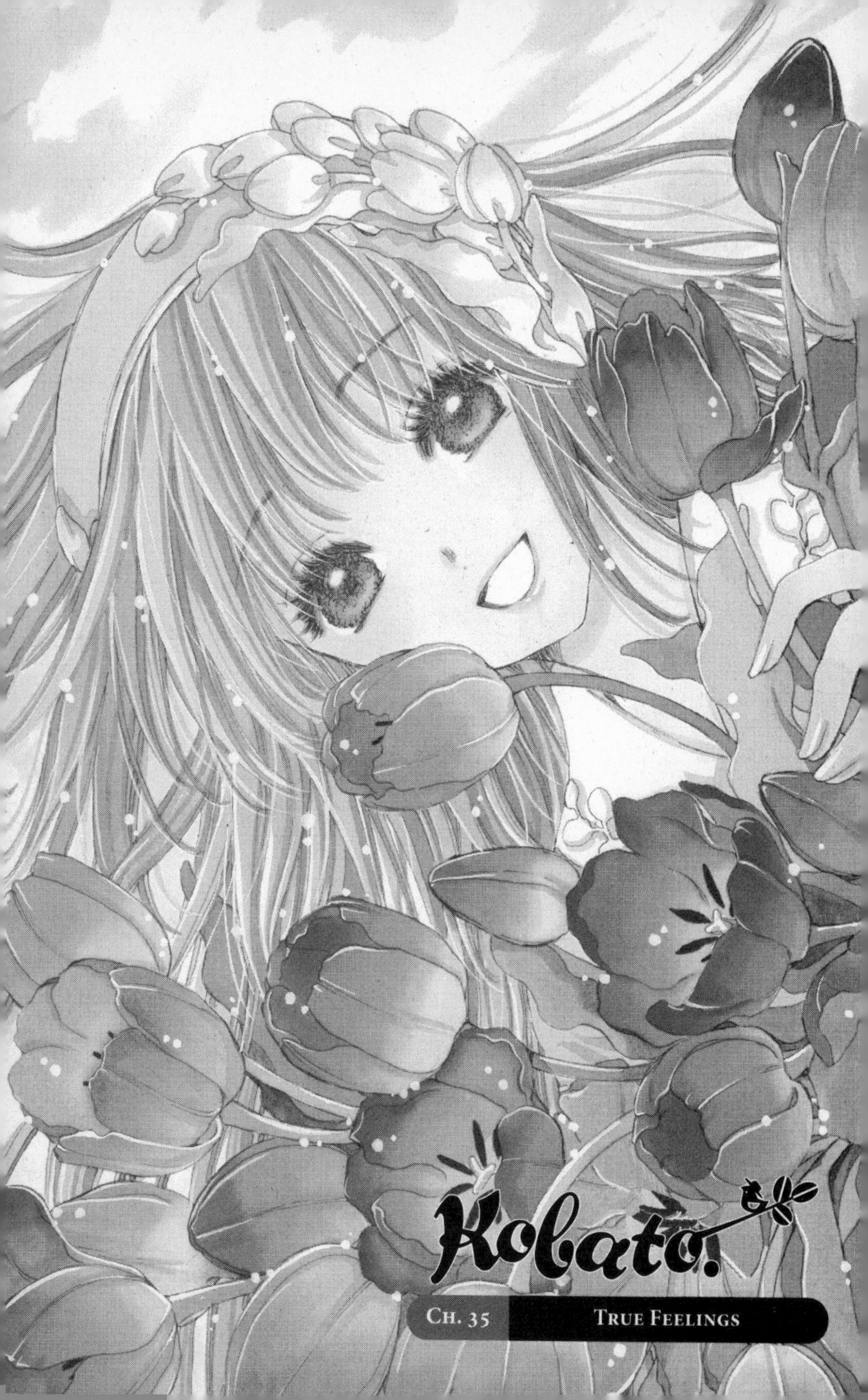
Kobato.
Ch. 35
True Feelings

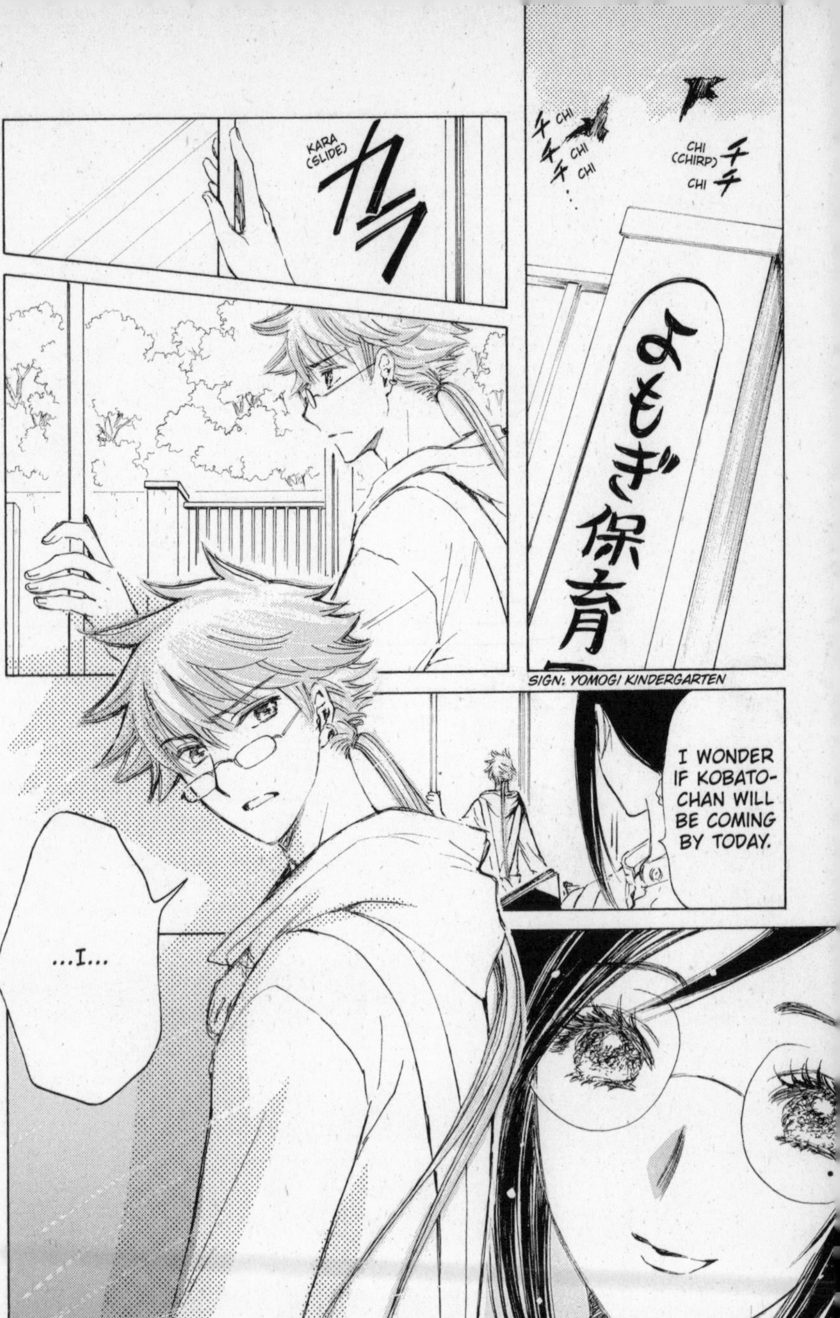

チチチ…
CHI CHI CHI...
チチ
CHI (CHIRP) CHI
よもぎ保育
SIGN: YOMOGI KINDERGARTEN
カラ
KARA (SLIDE)
I WONDER IF KOBATO-CHAN WILL BE COMING BY TODAY.
...I...

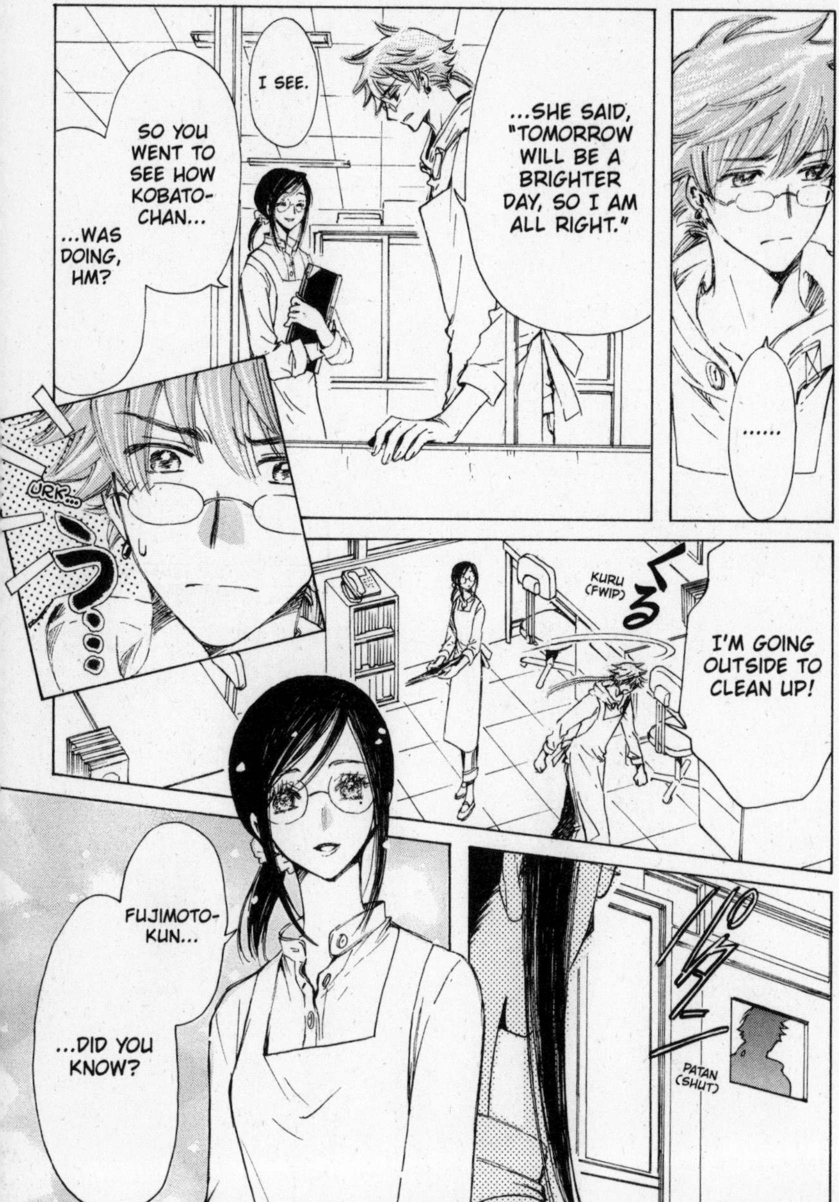
......
...SHE SAID, "TOMORROW WILL BE A BRIGHTER DAY, SO I AM ALL RIGHT."
I SEE.
SO YOU WENT TO SEE HOW KOBATO-CHAN...
...WAS DOING, HM?
I'M GOING OUTSIDE TO CLEAN UP!
くる
KURU (FWIP)
URK...
う…
パタン
PATAN (SHUT)
FUJIMOTO-KUN...
...DID YOU KNOW?

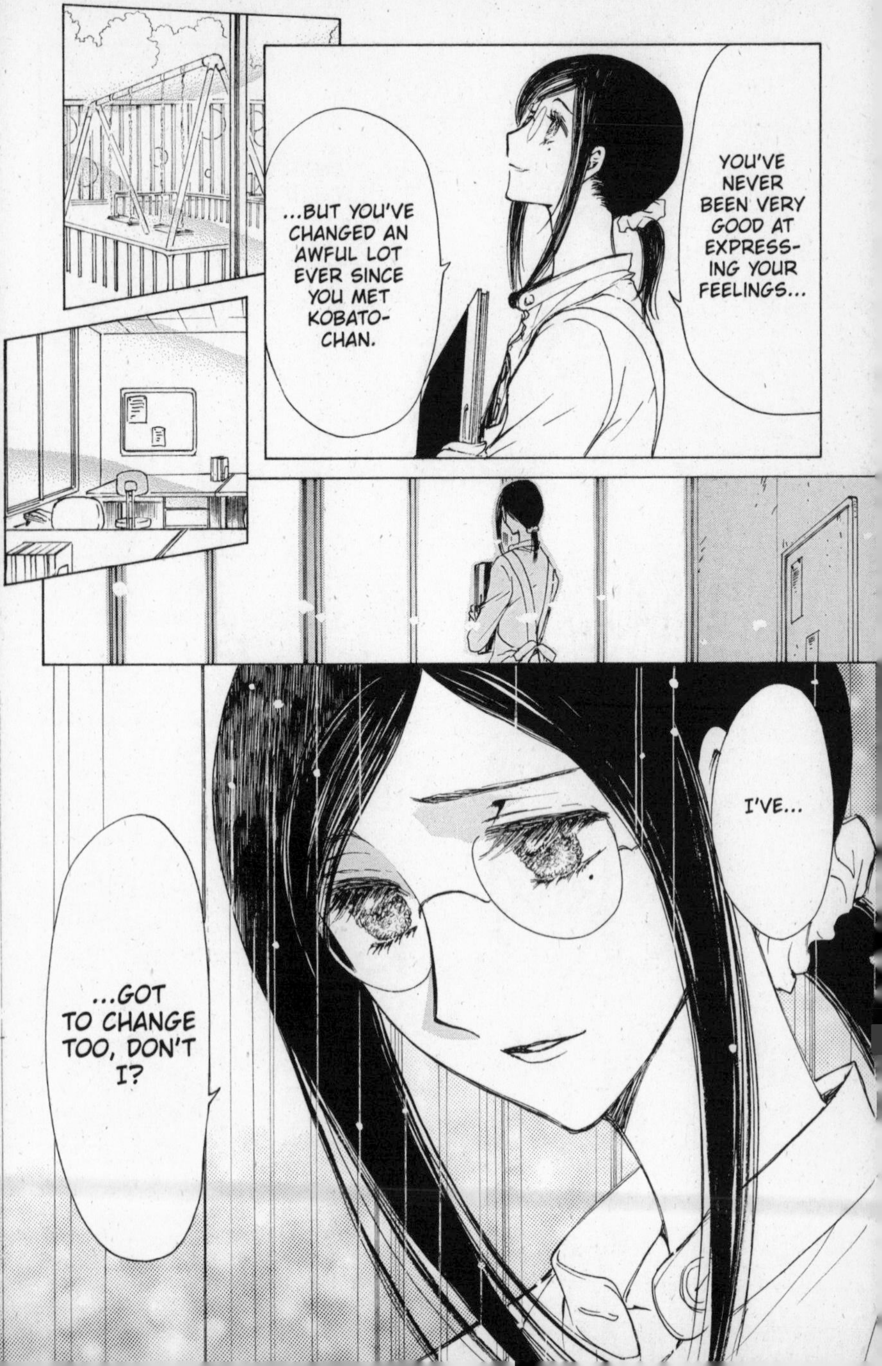
YOU'VE NEVER BEEN VERY GOOD AT EXPRESSING YOUR FEELINGS...
...BUT YOU'VE CHANGED AN AWFUL LOT EVER SINCE YOU MET KOBATO-CHAN.
I'VE...
...GOT TO CHANGE TOO, DON'T I?

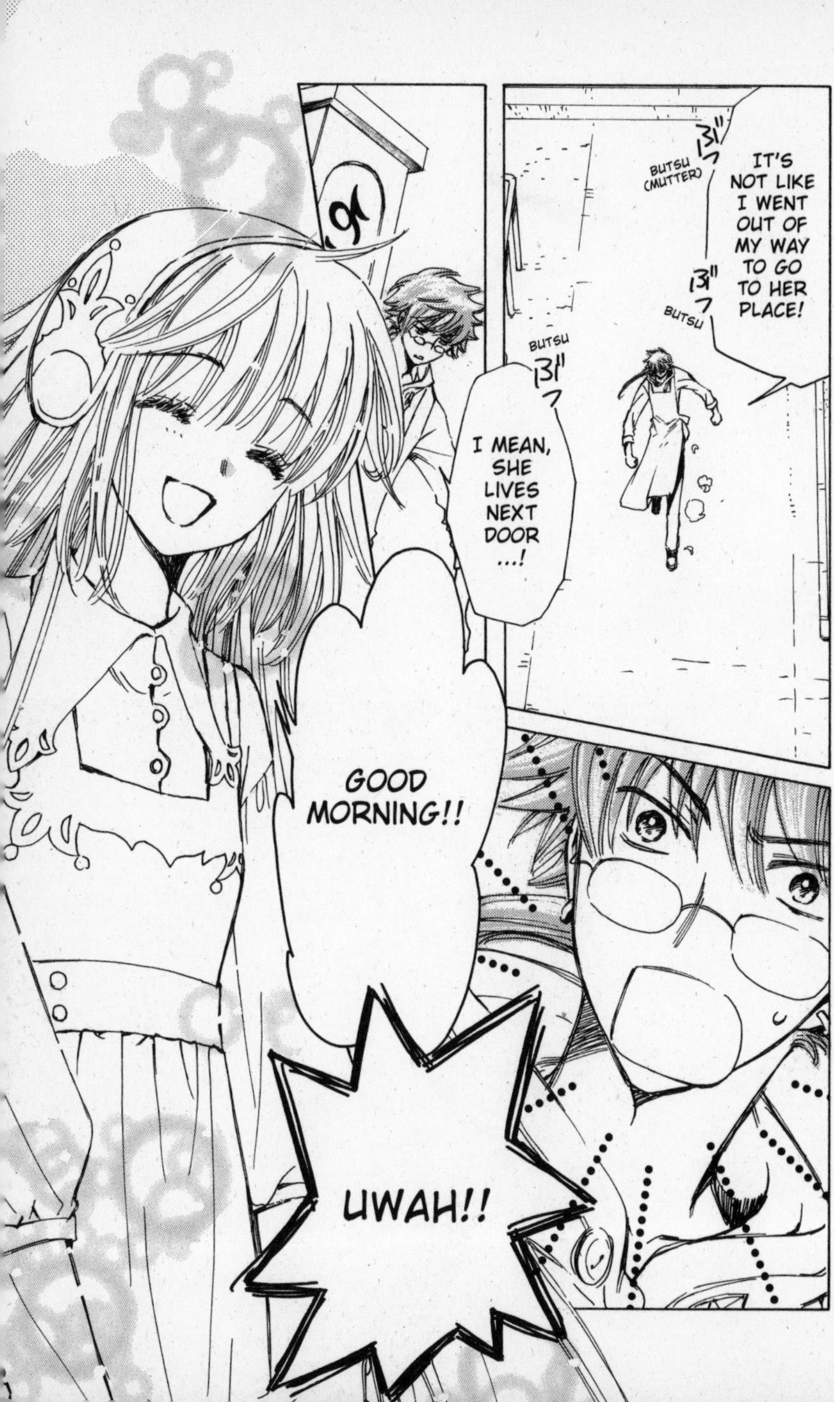

IT'S NOT LIKE I WENT OUT OF MY WAY TO GO TO HER PLACE!
BUTSU (MUTTER)
BUTSU
BUTSU
I MEAN, SHE LIVES NEXT DOOR ...!
GOOD MORNING!!
UWAH!!

SFX: DOKI (BADUM) DOKI

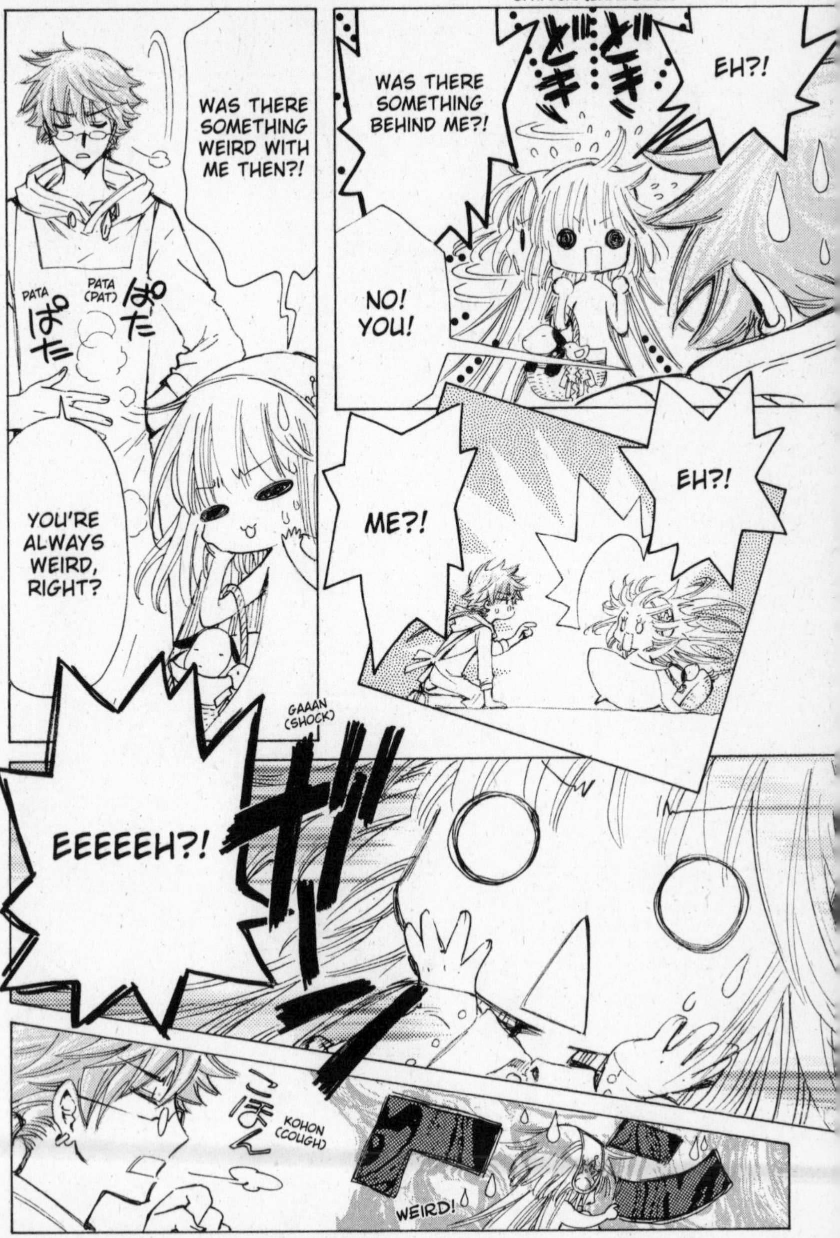
どきどき
EH?!
WAS THERE SOMETHING BEHIND ME?!
NO! YOU!
EH?!
ME?!
WAS THERE SOMETHING WEIRD WITH ME THEN?!
PATA (PAT) ぱた
PATA ぱた
YOU'RE ALWAYS WEIRD, RIGHT?
GAAAN (SHOCK)
EEEEEH?!
こほん
KOHON (COUGH)
WEIRD!

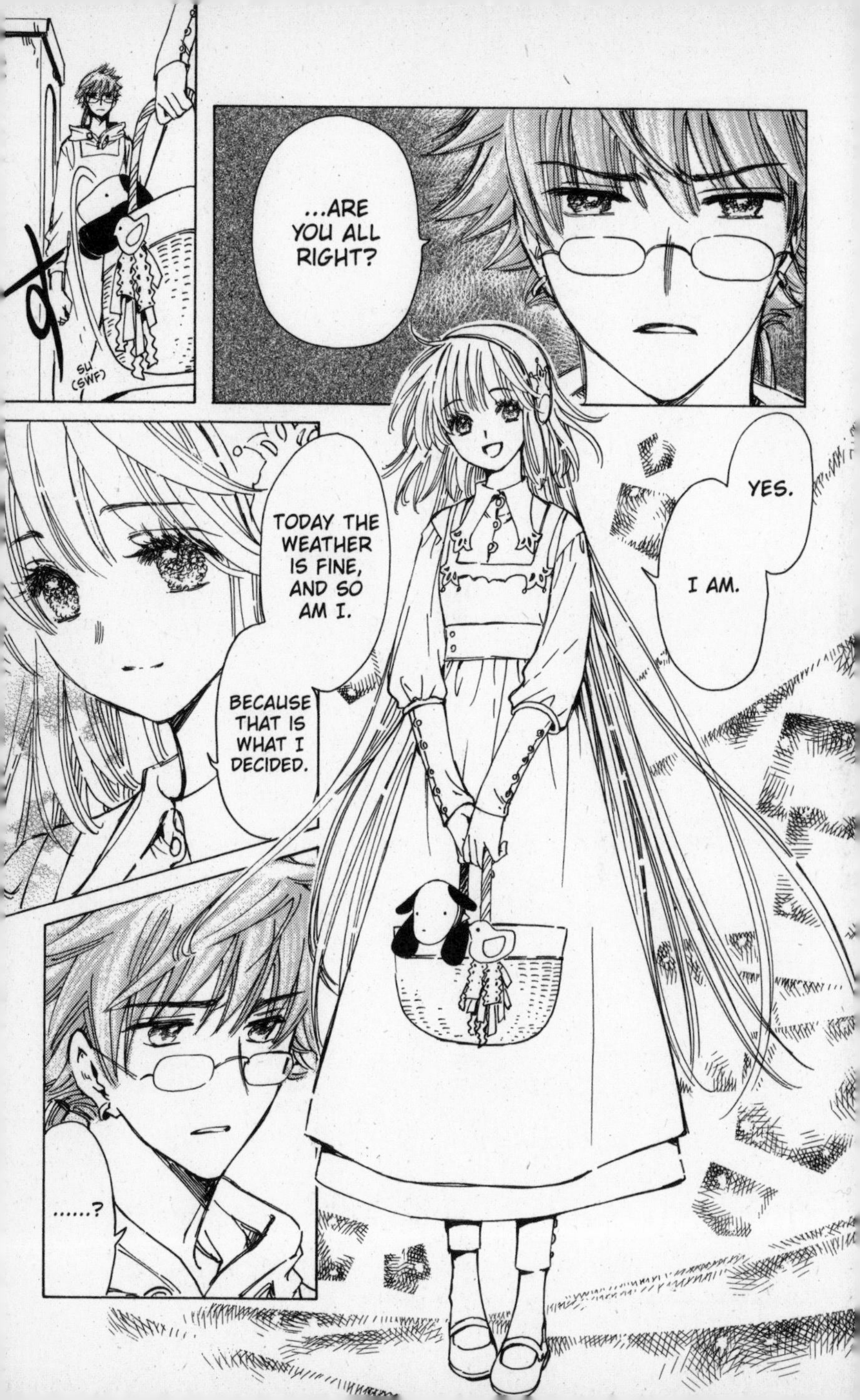
...ARE YOU ALL RIGHT?
SU (SWF)
YES.
I AM.
TODAY THE WEATHER IS FINE, AND SO AM I.
BECAUSE THAT IS WHAT I DECIDED.
......?

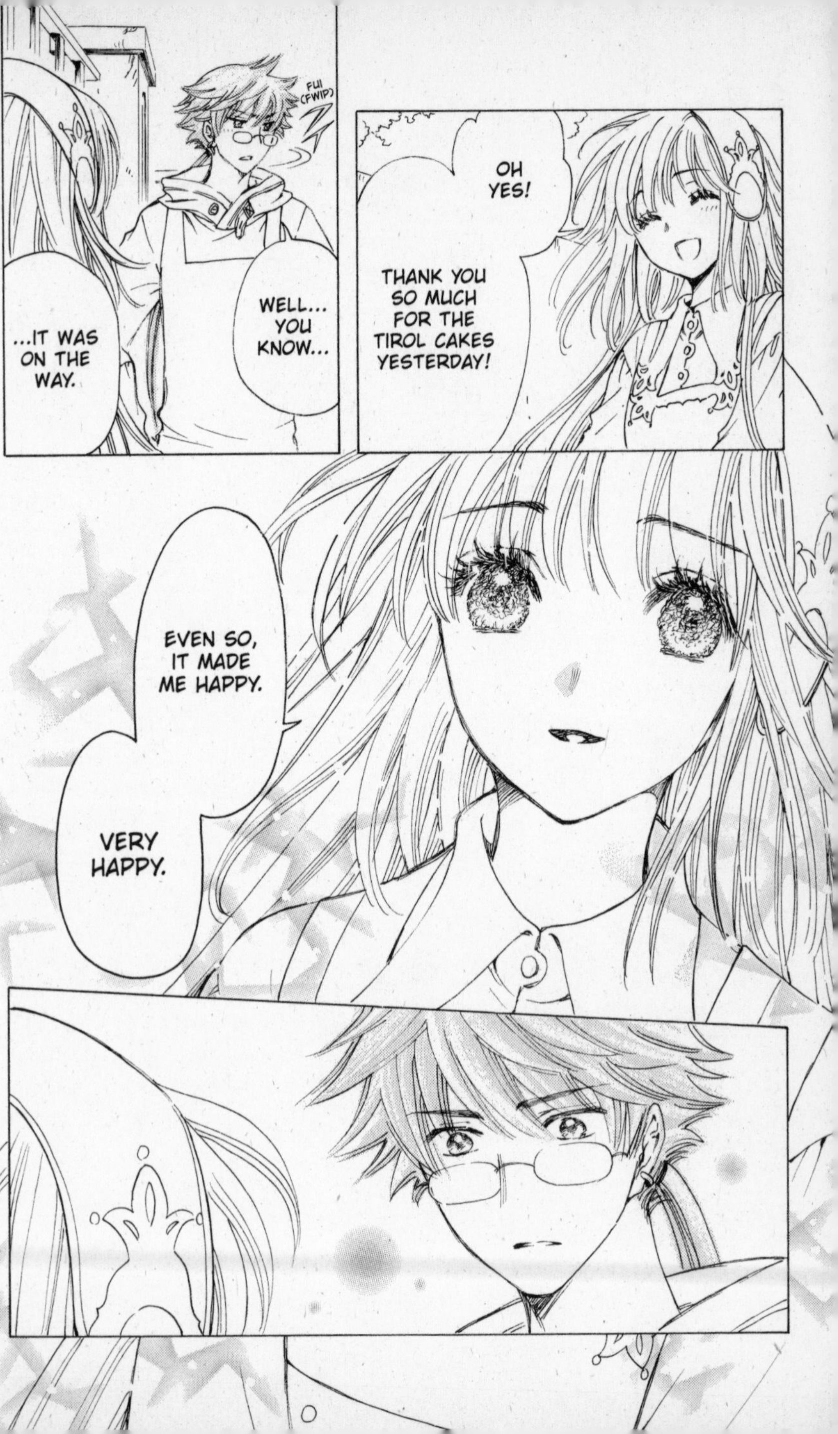
OH YES!
THANK YOU SO MUCH FOR THE TIROL CAKES YESTERDAY!
FUI (FWIP)
WELL... YOU KNOW...
...IT WAS ON THE WAY.
EVEN SO, IT MADE ME HAPPY.
VERY HAPPY.

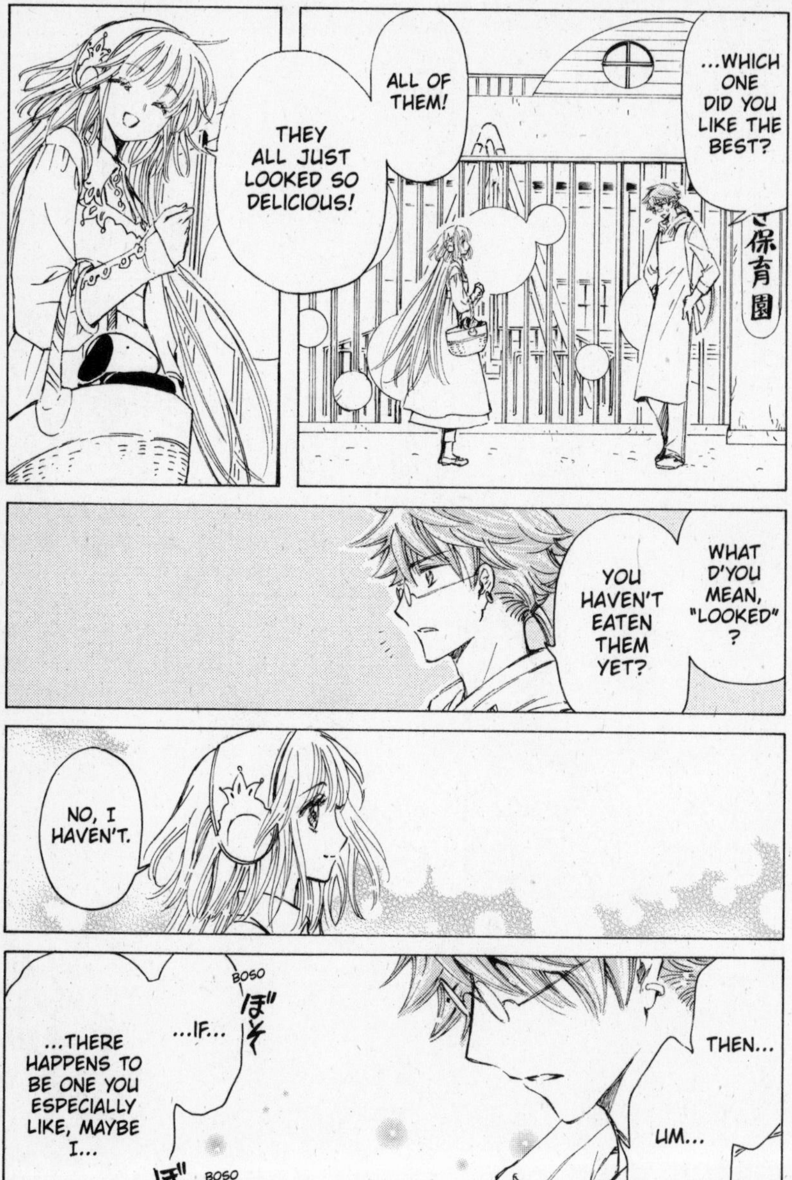
...WHICH ONE DID YOU LIKE THE BEST?
保育園
ALL OF THEM!
THEY ALL JUST LOOKED SO DELICIOUS!
WHAT D'YOU MEAN, "LOOKED"?
YOU HAVEN'T EATEN THEM YET?
NO, I HAVEN'T.
THEN...
UM...
BOSO
ぼそ
...IF...
...THERE HAPPENS TO BE ONE YOU ESPECIALLY LIKE, MAYBE I...
ぼそ
BOSO (MUMBLE)

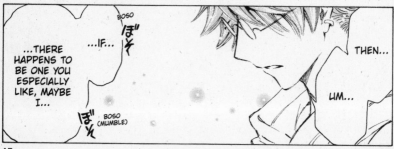

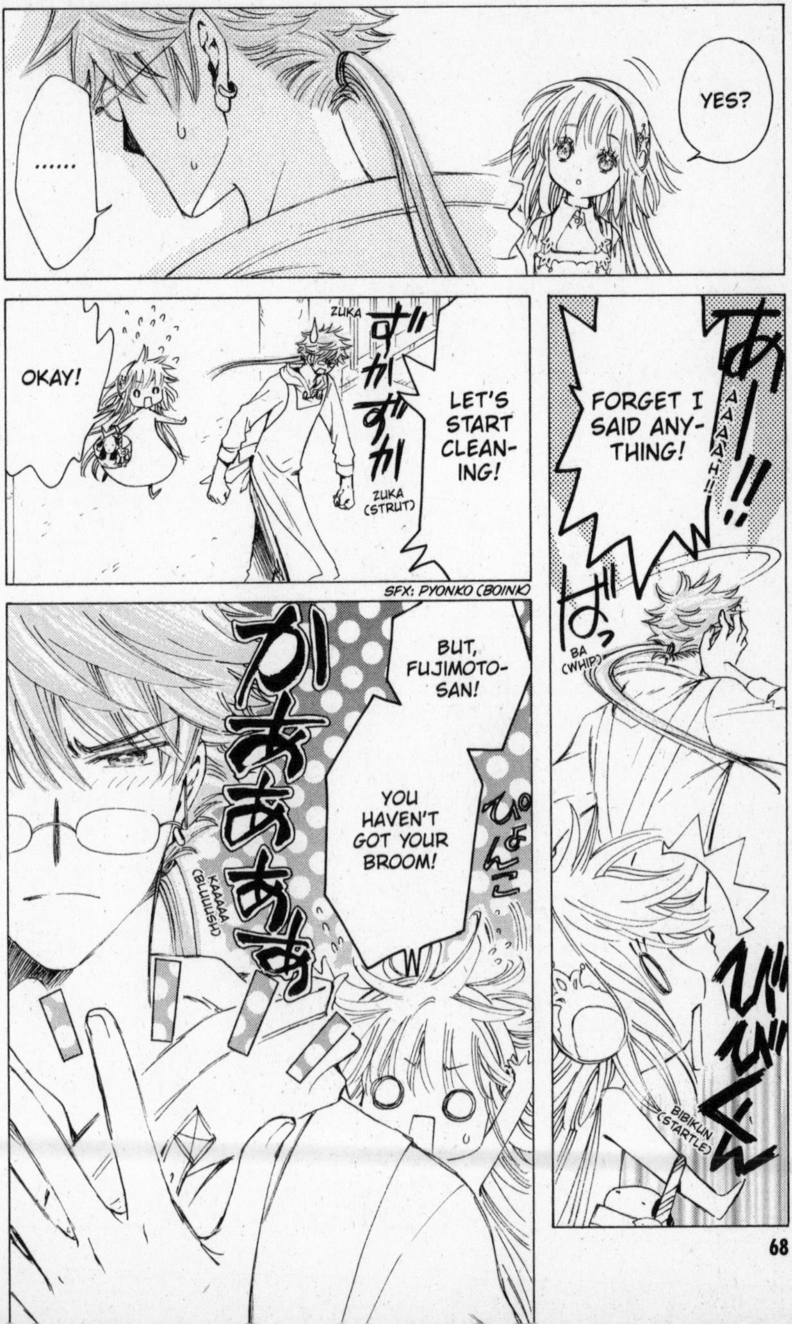
YES?
......
AAAAH!!
FORGET I SAID ANY-THING!
BA (WHIP)
BIBIKUN (STARTLE)
ZUKA
LET'S START CLEAN-ING!
ZUKA (STRUT)
OKAY!
SFX: PYONKO (BOINK)
BUT, FUJIMOTO-SAN!
YOU HAVEN'T GOT YOUR BROOM!
KAAAAA (BLUUUSH)

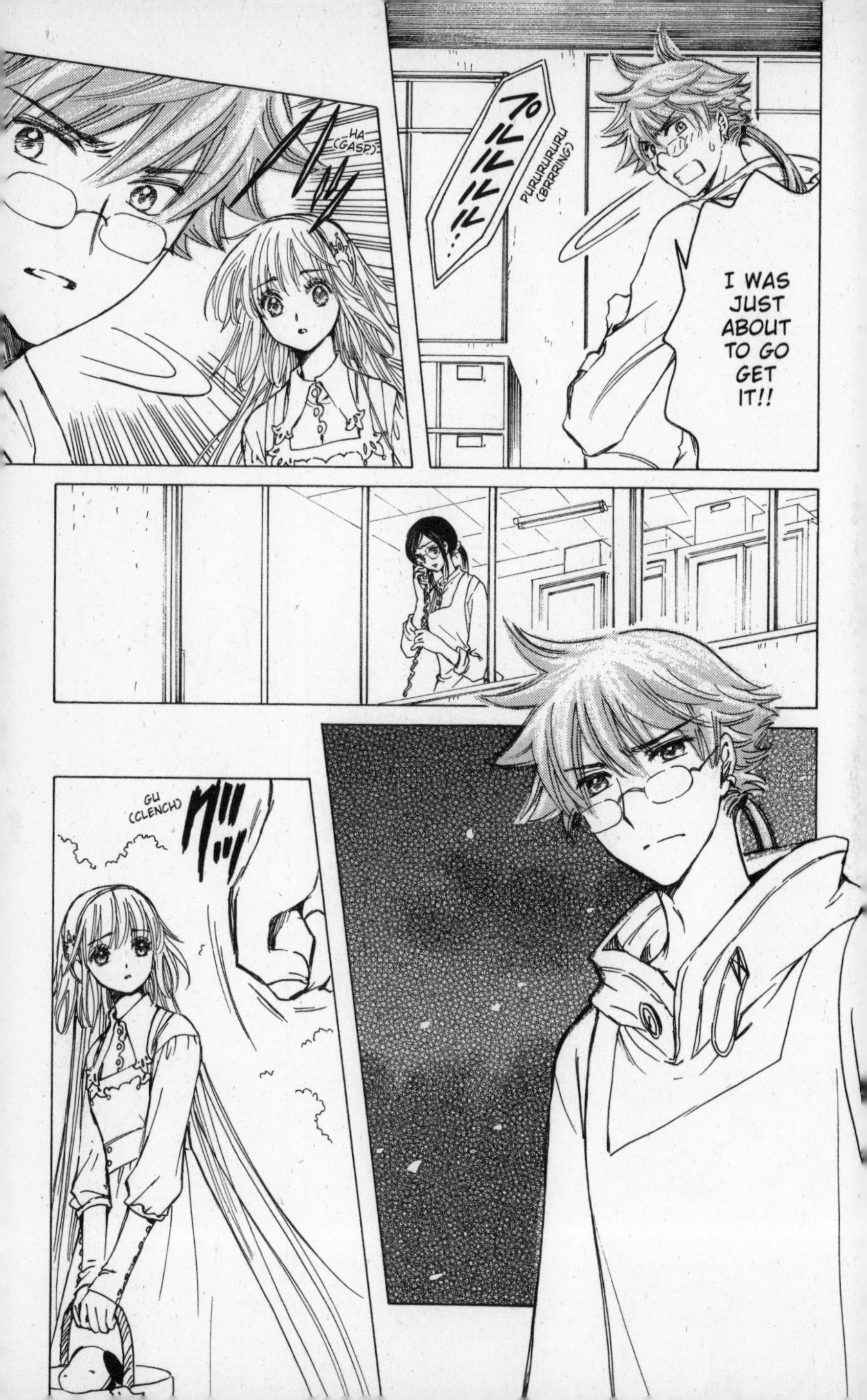
プルルルル…!!
PURURURURU (BRRRING)
I WAS JUST ABOUT TO GO GET IT!!
ハッ
HA (GASP)
グッ
GU (CLENCH)

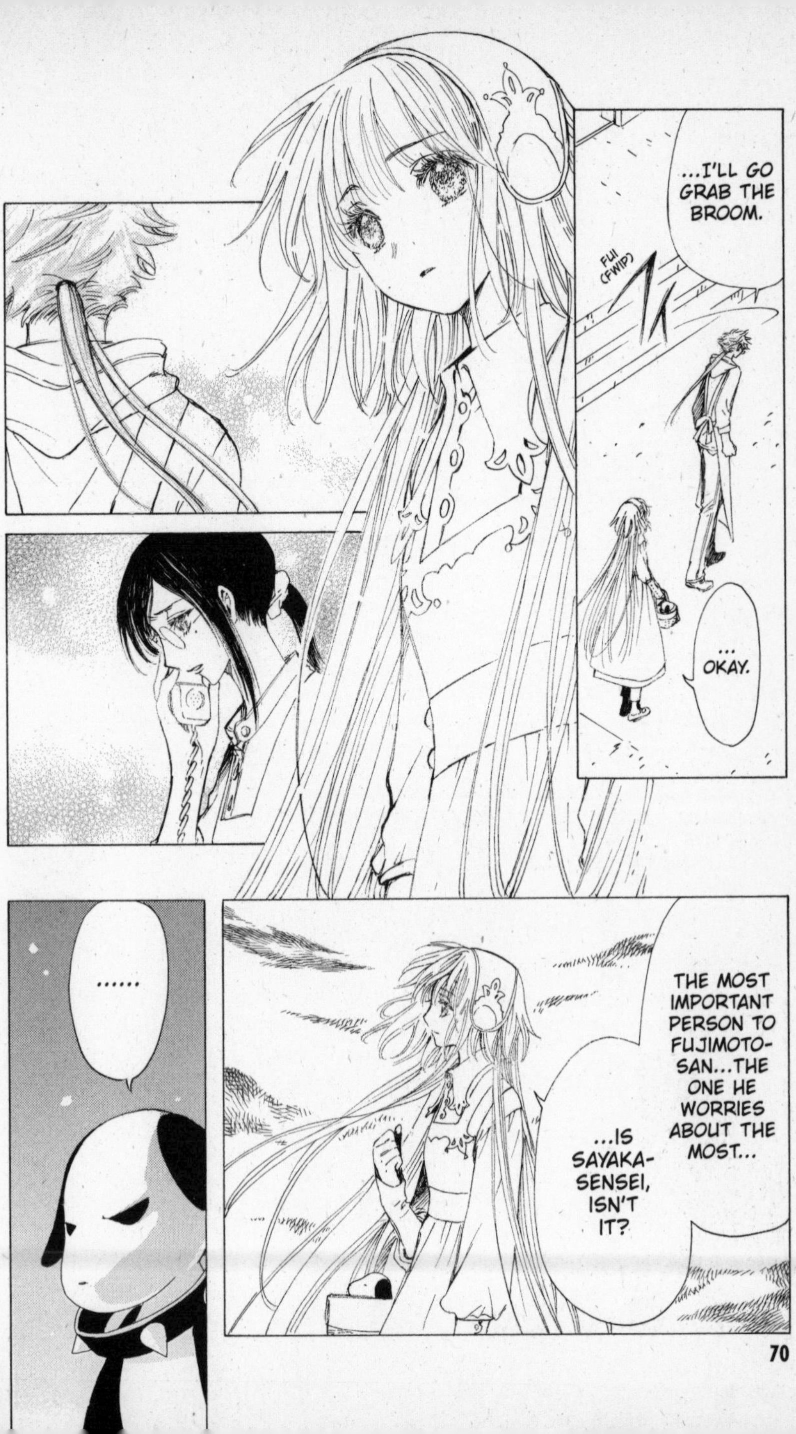
...I'LL GO GRAB THE BROOM.
FUI (FWIP)
... OKAY.
THE MOST IMPORTANT PERSON TO FUJIMOTO-SAN...THE ONE HE WORRIES ABOUT THE MOST...
...IS SAYAKA-SENSEI, ISN'T IT?
......

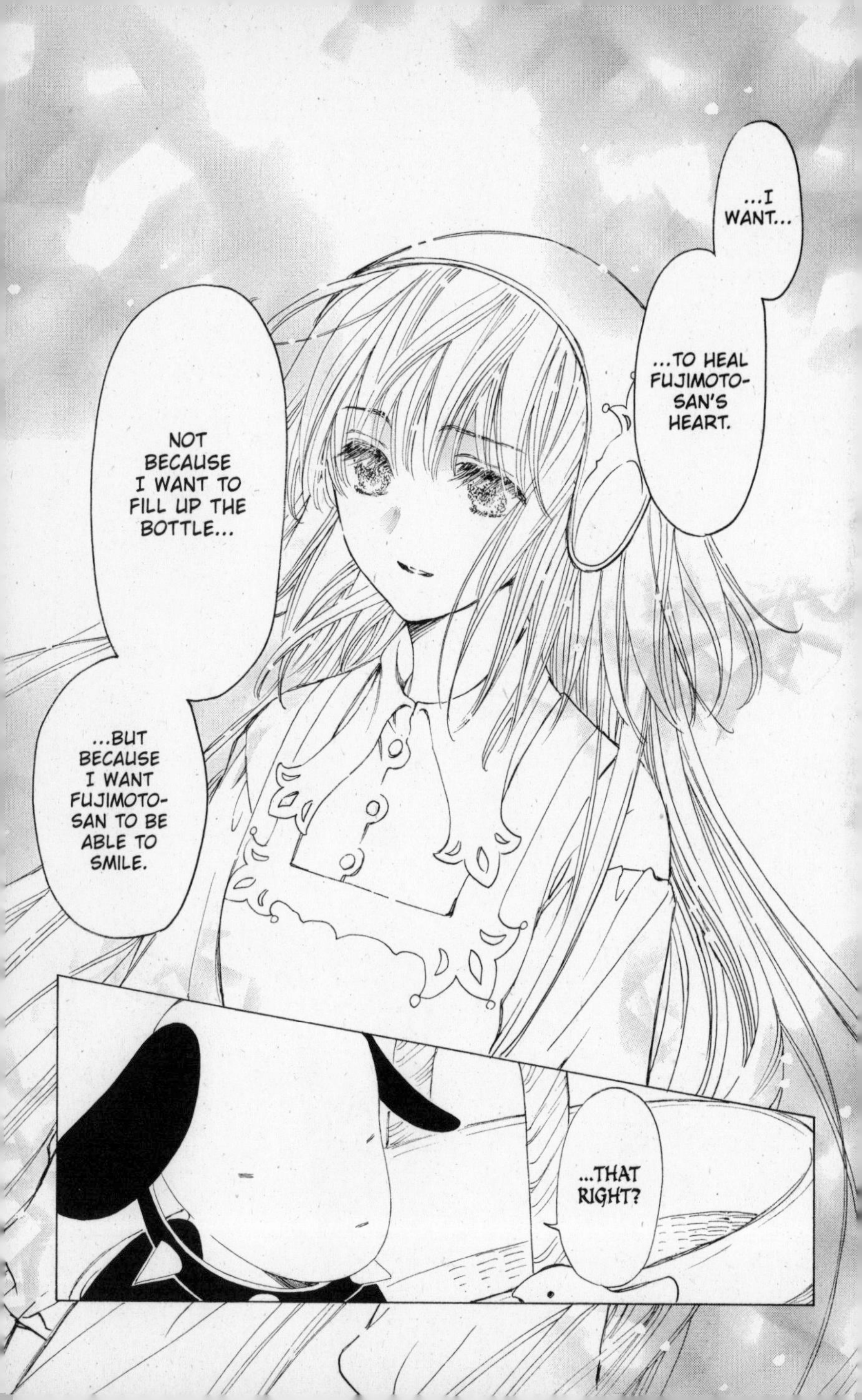
...I WANT...
...TO HEAL FUJIMOTO-SAN'S HEART.
NOT BECAUSE I WANT TO FILL UP THE BOTTLE...
...BUT BECAUSE I WANT FUJIMOTO-SAN TO BE ABLE TO SMILE.
...THAT RIGHT?

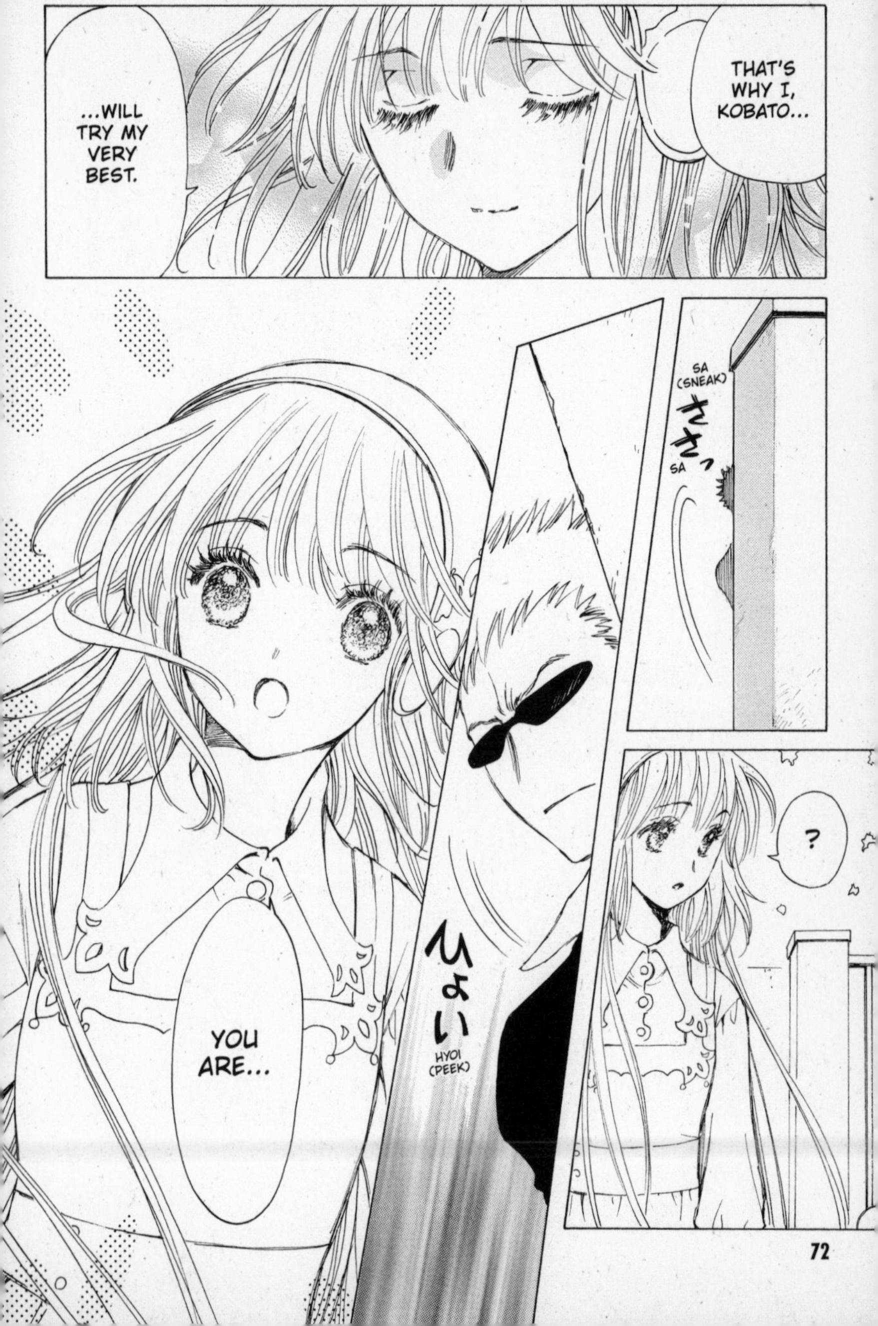
THAT'S WHY I, KOBATO...
...WILL TRY MY VERY BEST.
SA (SNEAK)
さ
さっ
SA
?
ひょい
HYOI (PEEK)
YOU ARE...

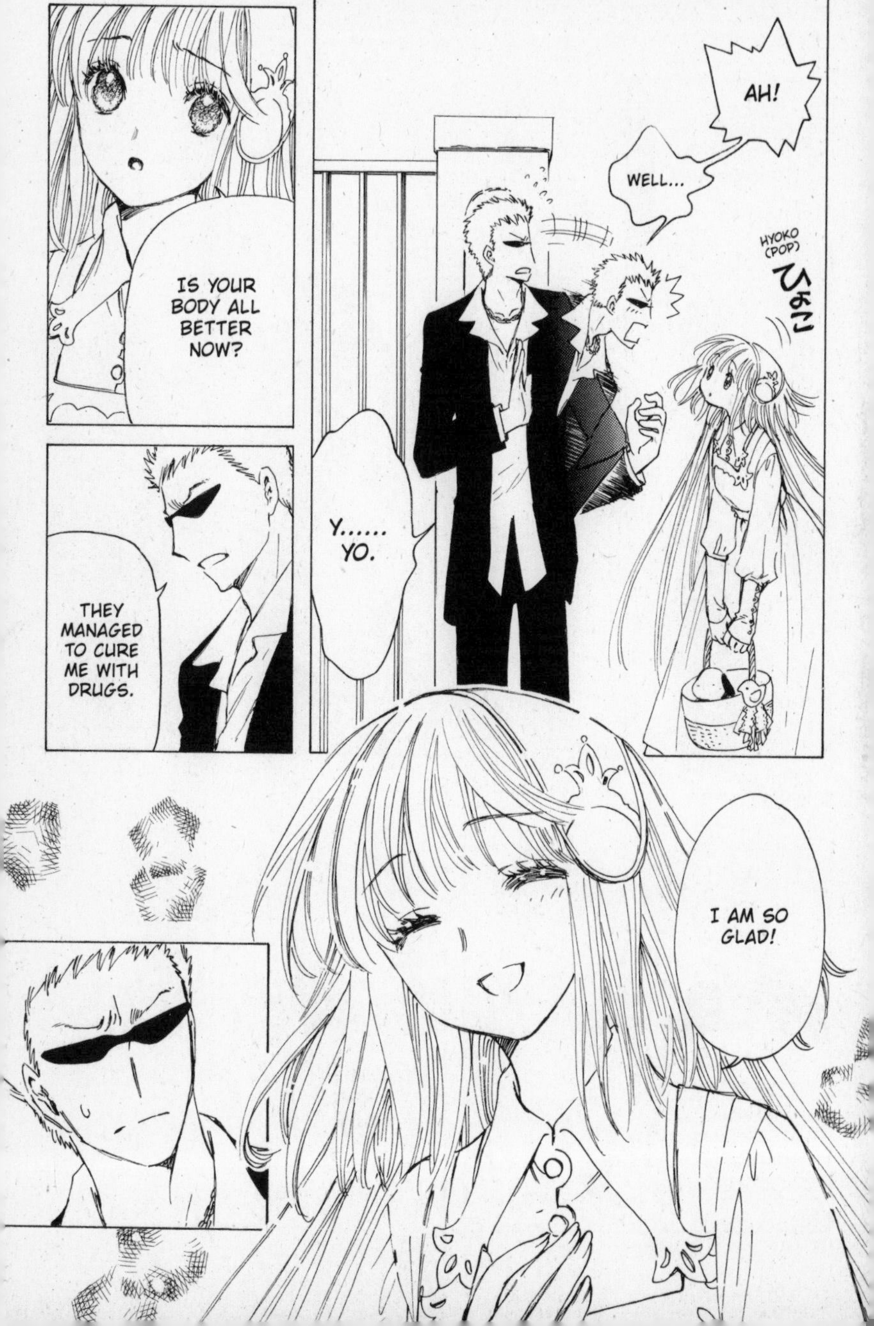
AH!
WELL...
HYOKO (POP)
ひょこ
Y...... YO.
IS YOUR BODY ALL BETTER NOW?
THEY MANAGED TO CURE ME WITH DRUGS.
I AM SO GLAD!

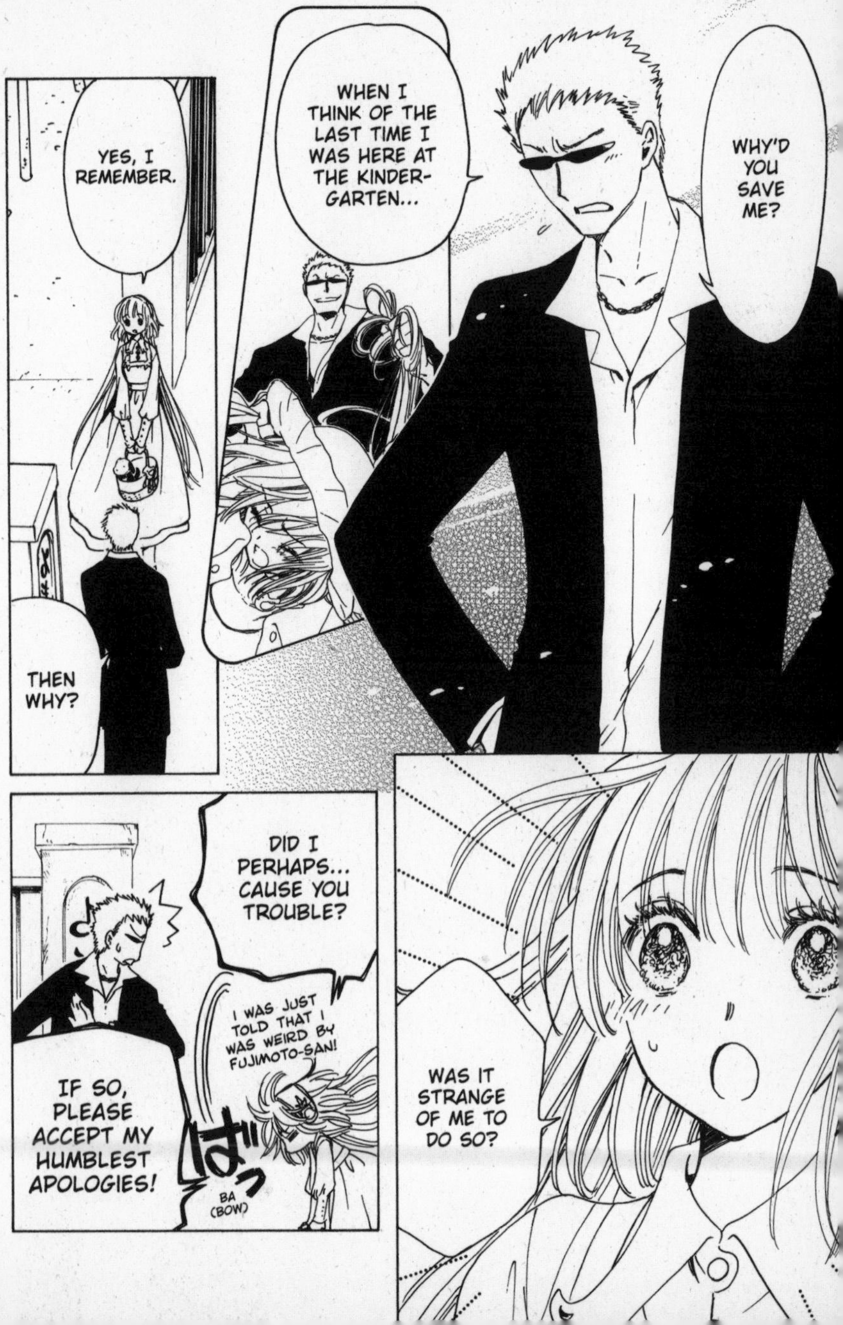
WHY'D YOU SAVE ME?
WHEN I THINK OF THE LAST TIME I WAS HERE AT THE KINDER-GARTEN...
YES, I REMEMBER.
THEN WHY?
WAS IT STRANGE OF ME TO DO SO?
DID I PERHAPS... CAUSE YOU TROUBLE?
I WAS JUST TOLD THAT I WAS WEIRD BY FUJIMOTO-SAN!
IF SO, PLEASE ACCEPT MY HUMBLEST APOLOGIES!
BA (BOW)

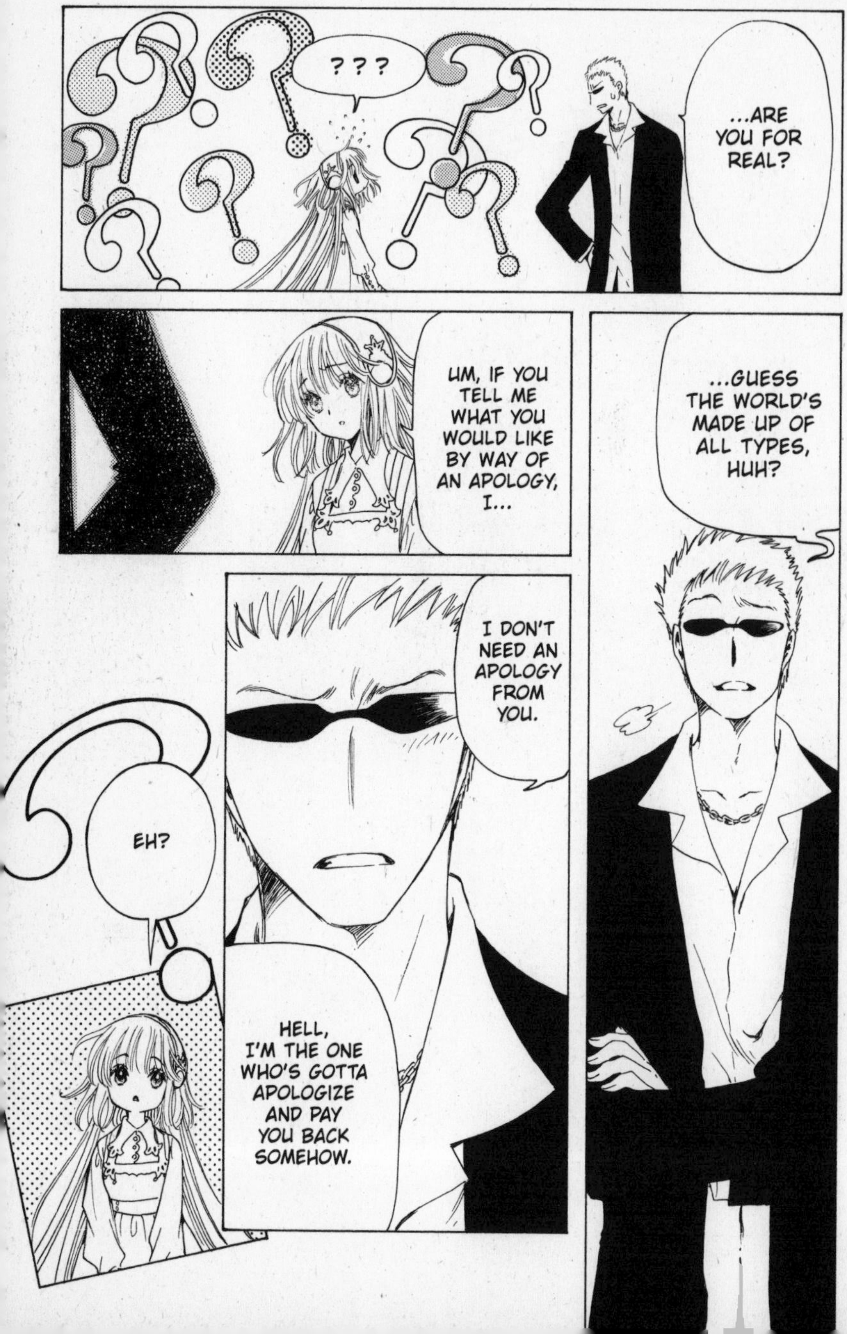
...ARE YOU FOR REAL?
???
...GUESS THE WORLD'S MADE UP OF ALL TYPES, HUH?
UM, IF YOU TELL ME WHAT YOU WOULD LIKE BY WAY OF AN APOLOGY, I...
I DON'T NEED AN APOLOGY FROM YOU.
HELL, I'M THE ONE WHO'S GOTTA APOLOGIZE AND PAY YOU BACK SOMEHOW.
EH?

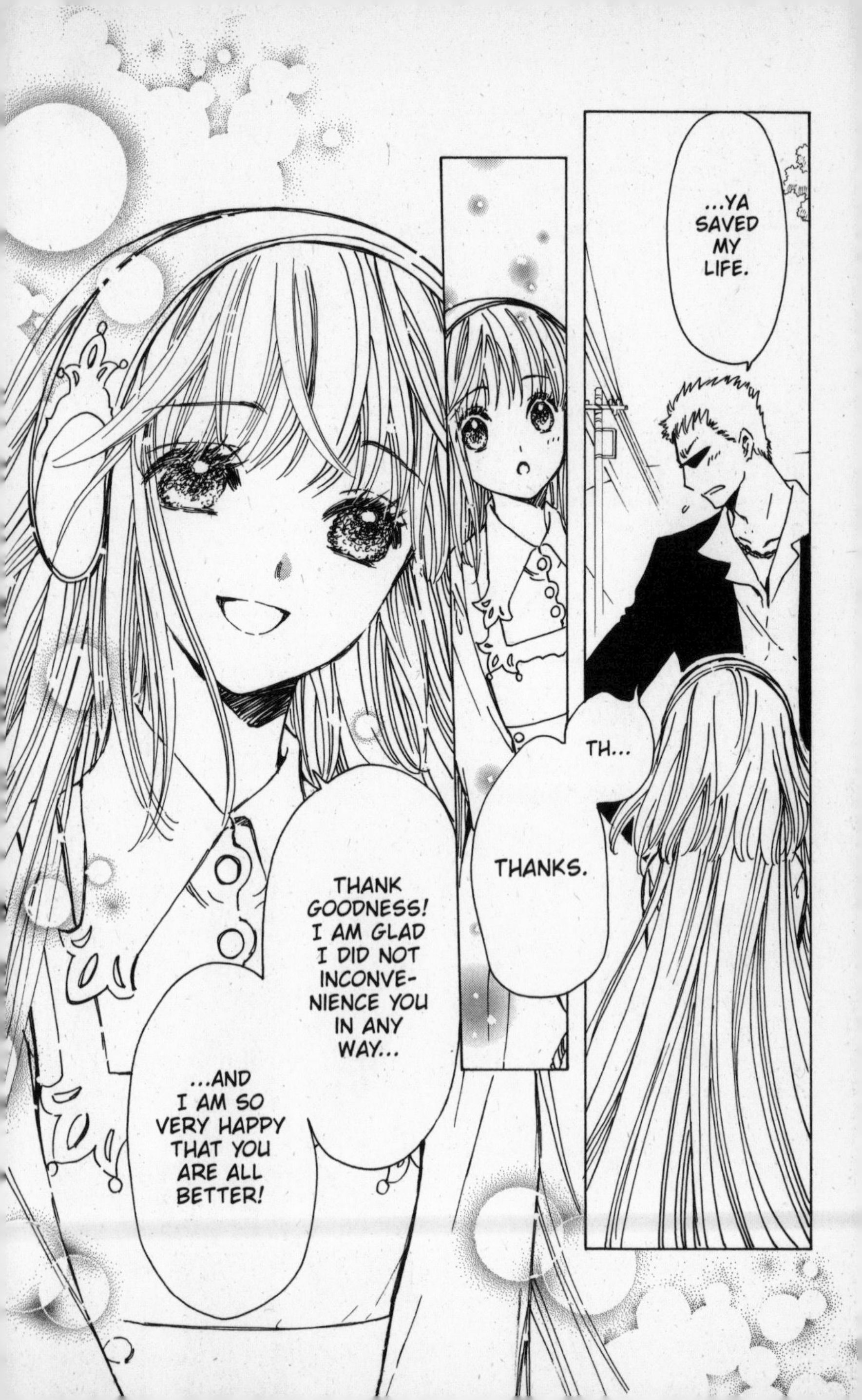
...YA SAVED MY LIFE.
TH...
THANKS.
THANK GOODNESS! I AM GLAD I DID NOT INCONVE-NIENCE YOU IN ANY WAY...
...AND I AM SO VERY HAPPY THAT YOU ARE ALL BETTER!

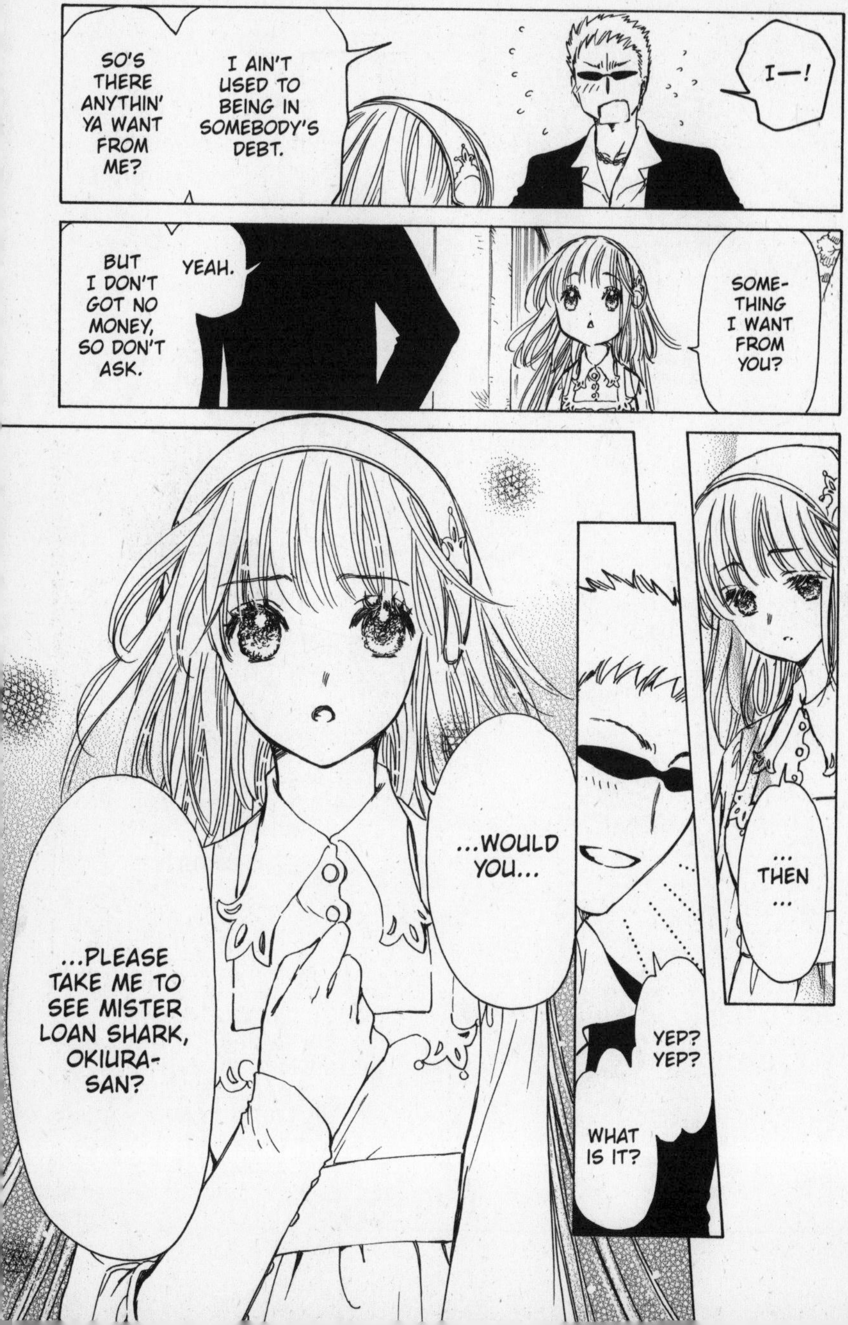
I—!
I AIN'T USED TO BEING IN SOMEBODY'S DEBT.
SO'S THERE ANYTHIN' YA WANT FROM ME?
SOME-THING I WANT FROM YOU?
YEAH.
BUT I DON'T GOT NO MONEY, SO DON'T ASK.
...THEN...
YEP? YEP?
WHAT IS IT?
...WOULD YOU...
...PLEASE TAKE ME TO SEE MISTER LOAN SHARK, OKIURA-SAN?

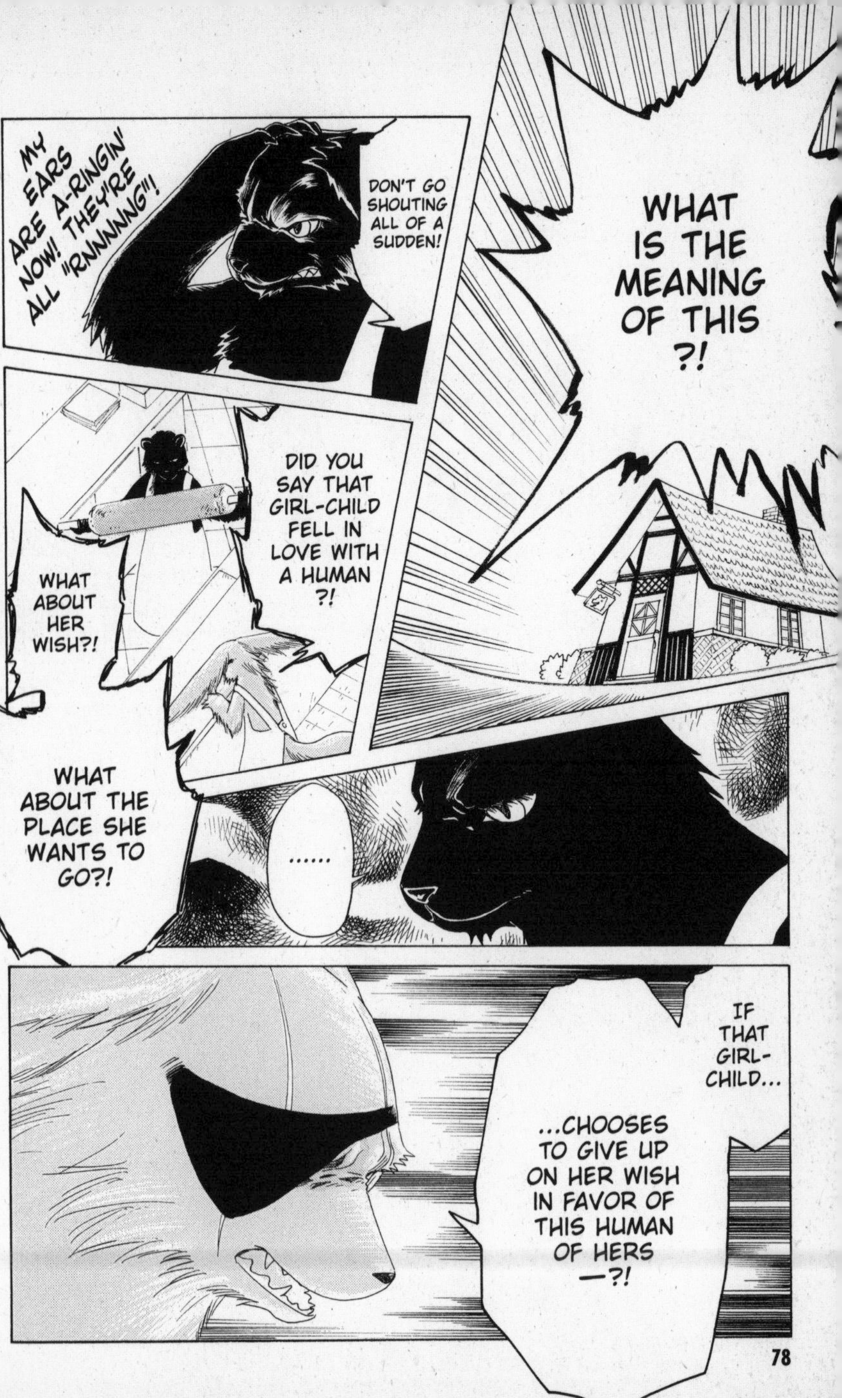

WHAT IS THE MEANING OF THIS?!
DON'T GO SHOUTING ALL OF A SUDDEN!
MY EARS ARE A-RINGIN' NOW! THEY'RE ALL "RNNNNNG"!
DID YOU SAY THAT GIRL-CHILD FELL IN LOVE WITH A HUMAN?!
WHAT ABOUT HER WISH?!
WHAT ABOUT THE PLACE SHE WANTS TO GO?!
......
IF THAT GIRL-CHILD...
...CHOOSES TO GIVE UP ON HER WISH IN FAVOR OF THIS HUMAN OF HERS—?!

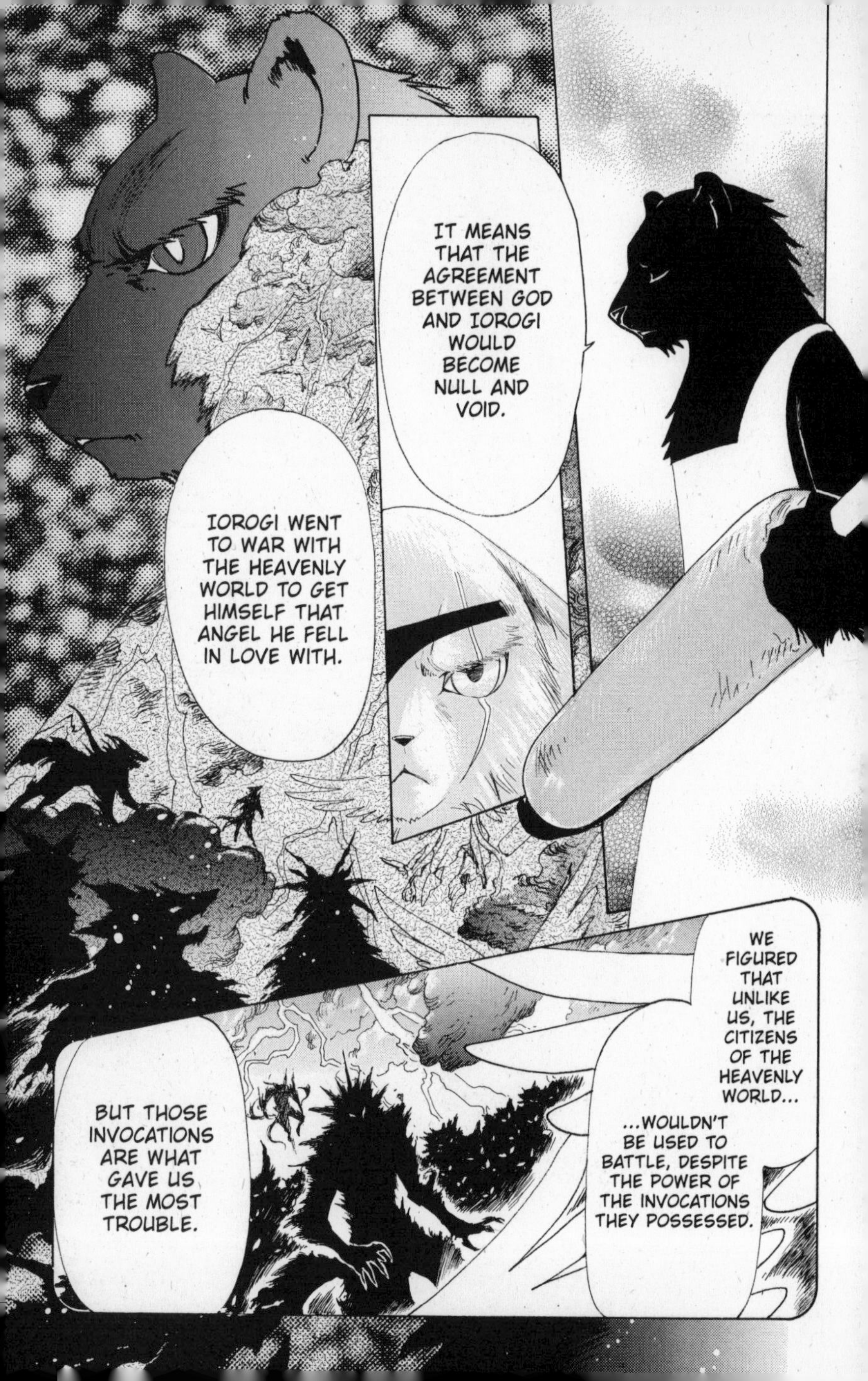
IT MEANS THAT THE AGREEMENT BETWEEN GOD AND IOROGI WOULD BECOME NULL AND VOID.
IOROGI WENT TO WAR WITH THE HEAVENLY WORLD TO GET HIMSELF THAT ANGEL HE FELL IN LOVE WITH.
WE FIGURED THAT UNLIKE US, THE CITIZENS OF THE HEAVENLY WORLD...
...WOULDN'T BE USED TO BATTLE, DESPITE THE POWER OF THE INVOCATIONS THEY POSSESSED.
BUT THOSE INVOCATIONS ARE WHAT GAVE US THE MOST TROUBLE.

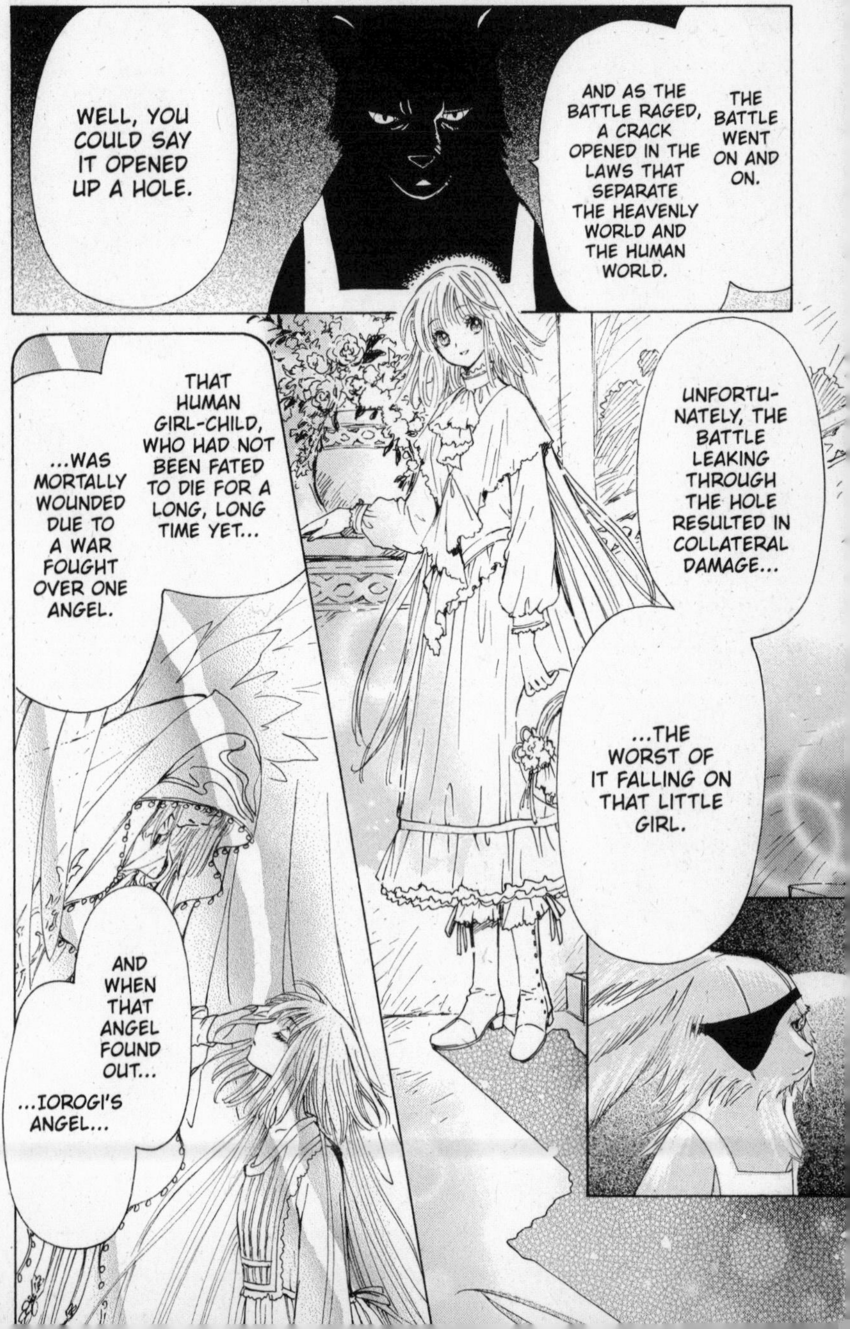
THE BATTLE WENT ON AND ON.
AND AS THE BATTLE RAGED, A CRACK OPENED IN THE LAWS THAT SEPARATE THE HEAVENLY WORLD AND THE HUMAN WORLD.
WELL, YOU COULD SAY IT OPENED UP A HOLE.
UNFORTUNATELY, THE BATTLE LEAKING THROUGH THE HOLE RESULTED IN COLLATERAL DAMAGE...
...THE WORST OF IT FALLING ON THAT LITTLE GIRL.
THAT HUMAN GIRL-CHILD, WHO HAD NOT BEEN FATED TO DIE FOR A LONG, LONG TIME YET...
...WAS MORTALLY WOUNDED DUE TO A WAR FOUGHT OVER ONE ANGEL.
AND WHEN THAT ANGEL FOUND OUT...
...IOROGI'S ANGEL...

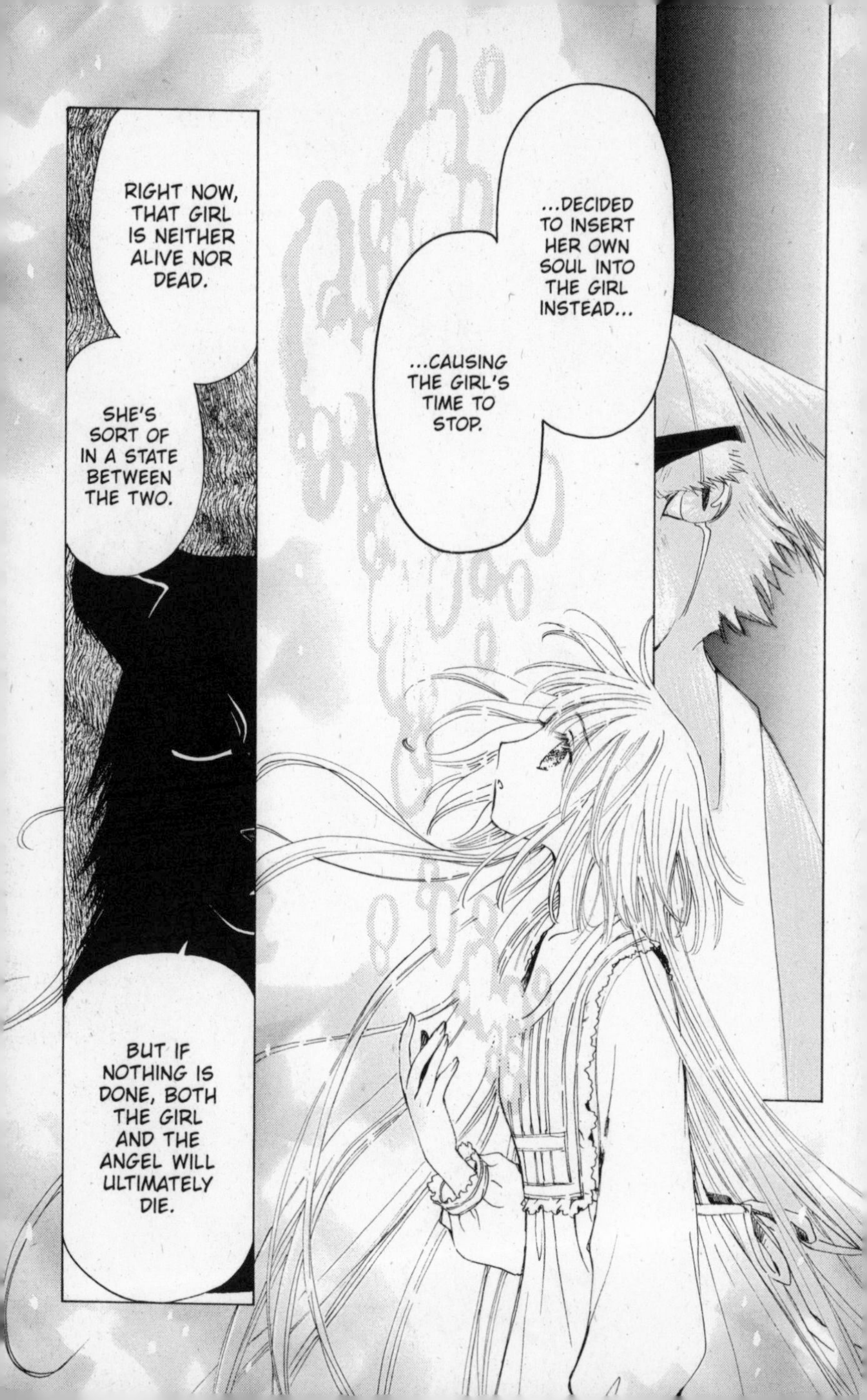
...DECIDED TO INSERT HER OWN SOUL INTO THE GIRL INSTEAD...
...CAUSING THE GIRL'S TIME TO STOP.
RIGHT NOW, THAT GIRL IS NEITHER ALIVE NOR DEAD.
SHE'S SORT OF IN A STATE BETWEEN THE TWO.
BUT IF NOTHING IS DONE, BOTH THE GIRL AND THE ANGEL WILL ULTIMATELY DIE.

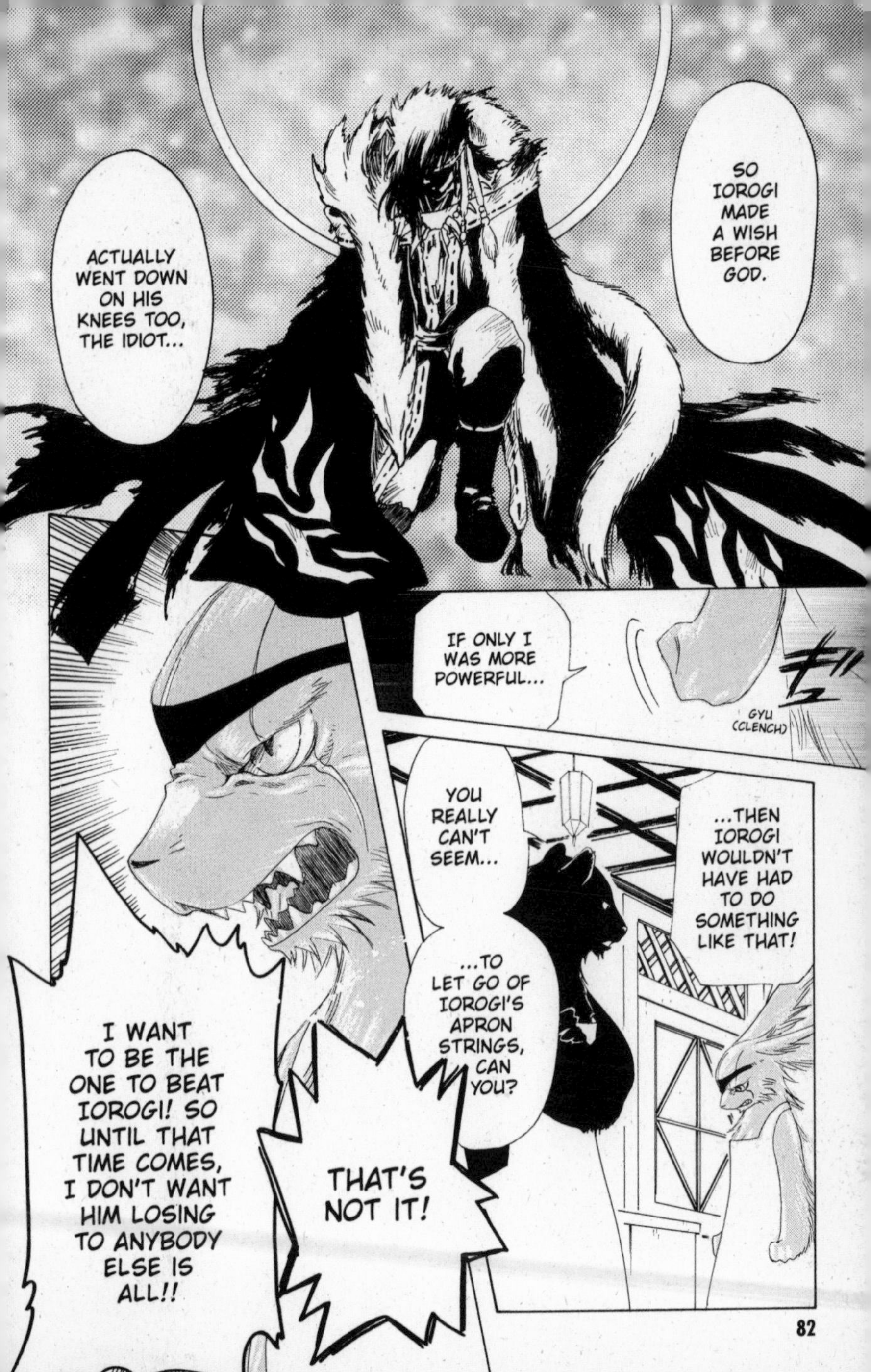
SO IOROGI MADE A WISH BEFORE GOD.
ACTUALLY WENT DOWN ON HIS KNEES TOO, THE IDIOT...
GYU (CLENCH)
IF ONLY I WAS MORE POWERFUL...
...THEN IOROGI WOULDN'T HAVE HAD TO DO SOMETHING LIKE THAT!
YOU REALLY CAN'T SEEM...
...TO LET GO OF IOROGI'S APRON STRINGS, CAN YOU?
THAT'S NOT IT!
I WANT TO BE THE ONE TO BEAT IOROGI! SO UNTIL THAT TIME COMES, I DON'T WANT HIM LOSING TO ANYBODY ELSE IS ALL!!

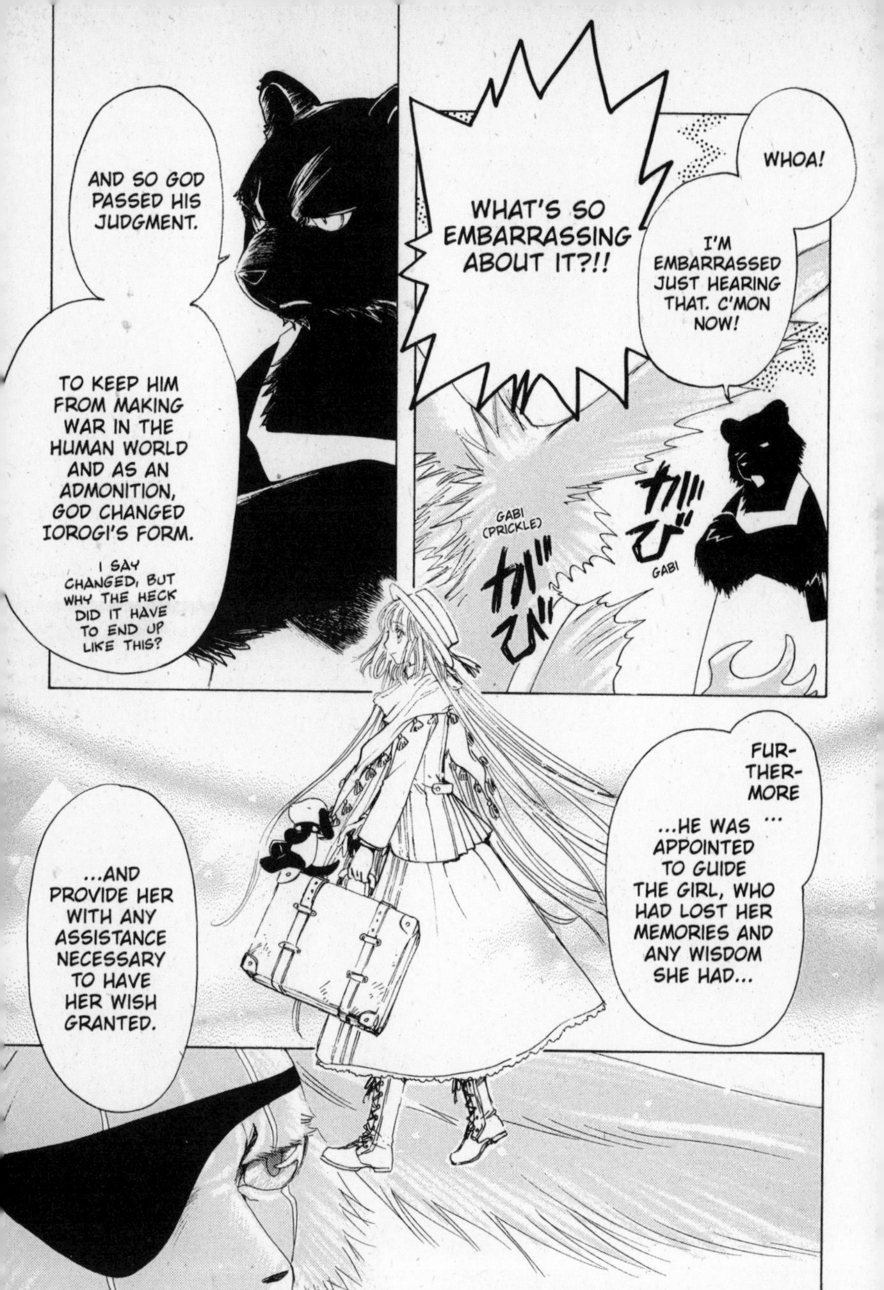
WHOA!
I'M EMBARRASSED JUST HEARING THAT. C'MON NOW!
WHAT'S SO EMBARRASSING ABOUT IT?!!
GABI
GABI (PRICKLE)
AND SO GOD PASSED HIS JUDGMENT.
TO KEEP HIM FROM MAKING WAR IN THE HUMAN WORLD AND AS AN ADMONITION, GOD CHANGED IOROGI'S FORM.
I SAY CHANGED, BUT WHY THE HECK DID IT HAVE TO END UP LIKE THIS?
FURTHERMORE...
...HE WAS APPOINTED TO GUIDE THE GIRL, WHO HAD LOST HER MEMORIES AND ANY WISDOM SHE HAD...
...AND PROVIDE HER WITH ANY ASSISTANCE NECESSARY TO HAVE HER WISH GRANTED.

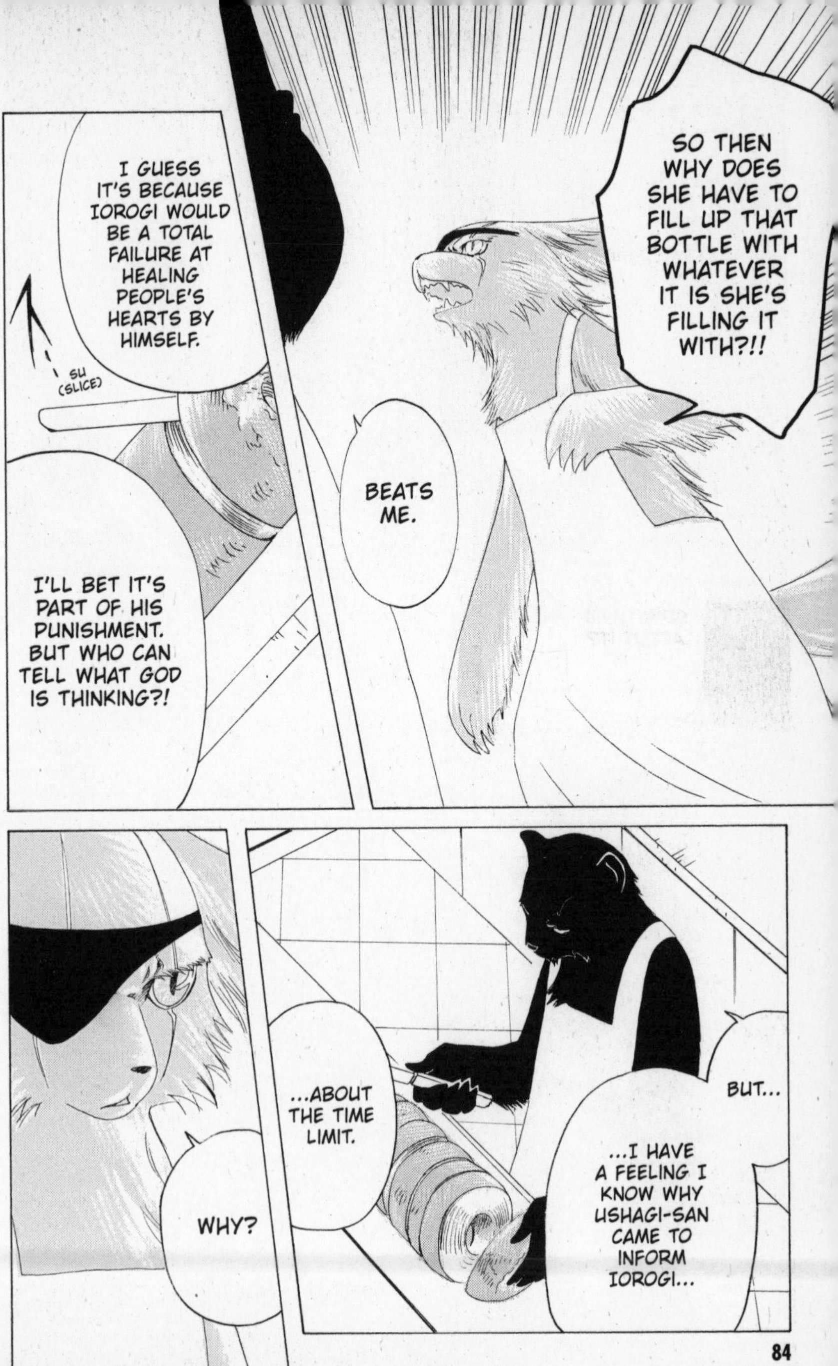
SO THEN WHY DOES SHE HAVE TO FILL UP THAT BOTTLE WITH WHATEVER IT IS SHE'S FILLING IT WITH?!!
BEATS ME.
I GUESS IT'S BECAUSE IOROGI WOULD BE A TOTAL FAILURE AT HEALING PEOPLE'S HEARTS BY HIMSELF.
SU (SLICE)
I'LL BET IT'S PART OF HIS PUNISHMENT. BUT WHO CAN TELL WHAT GOD IS THINKING?!
BUT...
...I HAVE A FEELING I KNOW WHY USHAGI-SAN CAME TO INFORM IOROGI...
...ABOUT THE TIME LIMIT.
WHY?

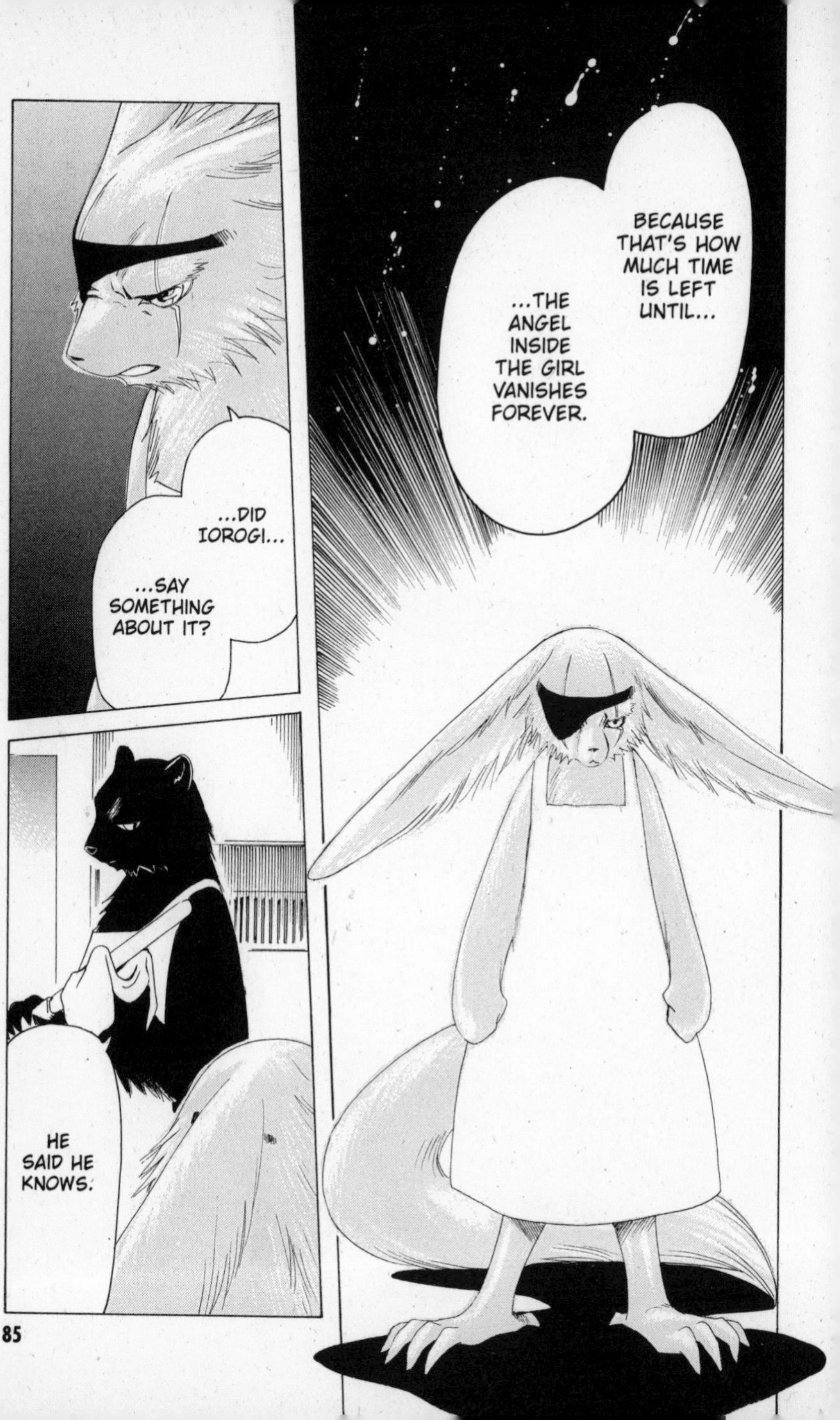
BECAUSE THAT'S HOW MUCH TIME IS LEFT UNTIL...
...THE ANGEL INSIDE THE GIRL VANISHES FOREVER.
...DID IOROGI...
...SAY SOMETHING ABOUT IT?
HE SAID HE KNOWS.

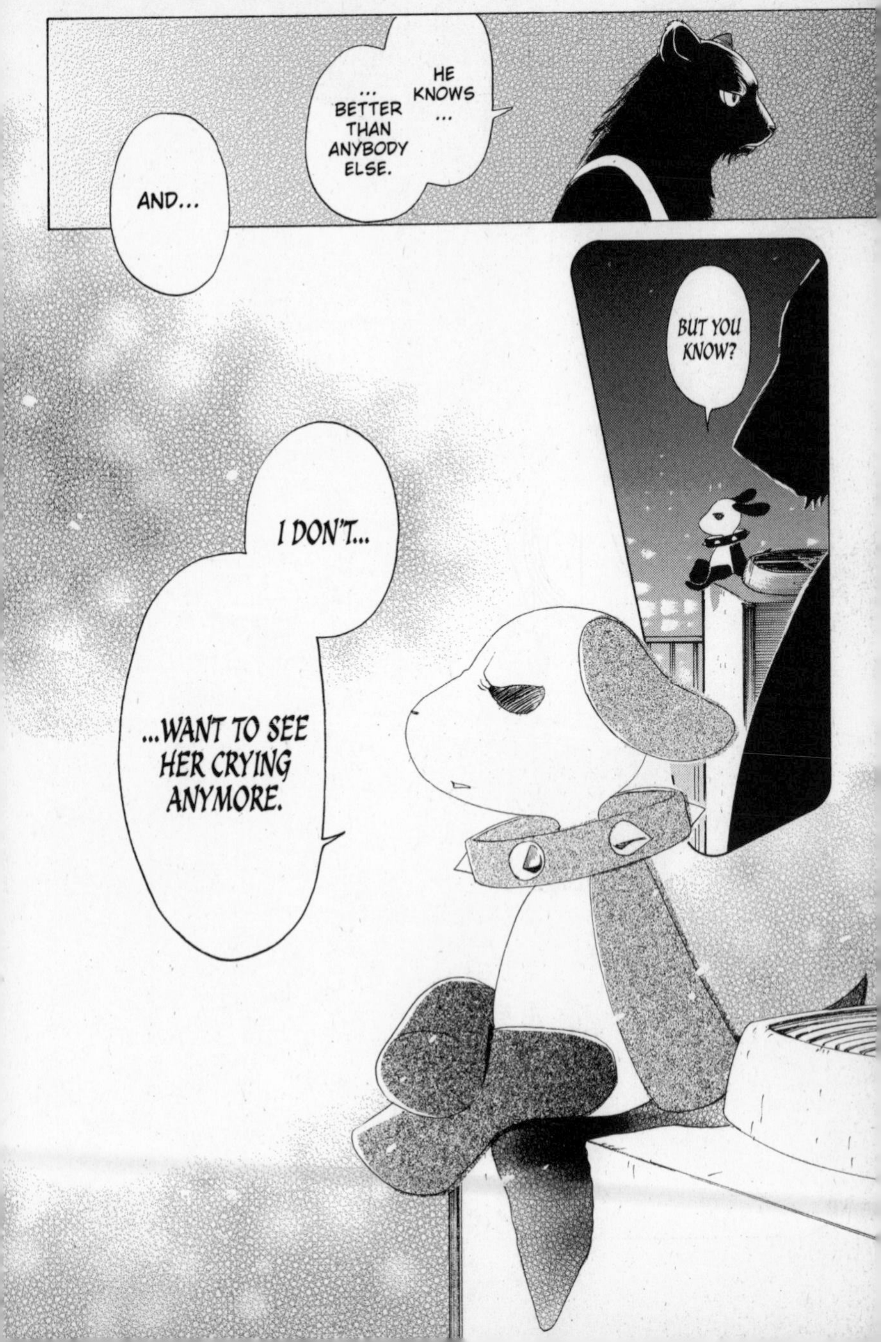
HE KNOWS ... ...BETTER THAN ANYBODY ELSE.
AND...
BUT YOU KNOW?
I DON'T...
...WANT TO SEE HER CRYING ANYMORE.

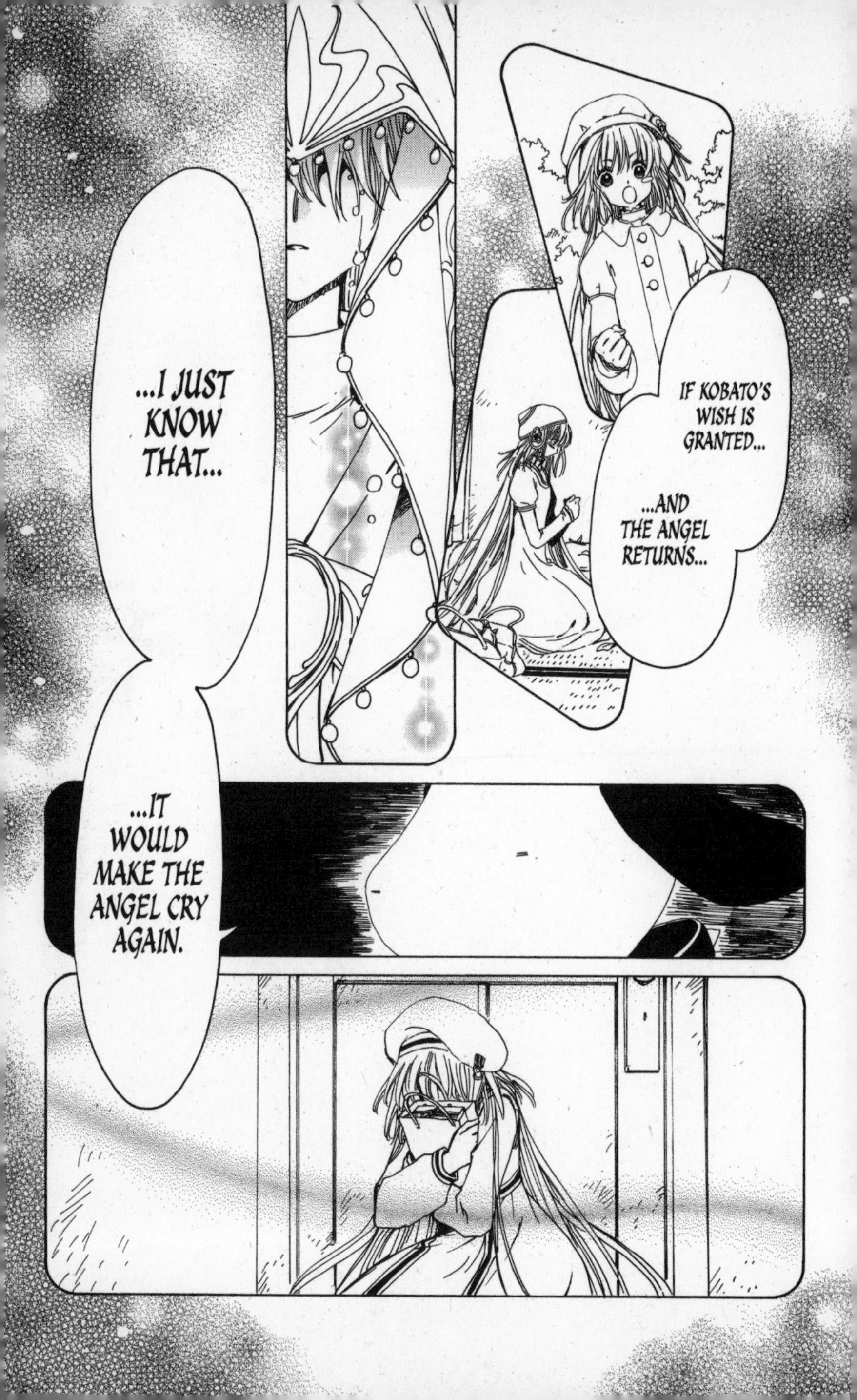
IF KOBATO'S WISH IS GRANTED...
...AND THE ANGEL RETURNS...
...I JUST KNOW THAT...
...IT WOULD MAKE THE ANGEL CRY AGAIN.

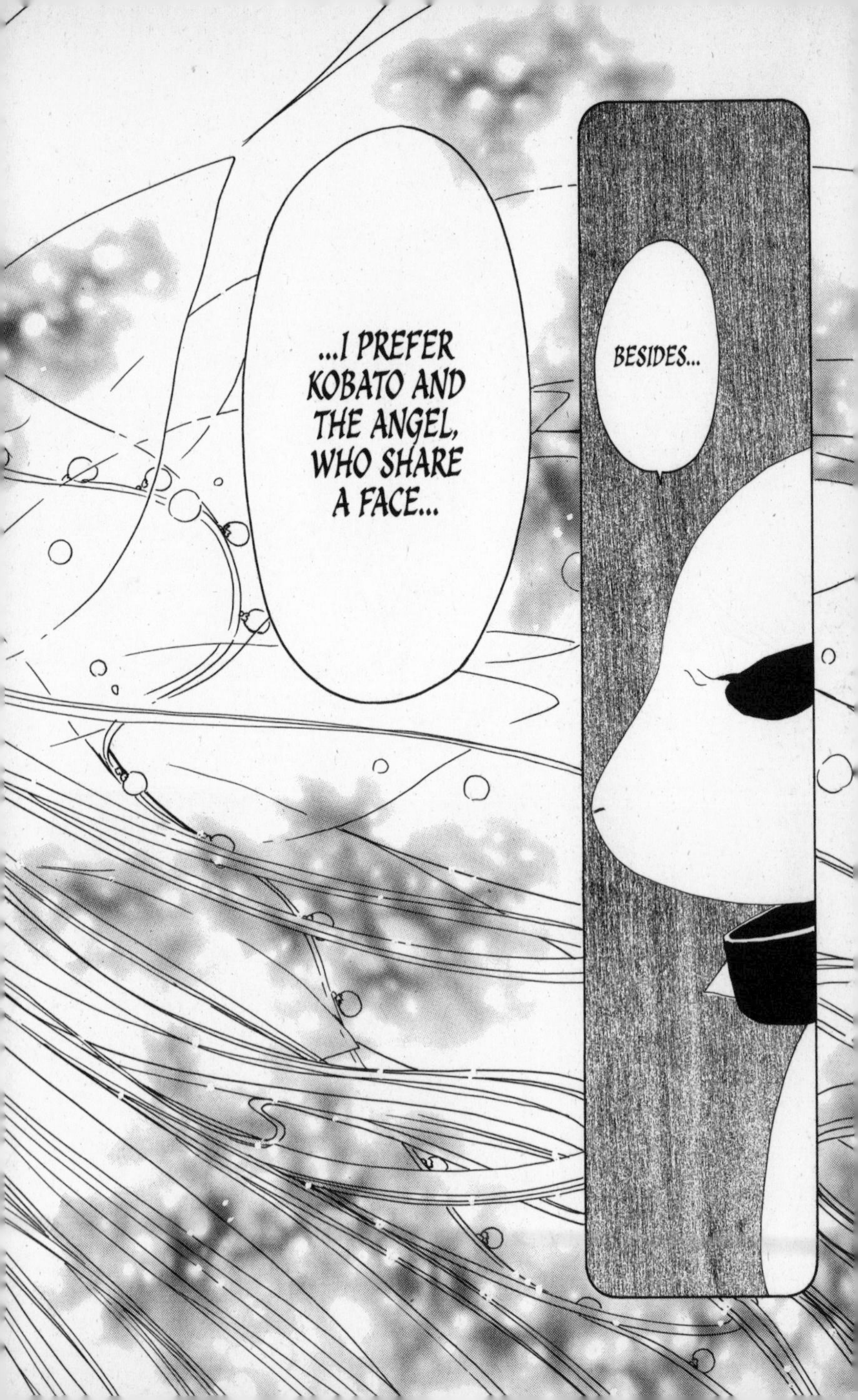
BESIDES...
...I PREFER KOBATO AND THE ANGEL, WHO SHARE A FACE...

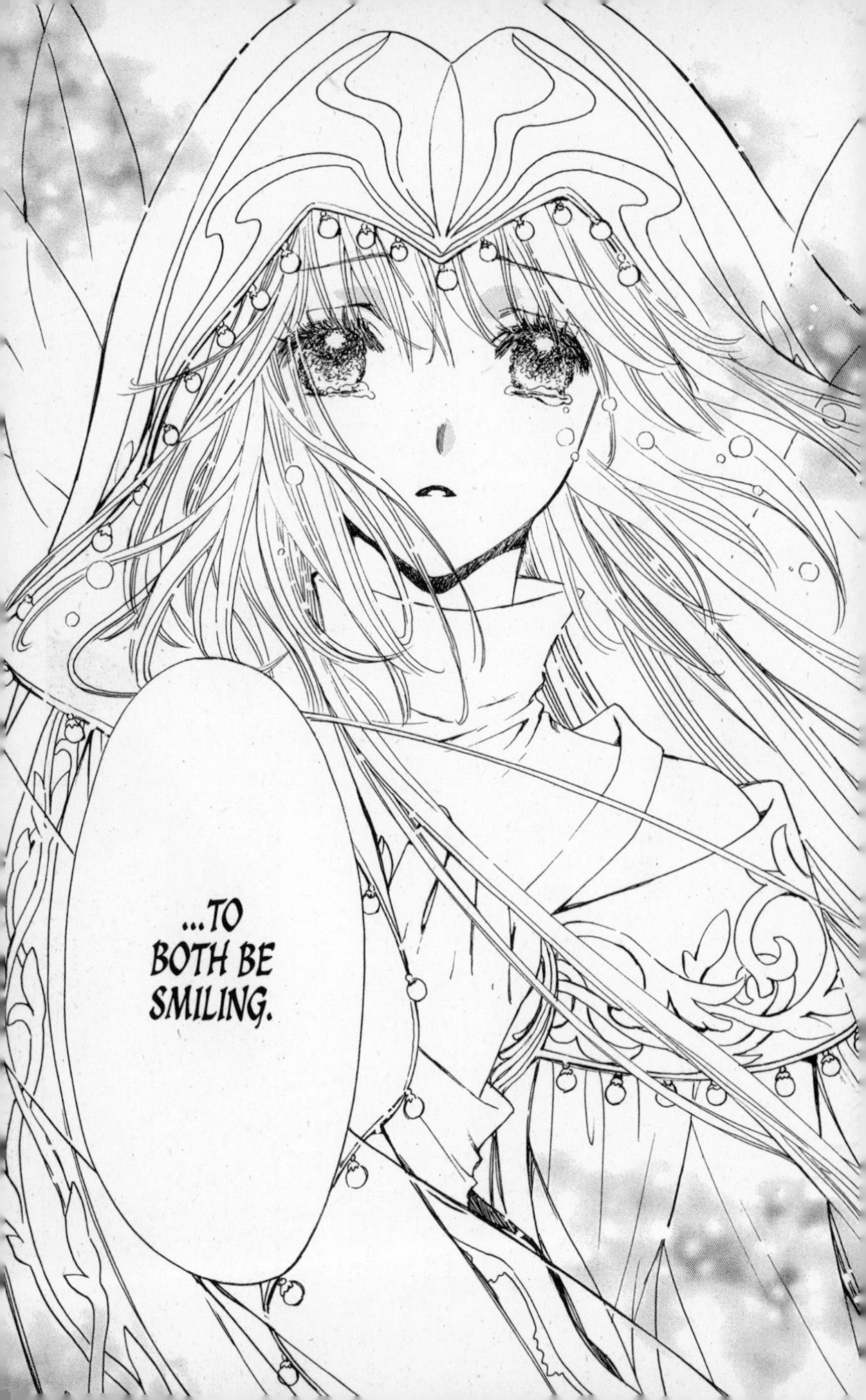
...TO BOTH BE SMILING.

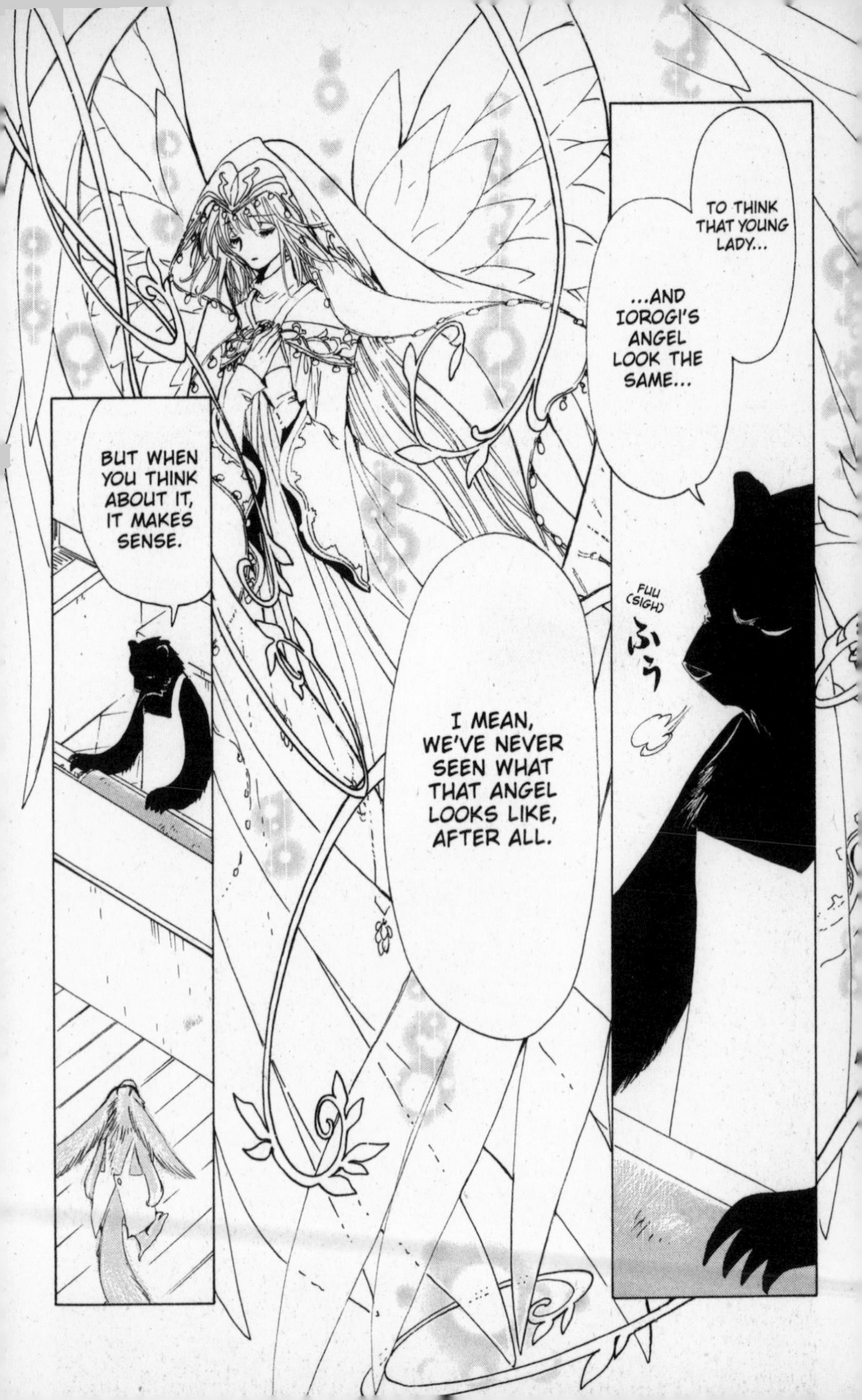
TO THINK THAT YOUNG LADY...
...AND IOROGI'S ANGEL LOOK THE SAME...
FUU (SIGH)
ふぅ
BUT WHEN YOU THINK ABOUT IT, IT MAKES SENSE.
I MEAN, WE'VE NEVER SEEN WHAT THAT ANGEL LOOKS LIKE, AFTER ALL.

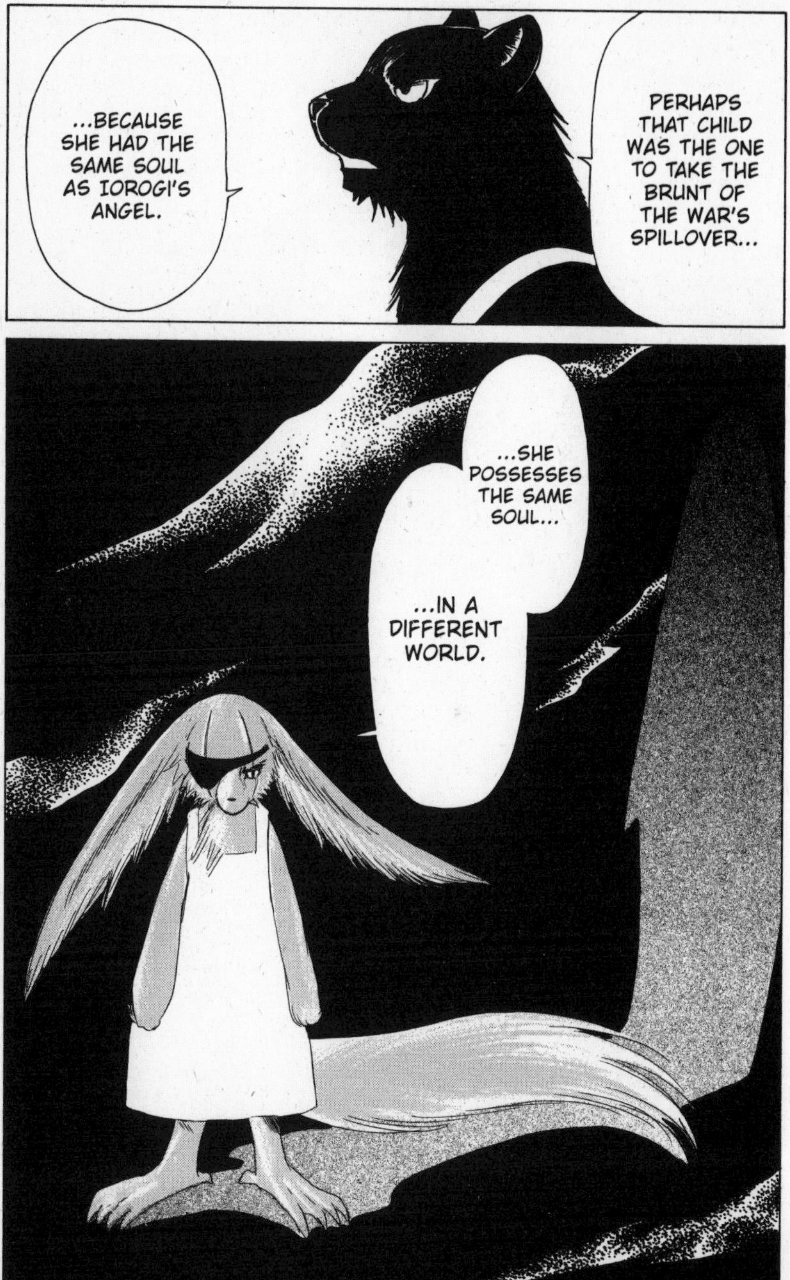
PERHAPS THAT CHILD WAS THE ONE TO TAKE THE BRUNT OF THE WAR'S SPILLOVER...
...BECAUSE SHE HAD THE SAME SOUL AS IOROGI'S ANGEL.
...SHE POSSESSES THE SAME SOUL...
...IN A DIFFERENT WORLD.

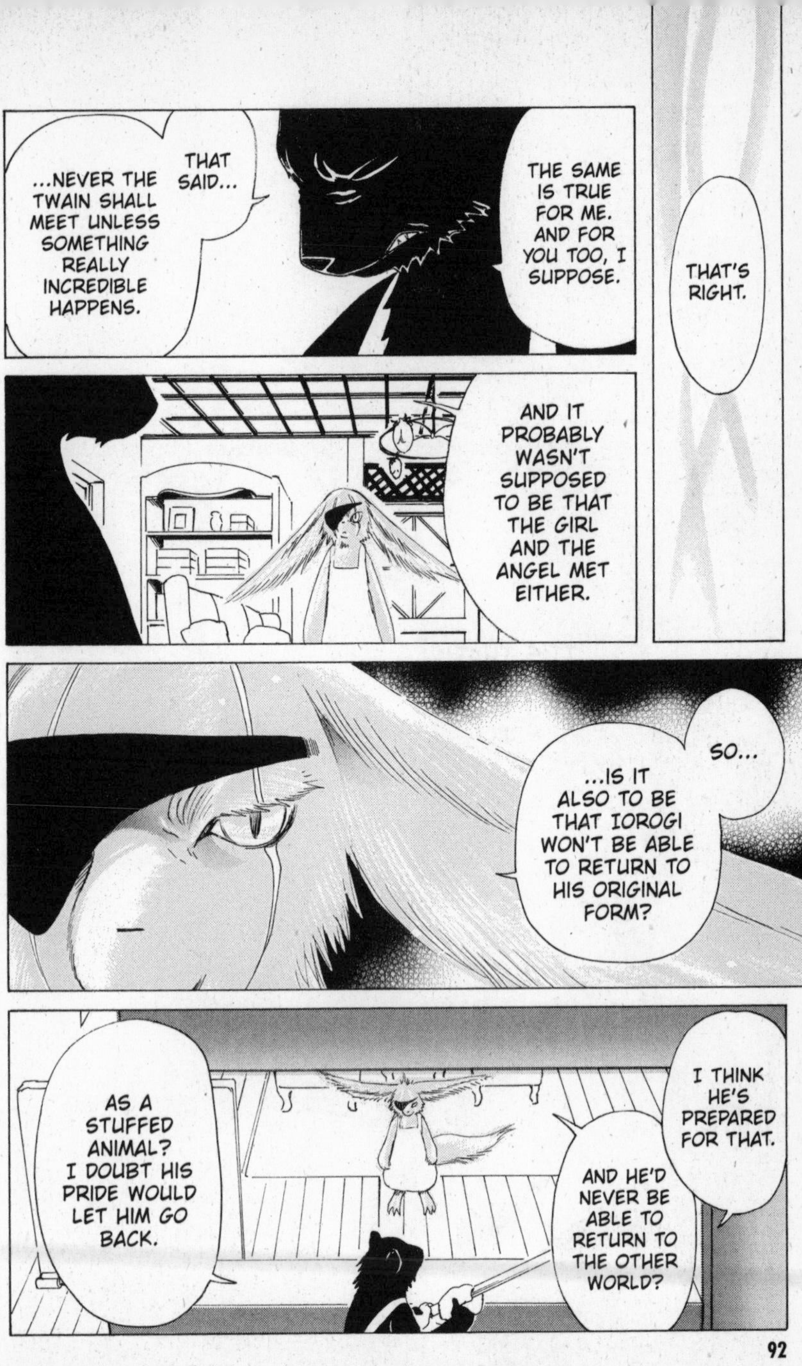
THAT'S RIGHT.
THE SAME IS TRUE FOR ME. AND FOR YOU TOO, I SUPPOSE.
THAT SAID...
...NEVER THE TWAIN SHALL MEET UNLESS SOMETHING REALLY INCREDIBLE HAPPENS.
AND IT PROBABLY WASN'T SUPPOSED TO BE THAT THE GIRL AND THE ANGEL MET EITHER.
SO...
...IS IT ALSO TO BE THAT IOROGI WON'T BE ABLE TO RETURN TO HIS ORIGINAL FORM?
I THINK HE'S PREPARED FOR THAT.
AND HE'D NEVER BE ABLE TO RETURN TO THE OTHER WORLD?
AS A STUFFED ANIMAL? I DOUBT HIS PRIDE WOULD LET HIM GO BACK.

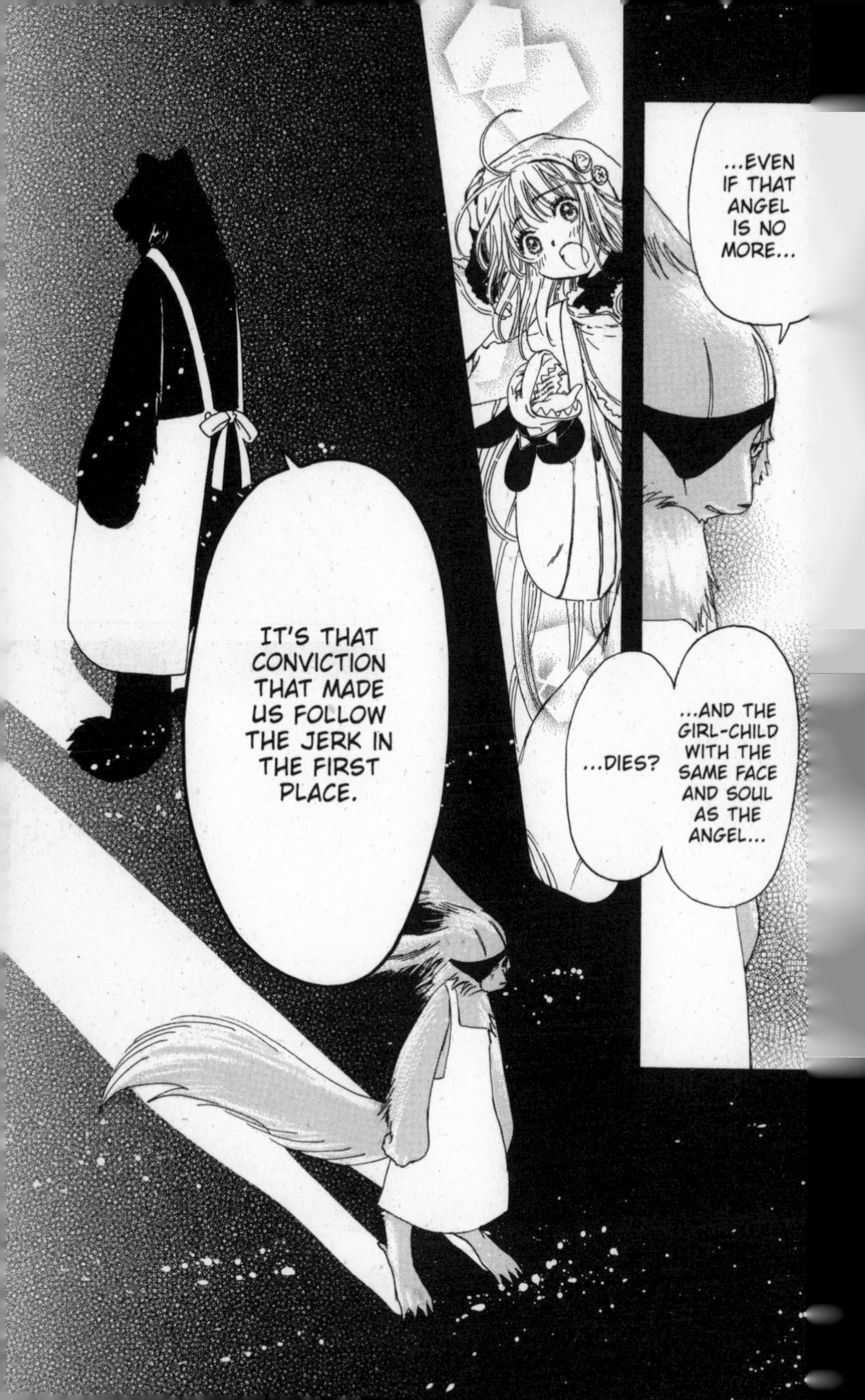
...EVEN IF THAT ANGEL IS NO MORE...
...AND THE GIRL-CHILD WITH THE SAME FACE AND SOUL AS THE ANGEL...
...DIES?
IT'S THAT CONVICTION THAT MADE US FOLLOW THE JERK IN THE FIRST PLACE.

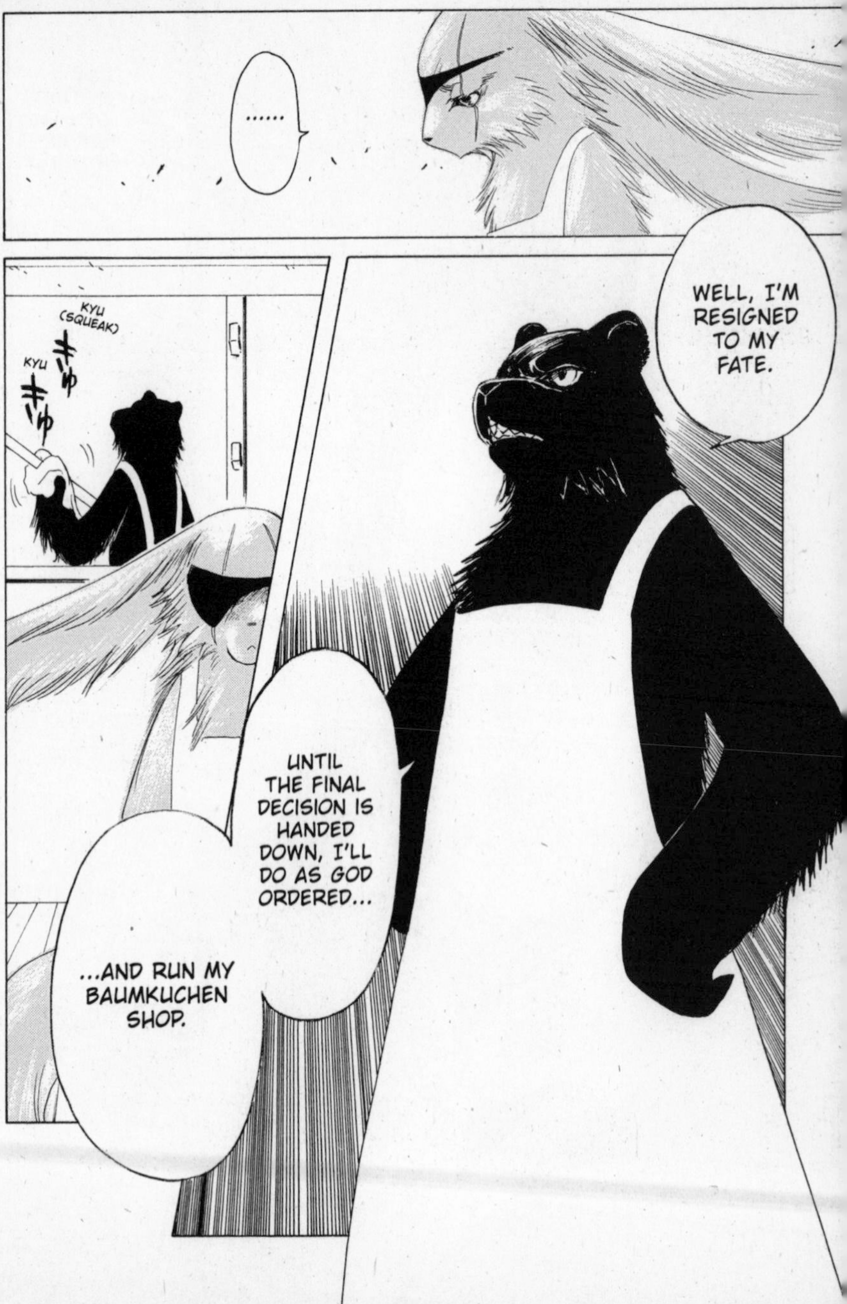
......
WELL, I'M RESIGNED TO MY FATE.
UNTIL THE FINAL DECISION IS HANDED DOWN, I'LL DO AS GOD ORDERED...
...AND RUN MY BAUMKUCHEN SHOP.
きゅ KYU (SQUEAK)
きゅ KYU

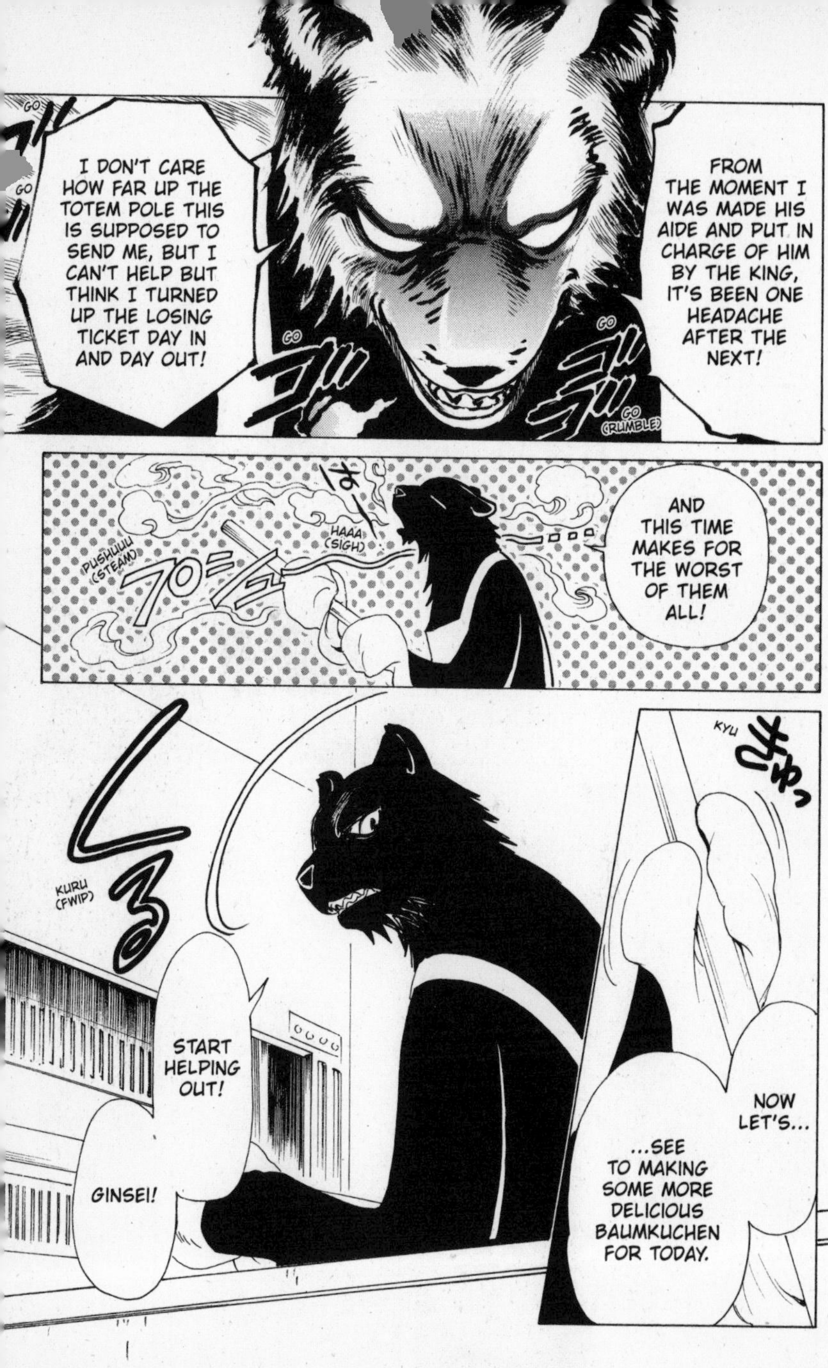
FROM THE MOMENT I WAS MADE HIS AIDE AND PUT IN CHARGE OF HIM BY THE KING, IT'S BEEN ONE HEADACHE AFTER THE NEXT!
GO
GO (RUMBLE)
GO
I DON'T CARE HOW FAR UP THE TOTEM POLE THIS IS SUPPOSED TO SEND ME, BUT I CAN'T HELP BUT THINK I TURNED UP THE LOSING TICKET DAY IN AND DAY OUT!
GO
GO
AND THIS TIME MAKES FOR THE WORST OF THEM ALL!
HAAA (SIGH)
PUSHUUU (STEAM)
KYU
NOW LET'S...
...SEE TO MAKING SOME MORE DELICIOUS BAUMKUCHEN FOR TODAY.
KURU (FWIP)
START HELPING OUT!
GINSEI!

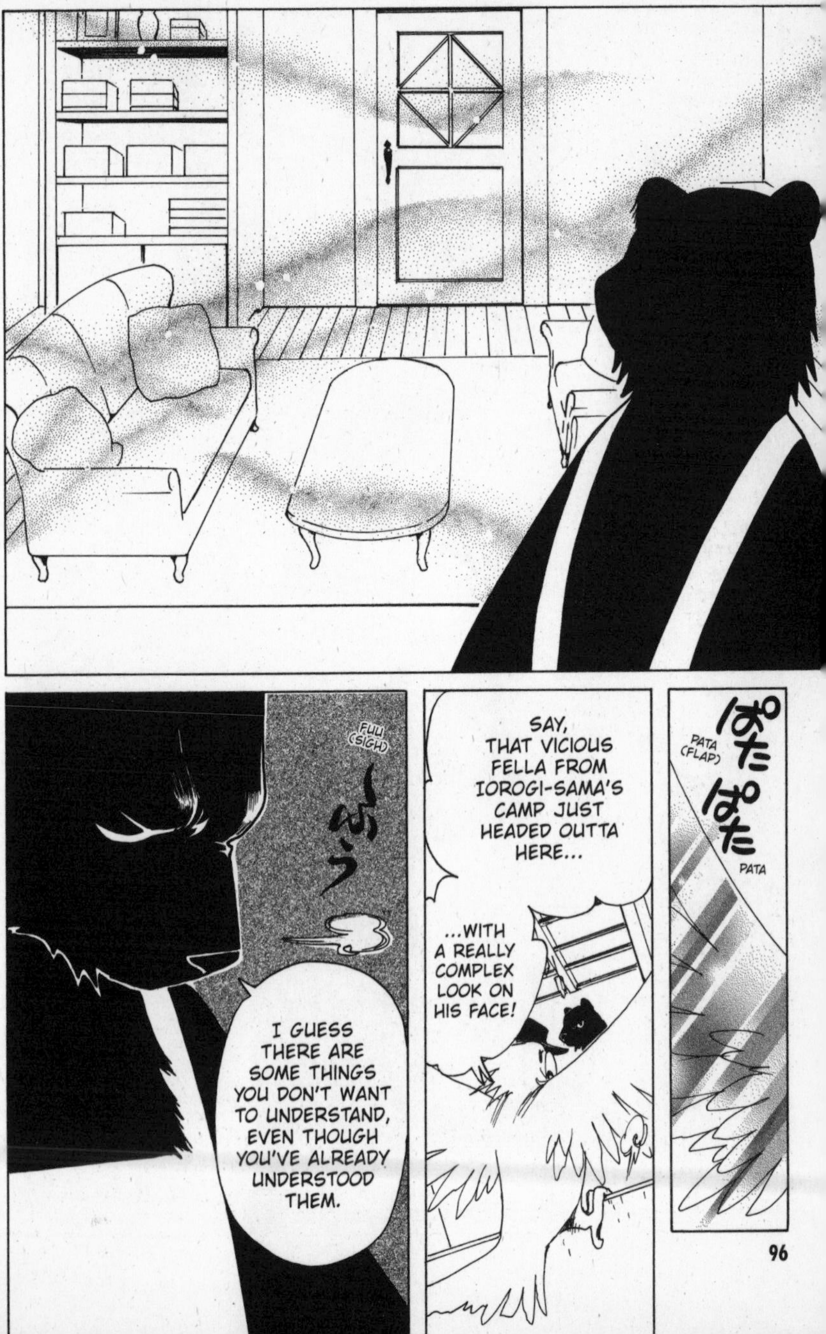
ぱた ぱた
PATA (FLAP)
PATA
SAY, THAT VICIOUS FELLA FROM IOROGI-SAMA'S CAMP JUST HEADED OUTTA HERE...
...WITH A REALLY COMPLEX LOOK ON HIS FACE!
ふう
FUU (SIGH)
I GUESS THERE ARE SOME THINGS YOU DON'T WANT TO UNDERSTAND, EVEN THOUGH YOU'VE ALREADY UNDERSTOOD THEM.

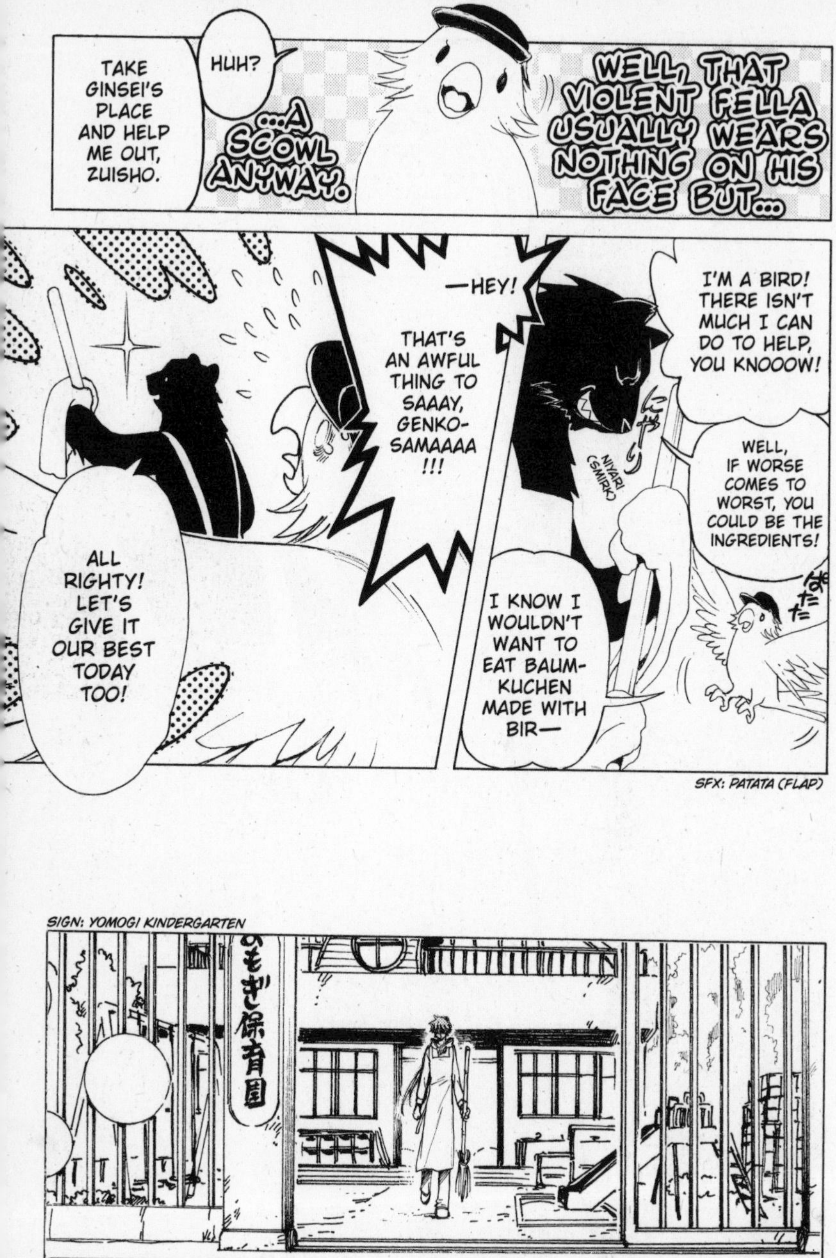
WELL, THAT VIOLENT FELLA USUALLY WEARS NOTHING ON HIS FACE BUT...
...A SCOWL ANYWAY.
HUH?
TAKE GINSEI'S PLACE AND HELP ME OUT, ZUISHO.
I'M A BIRD! THERE ISN'T MUCH I CAN DO TO HELP, YOU KNOOOW!
NIYARI (SMIRK)
WELL, IF WORSE COMES TO WORST, YOU COULD BE THE INGREDIENTS!
I KNOW I WOULDN'T WANT TO EAT BAUMKUCHEN MADE WITH BIR—
—HEY!
THAT'S AN AWFUL THING TO SAAAY, GENKO-SAMAAAA!!!
ALL RIGHTY! LET'S GIVE IT OUR BEST TODAY TOO!
よもぎ保育園

SFX: PATATA (FLAP)

SIGN: YOMOGI KINDERGARTEN

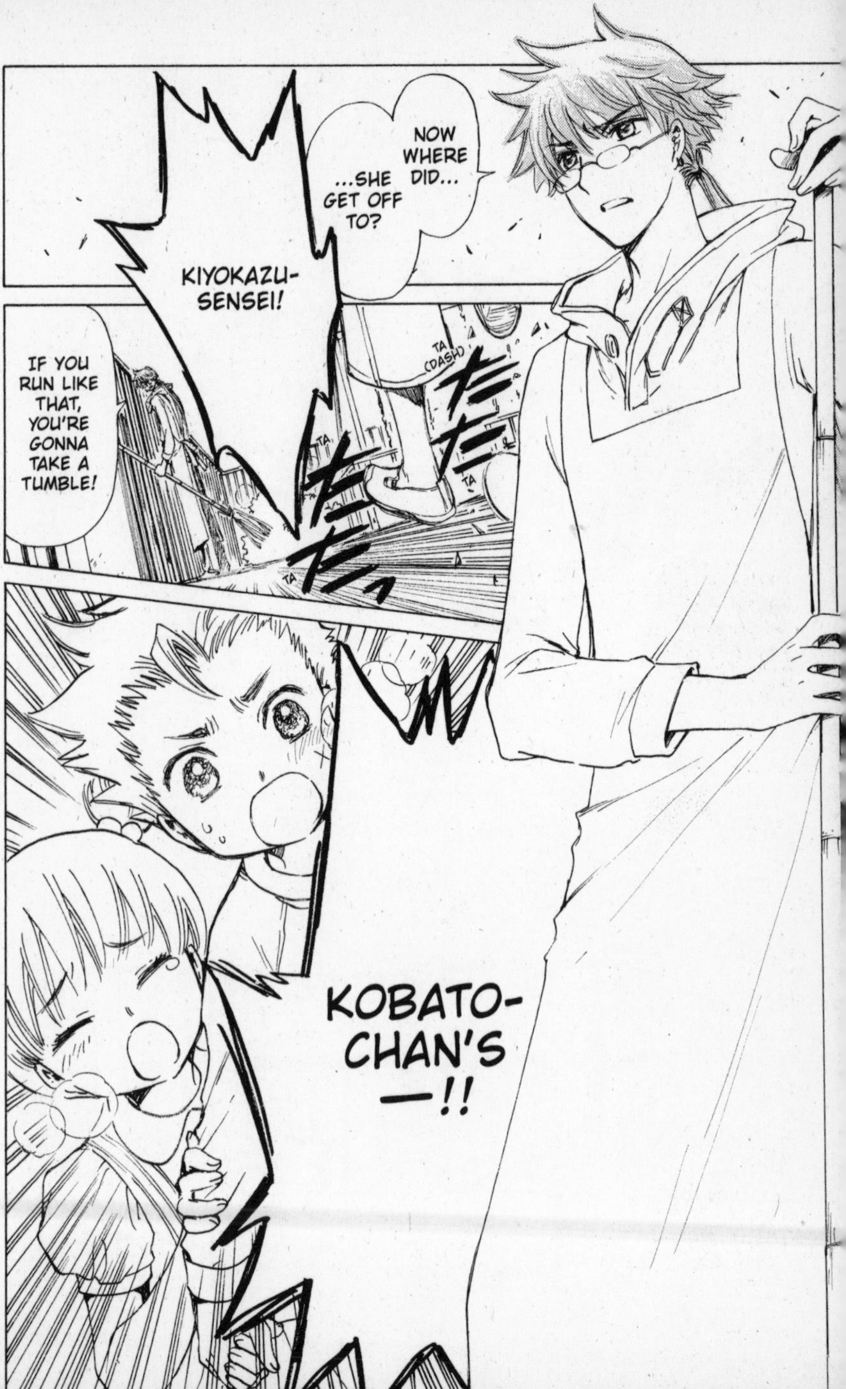
NOW WHERE DID...
...SHE GET OFF TO?
KIYOKAZU-SENSEI!
TA (DASH)
TA
TA
TA
IF YOU RUN LIKE THAT, YOU'RE GONNA TAKE A TUMBLE!
KOBATO-CHAN'S—!!

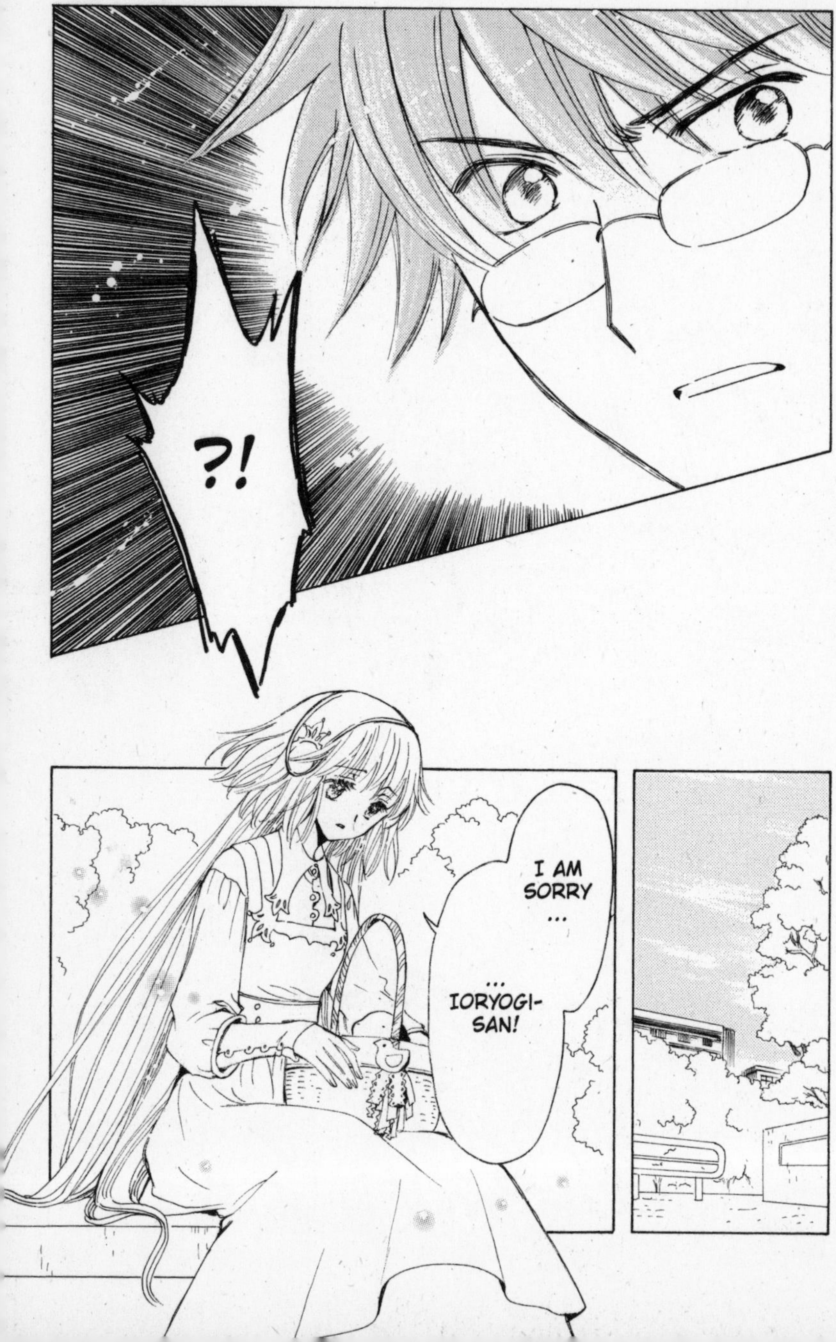
?!
I AM SORRY ...
... IORYOGI-SAN!

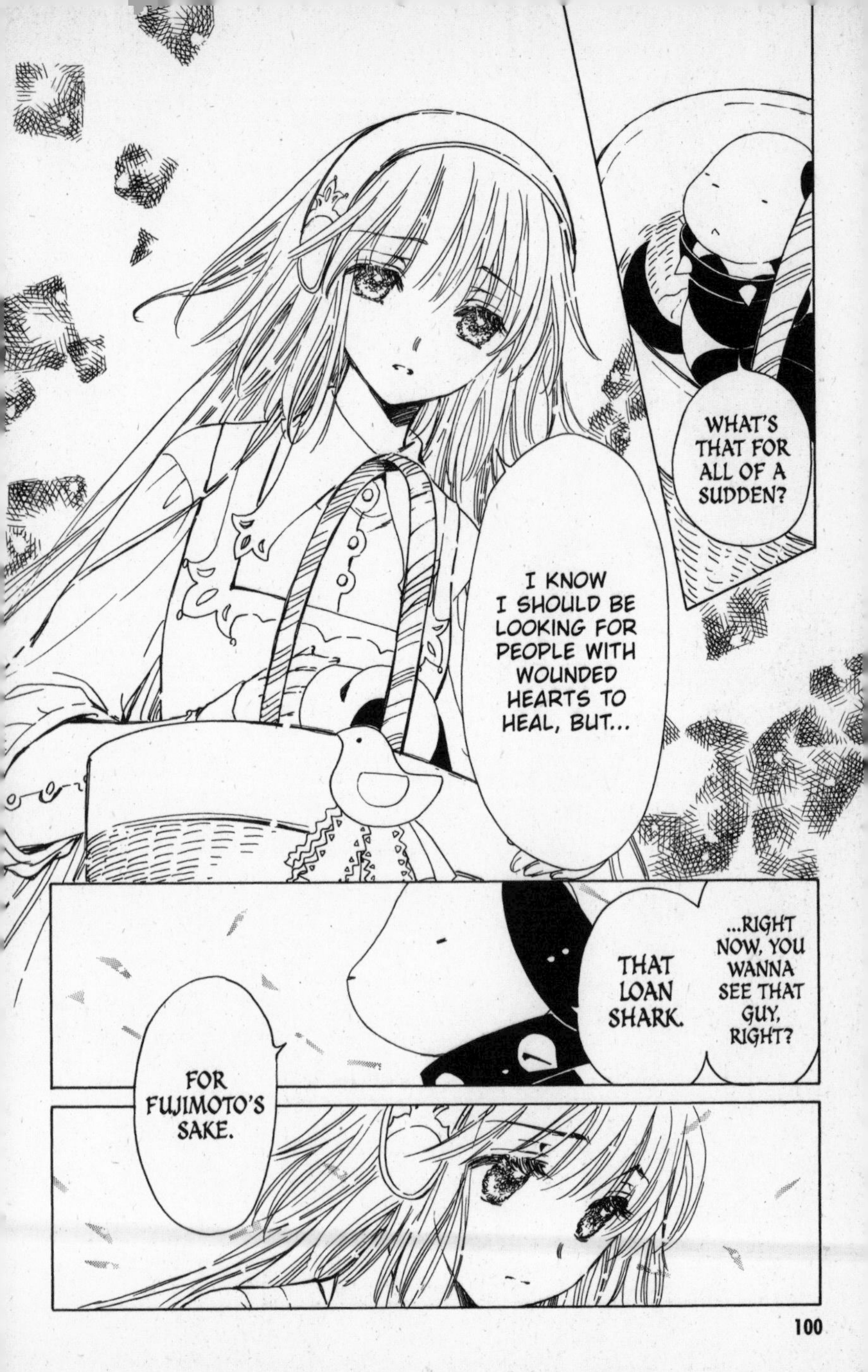
WHAT'S THAT FOR ALL OF A SUDDEN?
I KNOW I SHOULD BE LOOKING FOR PEOPLE WITH WOUNDED HEARTS TO HEAL, BUT...
...RIGHT NOW, YOU WANNA SEE THAT GUY, RIGHT?
THAT LOAN SHARK.
FOR FUJIMOTO'S SAKE.

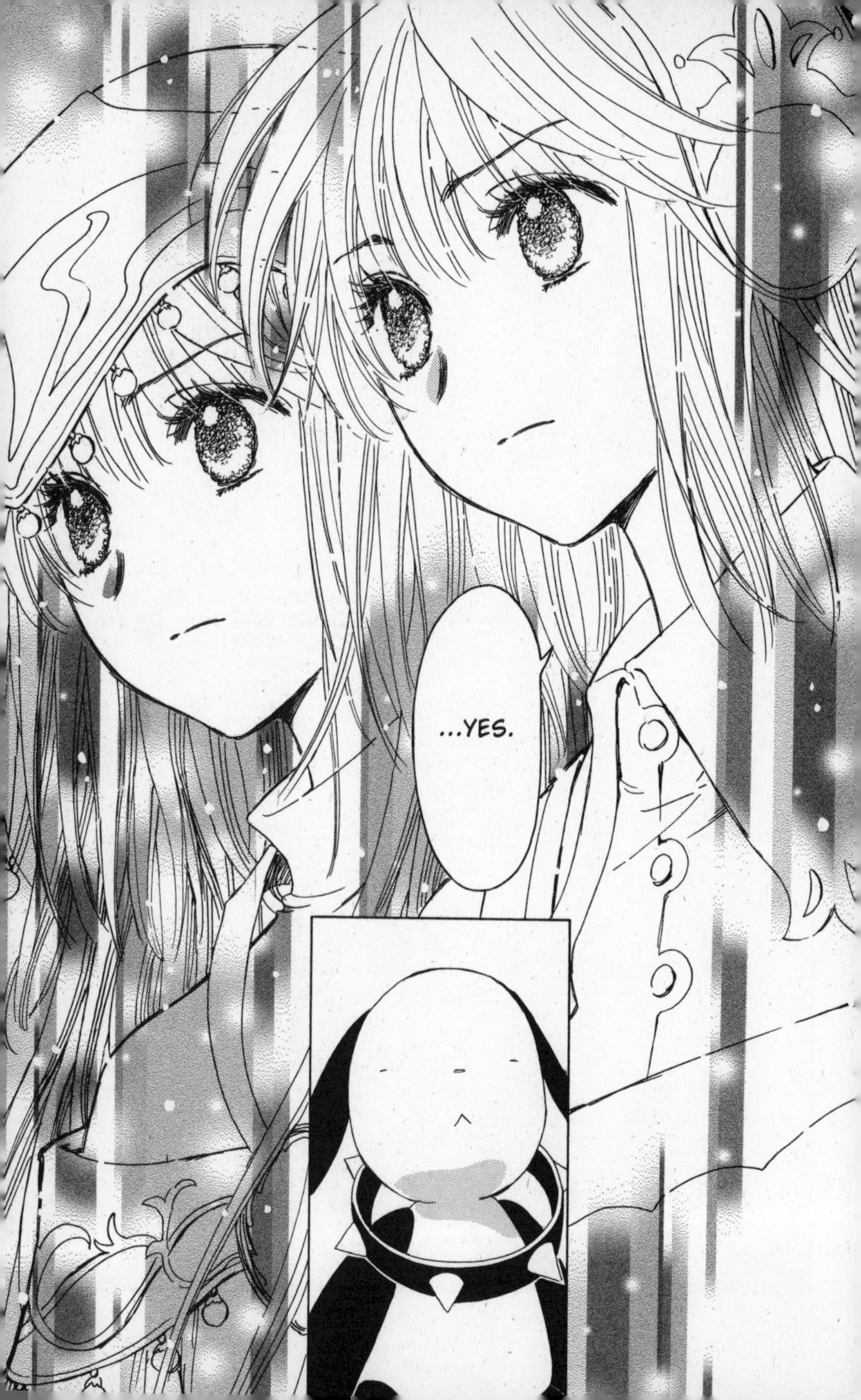
...YES.

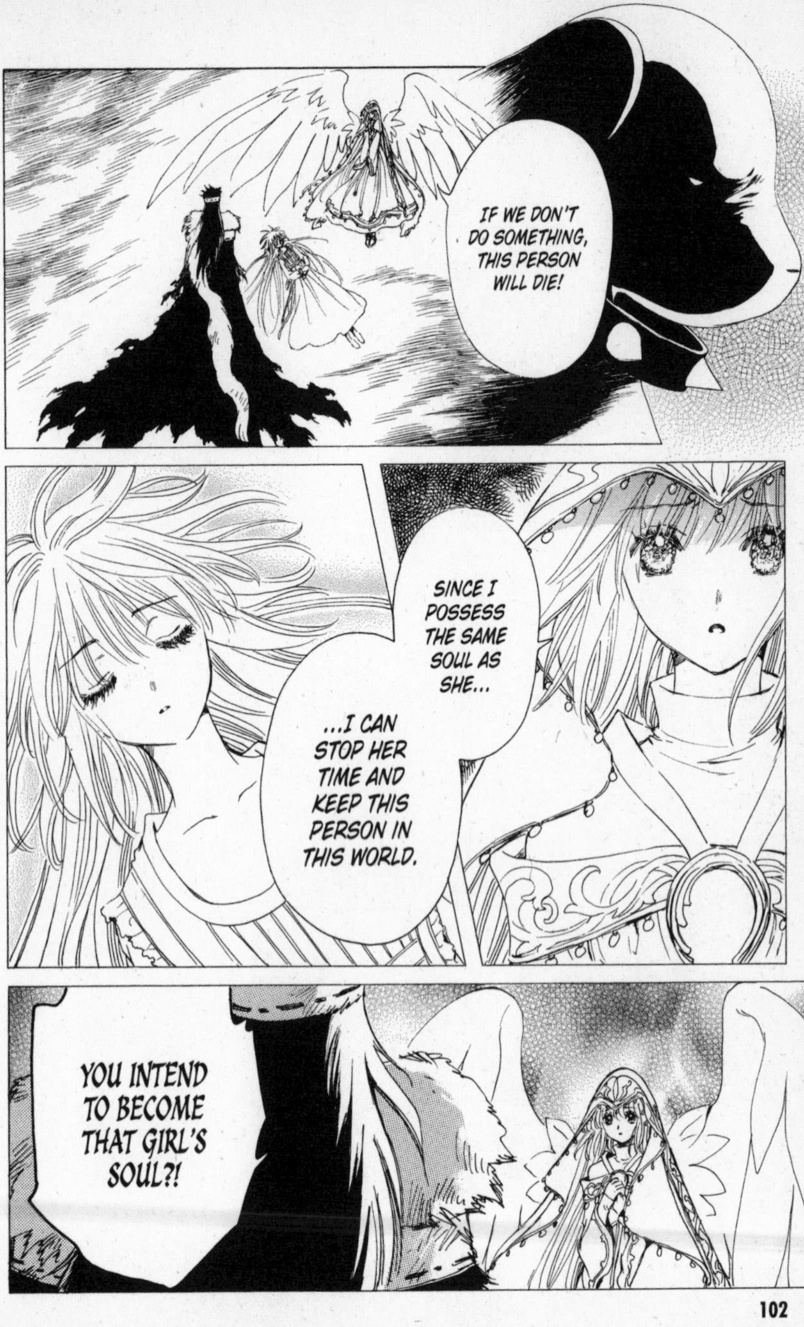
IF WE DON'T DO SOMETHING, THIS PERSON WILL DIE!
SINCE I POSSESS THE SAME SOUL AS SHE...
...I CAN STOP HER TIME AND KEEP THIS PERSON IN THIS WORLD.
YOU INTEND TO BECOME THAT GIRL'S SOUL?!

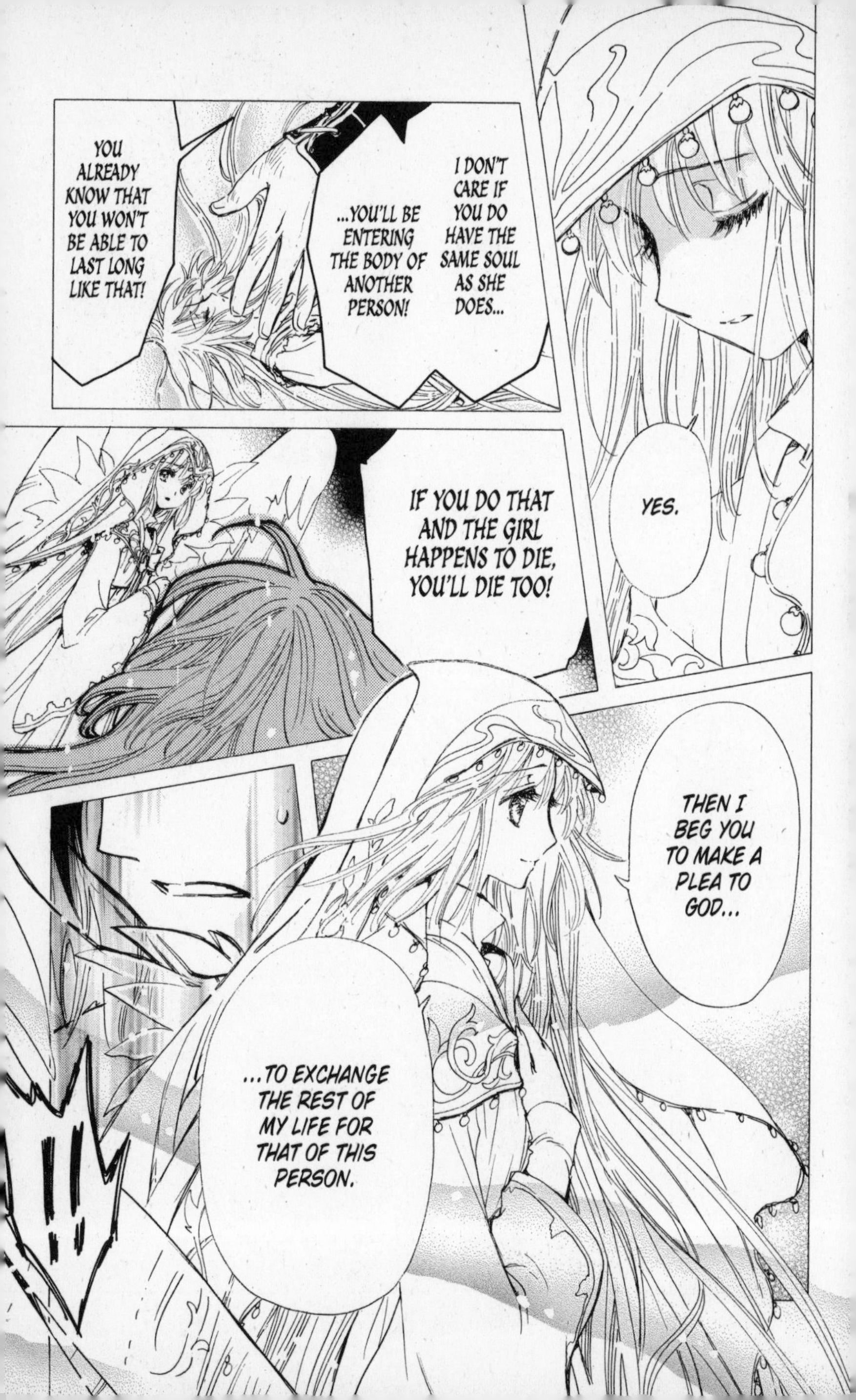
I DON'T CARE IF YOU DO HAVE THE SAME SOUL AS SHE DOES...
...YOU'LL BE ENTERING THE BODY OF ANOTHER PERSON!
YOU ALREADY KNOW THAT YOU WON'T BE ABLE TO LAST LONG LIKE THAT!
IF YOU DO THAT AND THE GIRL HAPPENS TO DIE, YOU'LL DIE TOO!
YES.
THEN I BEG YOU TO MAKE A PLEA TO GOD...
...TO EXCHANGE THE REST OF MY LIFE FOR THAT OF THIS PERSON.
!!

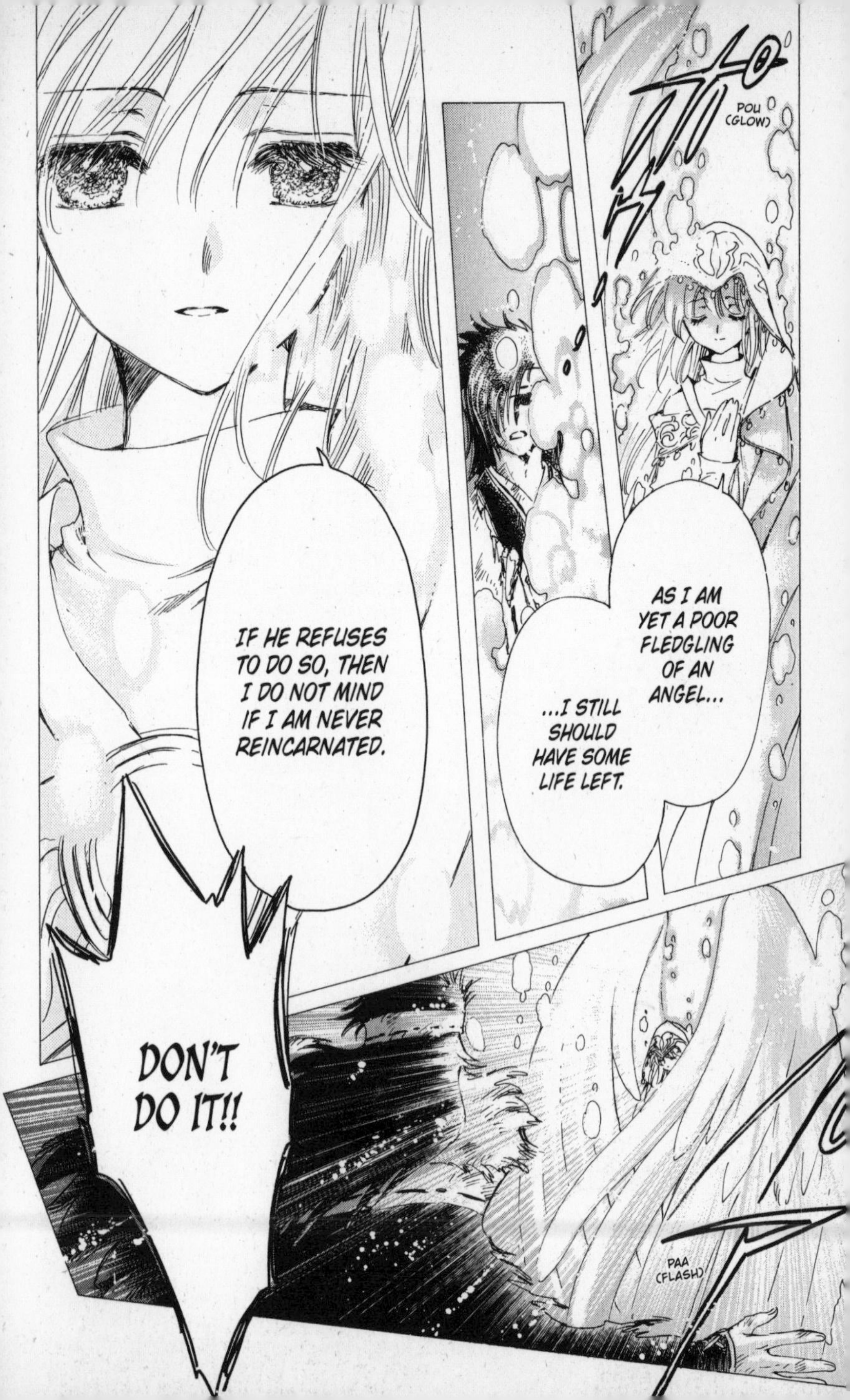
POU (GLOW)
AS I AM YET A POOR FLEDGLING OF AN ANGEL...
...I STILL SHOULD HAVE SOME LIFE LEFT.
IF HE REFUSES TO DO SO, THEN I DO NOT MIND IF I AM NEVER REINCARNATED.
PAA (FLASH)
DON'T DO IT!!

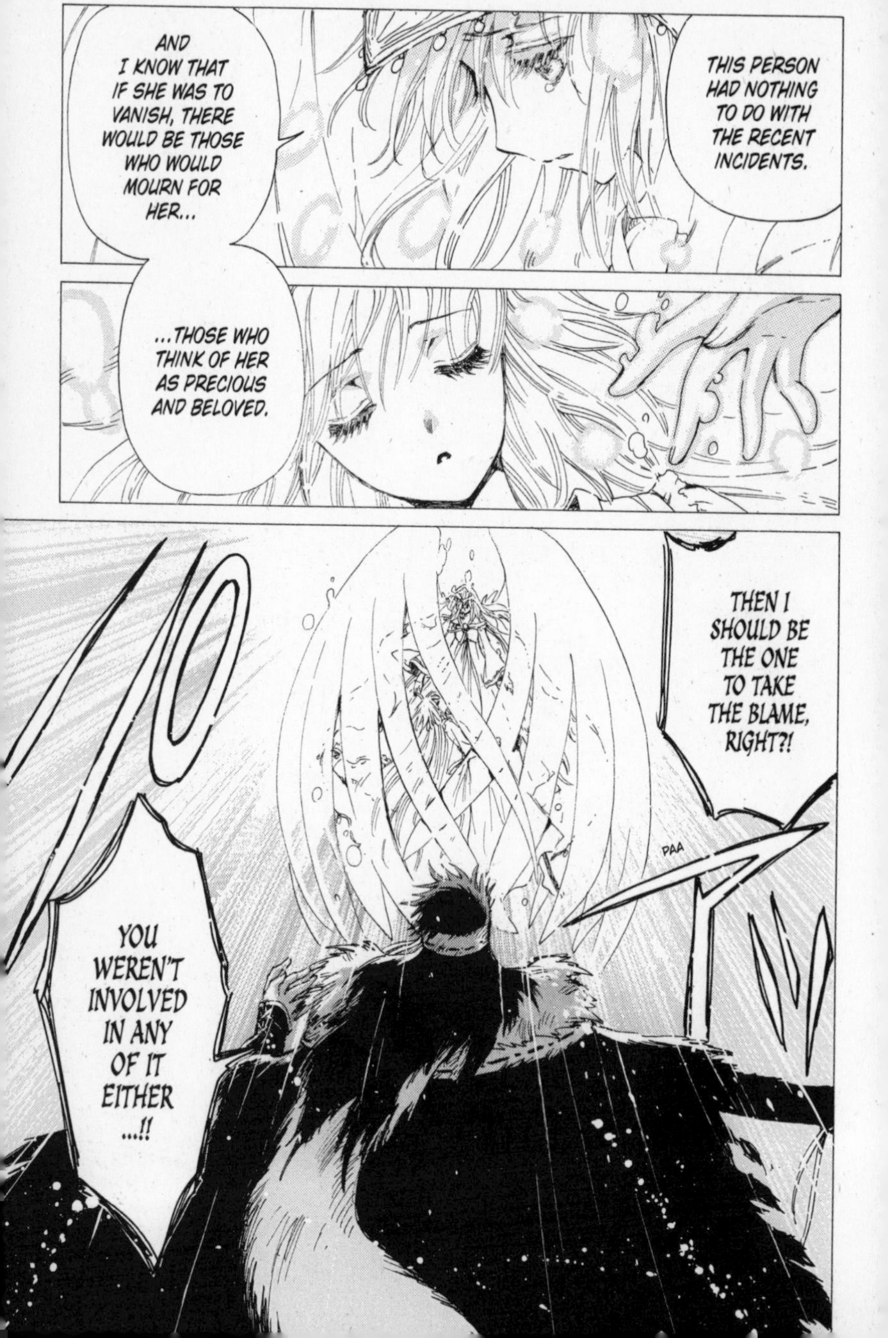
THIS PERSON HAD NOTHING TO DO WITH THE RECENT INCIDENTS.
AND I KNOW THAT IF SHE WAS TO VANISH, THERE WOULD BE THOSE WHO WOULD MOURN FOR HER...
...THOSE WHO THINK OF HER AS PRECIOUS AND BELOVED.
THEN I SHOULD BE THE ONE TO TAKE THE BLAME, RIGHT?!
PAA
YOU WEREN'T INVOLVED IN ANY OF IT EITHER ...!!

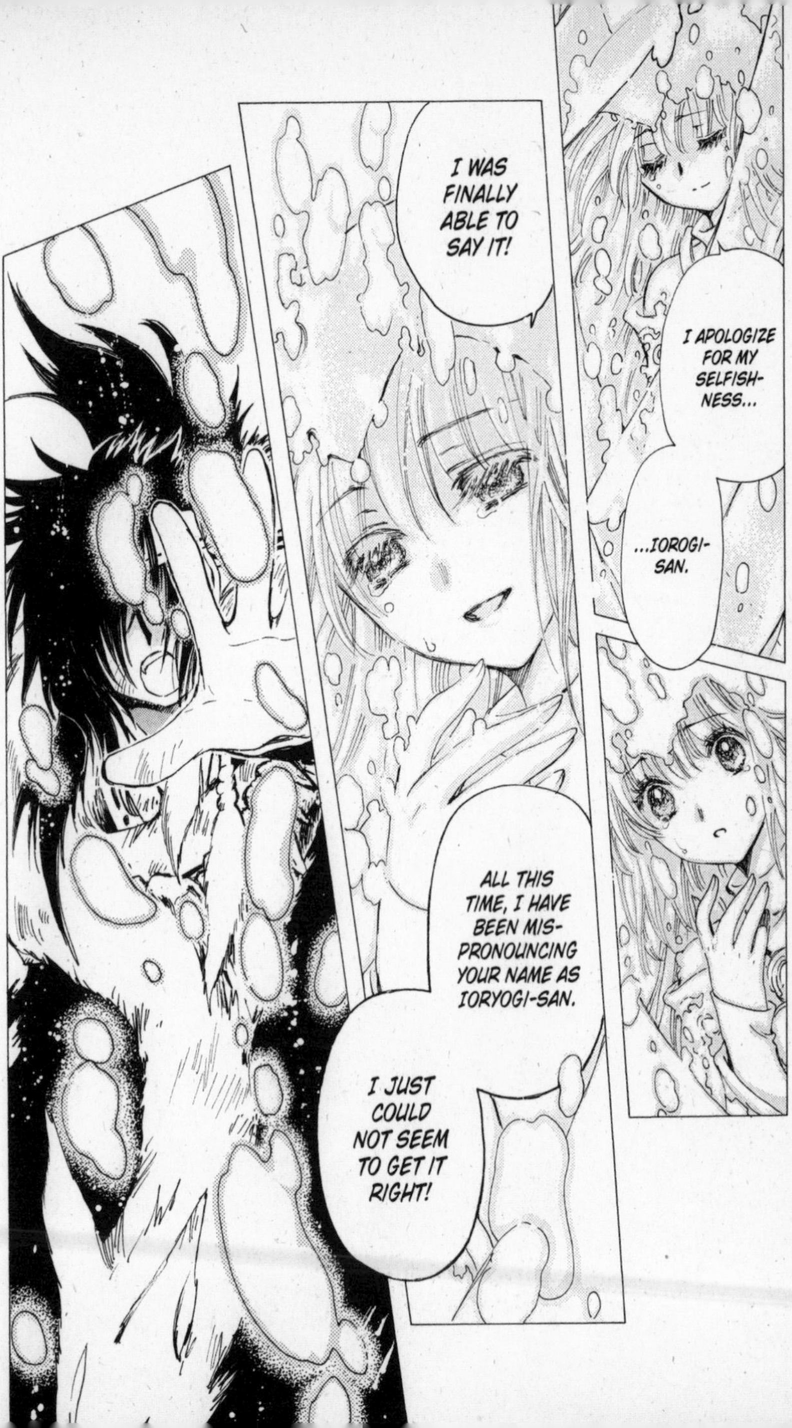
I APOLOGIZE FOR MY SELFISH-NESS...
...IOROGI-SAN.
I WAS FINALLY ABLE TO SAY IT!
ALL THIS TIME, I HAVE BEEN MIS-PRONOUNCING YOUR NAME AS IORYOGI-SAN.
I JUST COULD NOT SEEM TO GET IT RIGHT!

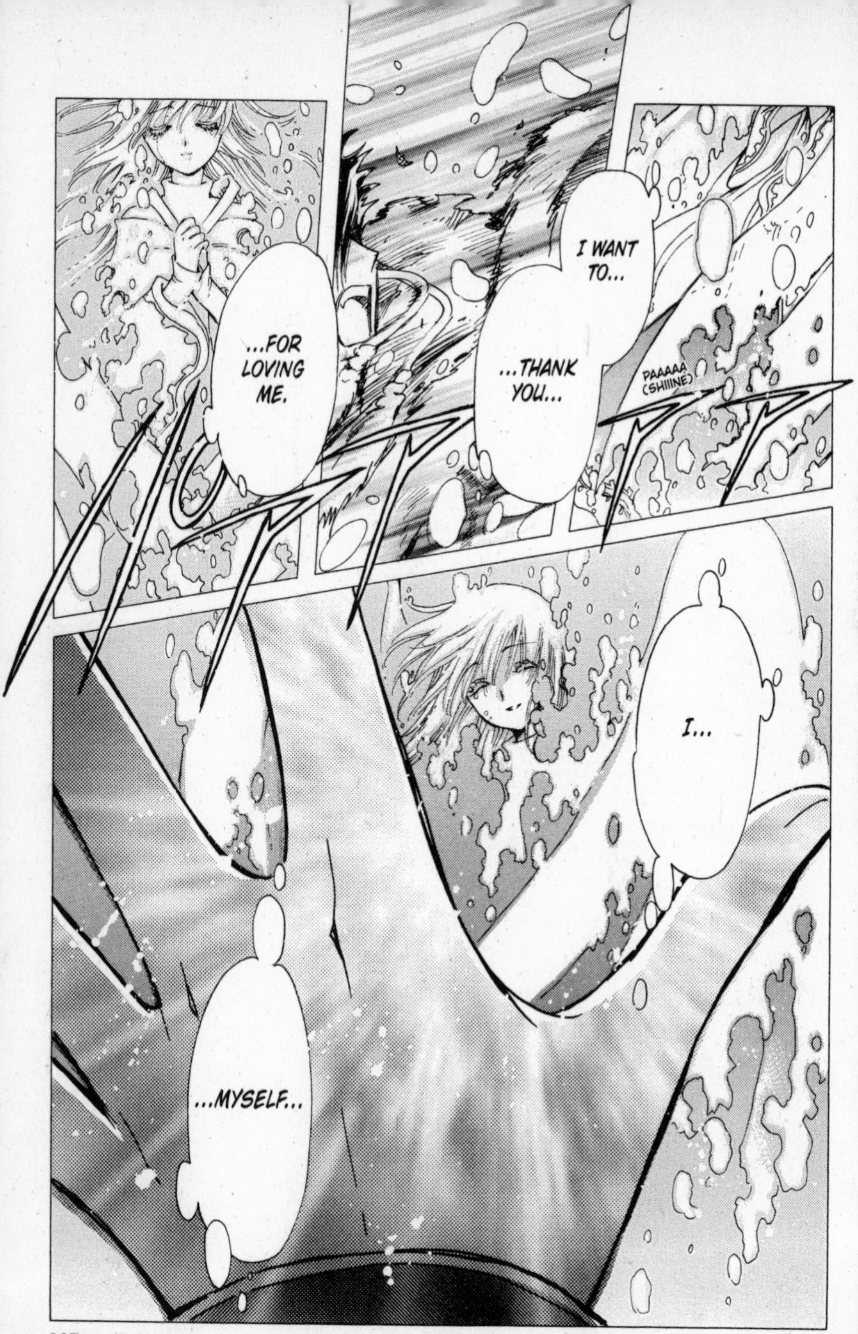
PAAAAA (SHIIINE)
I WANT TO...
...THANK YOU...
...FOR LOVING ME.
I...
...MYSELF...

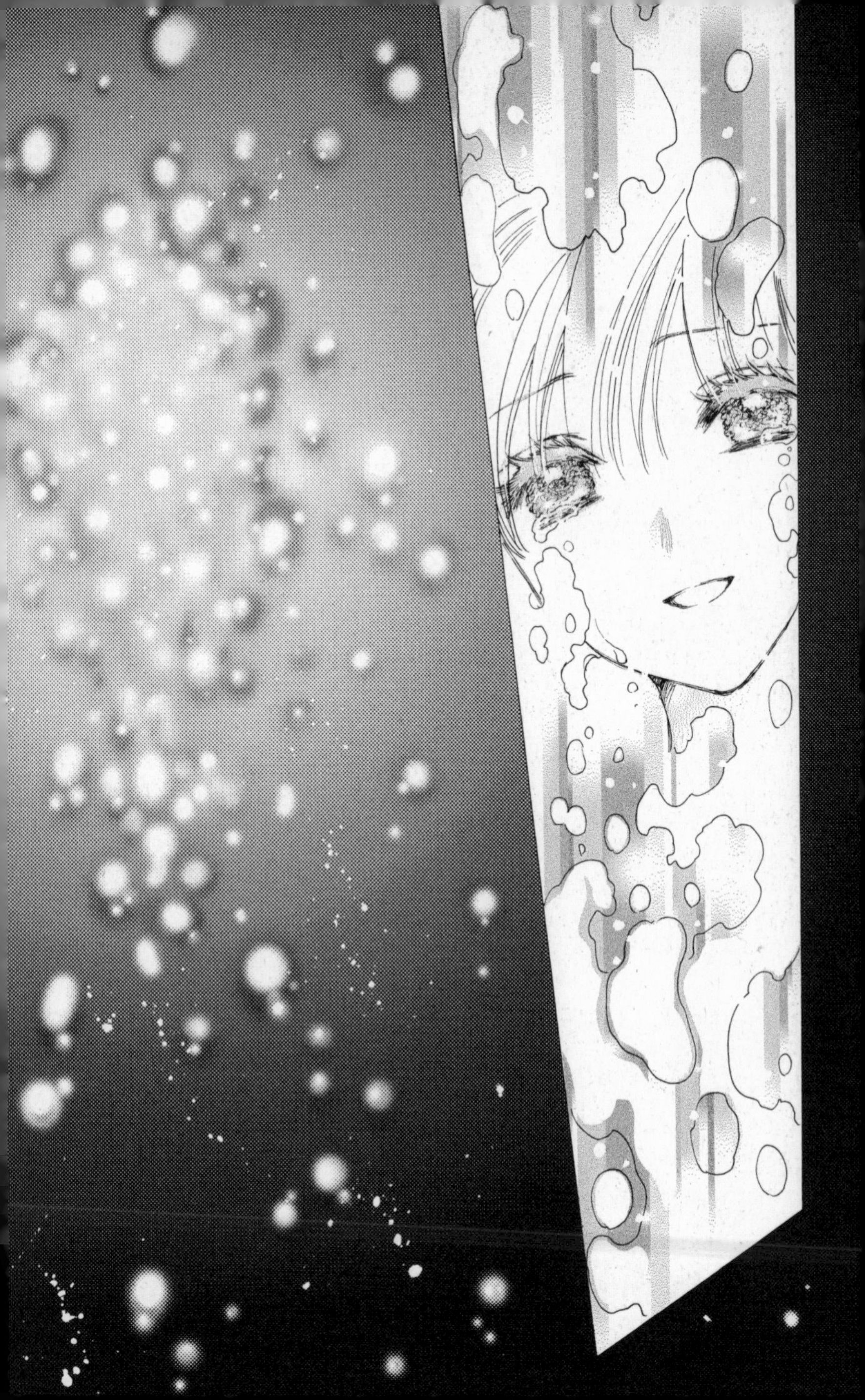

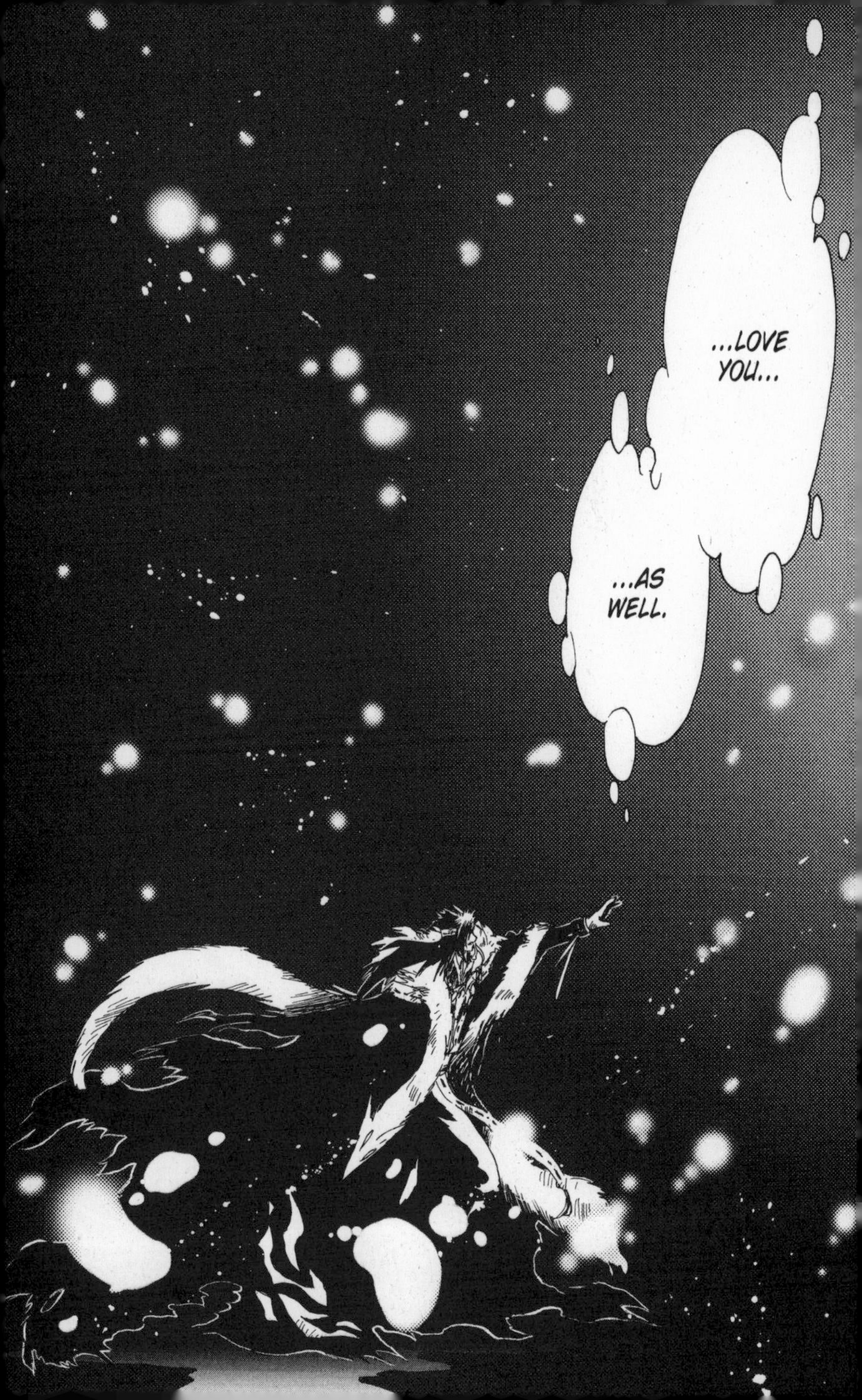
...LOVE YOU...
...AS WELL.

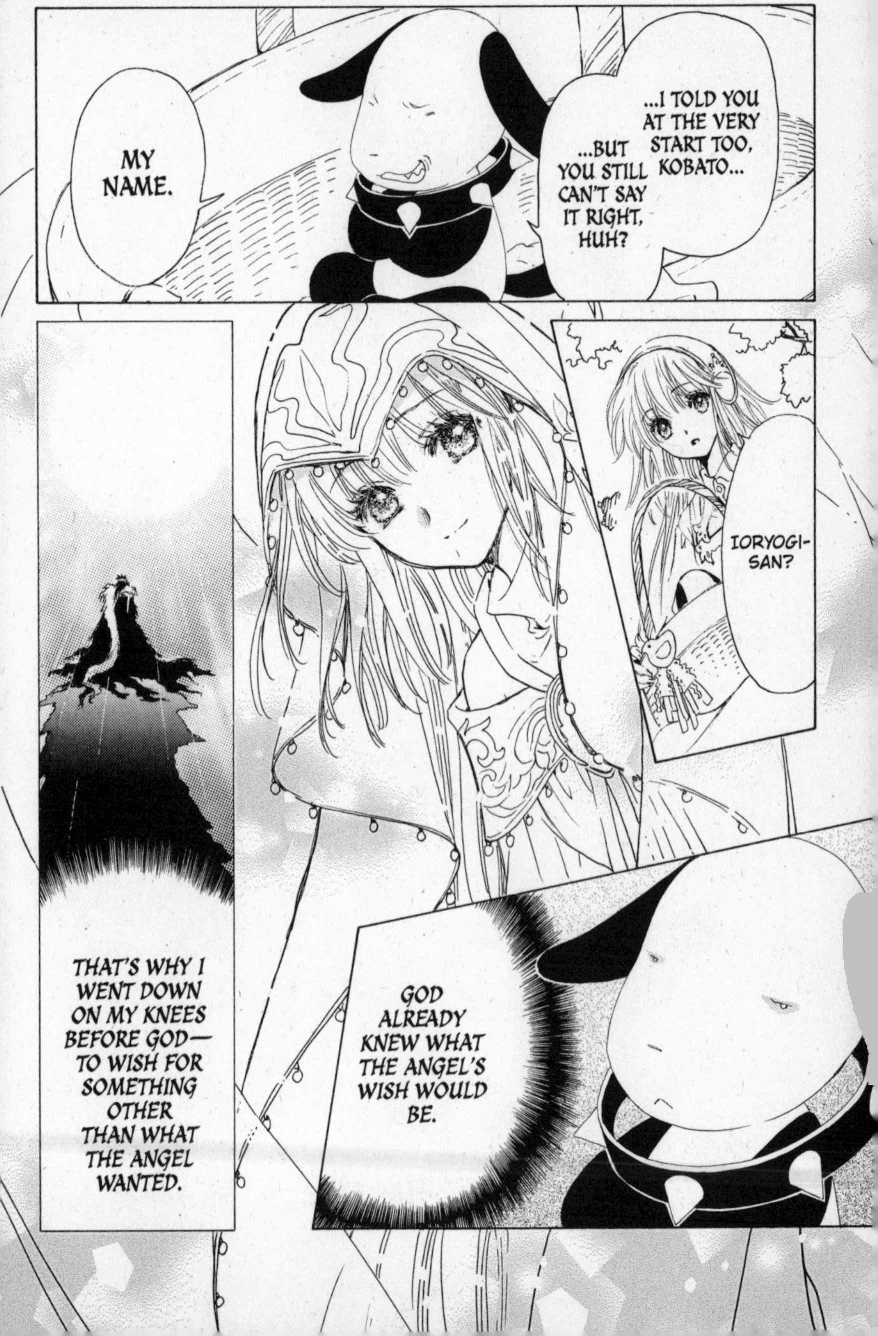
...I TOLD YOU AT THE VERY START TOO, KOBATO...
...BUT YOU STILL CAN'T SAY IT RIGHT, HUH?
MY NAME.
IORYOGI-SAN?
GOD ALREADY KNEW WHAT THE ANGEL'S WISH WOULD BE.
THAT'S WHY I WENT DOWN ON MY KNEES BEFORE GOD—TO WISH FOR SOMETHING OTHER THAN WHAT THE ANGEL WANTED.

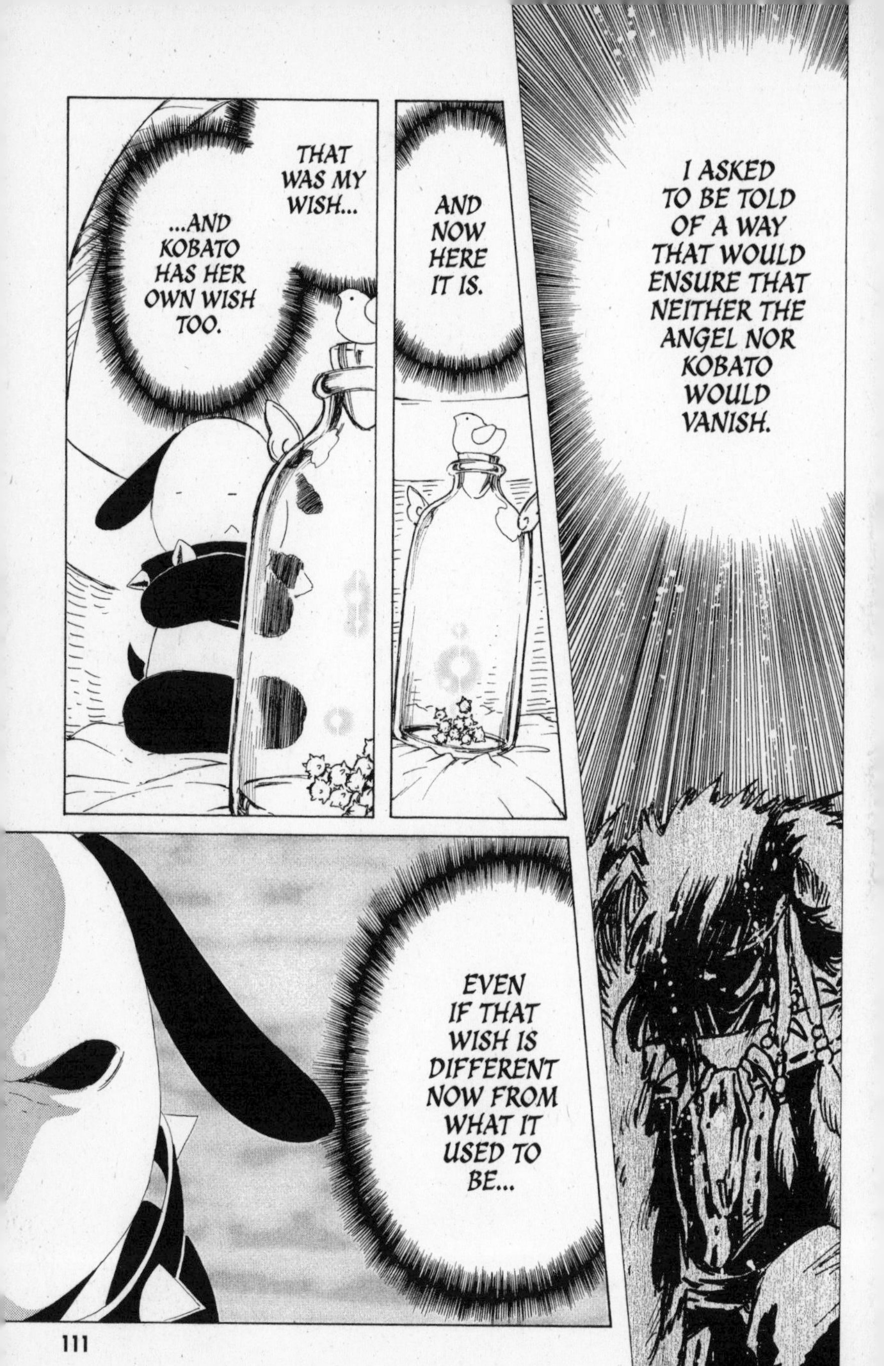
I ASKED TO BE TOLD OF A WAY THAT WOULD ENSURE THAT NEITHER THE ANGEL NOR KOBATO WOULD VANISH.
AND NOW HERE IT IS.
THAT WAS MY WISH...
...AND KOBATO HAS HER OWN WISH TOO.
EVEN IF THAT WISH IS DIFFERENT NOW FROM WHAT IT USED TO BE...

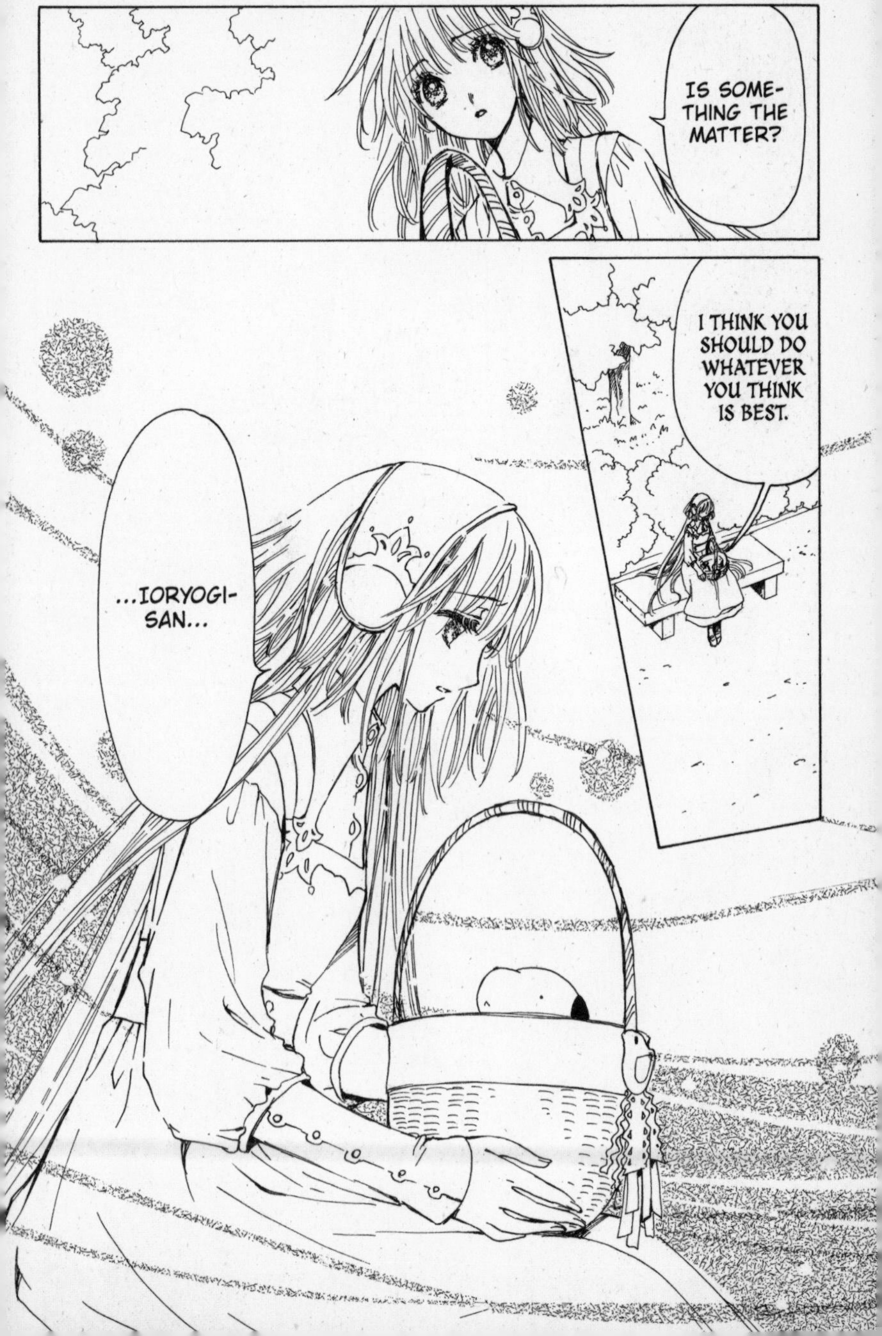
IS SOME-THING THE MATTER?
I THINK YOU SHOULD DO WHATEVER YOU THINK IS BEST.
...IORYOGI-SAN...

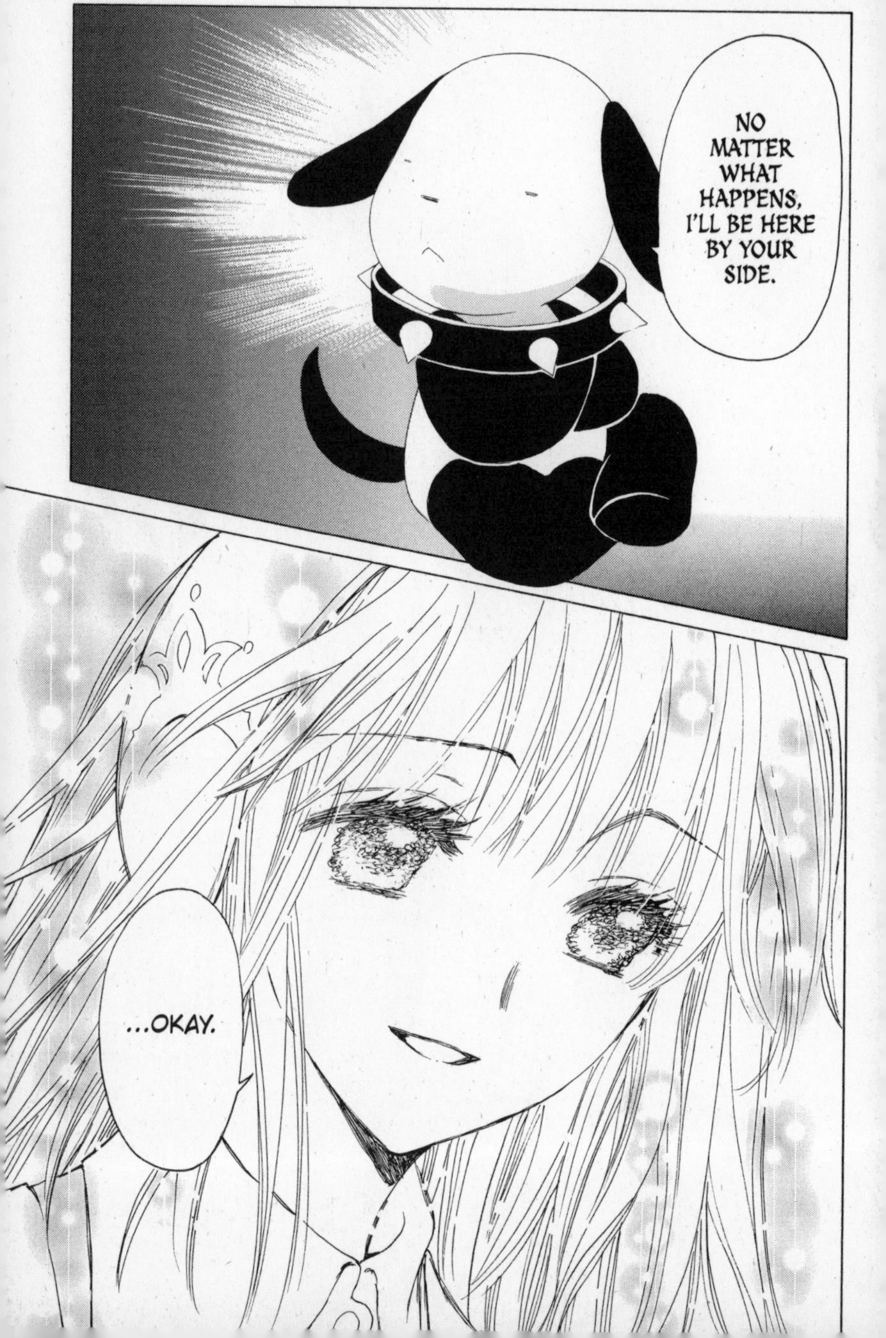
NO MATTER WHAT HAPPENS, I'LL BE HERE BY YOUR SIDE.
...OKAY.

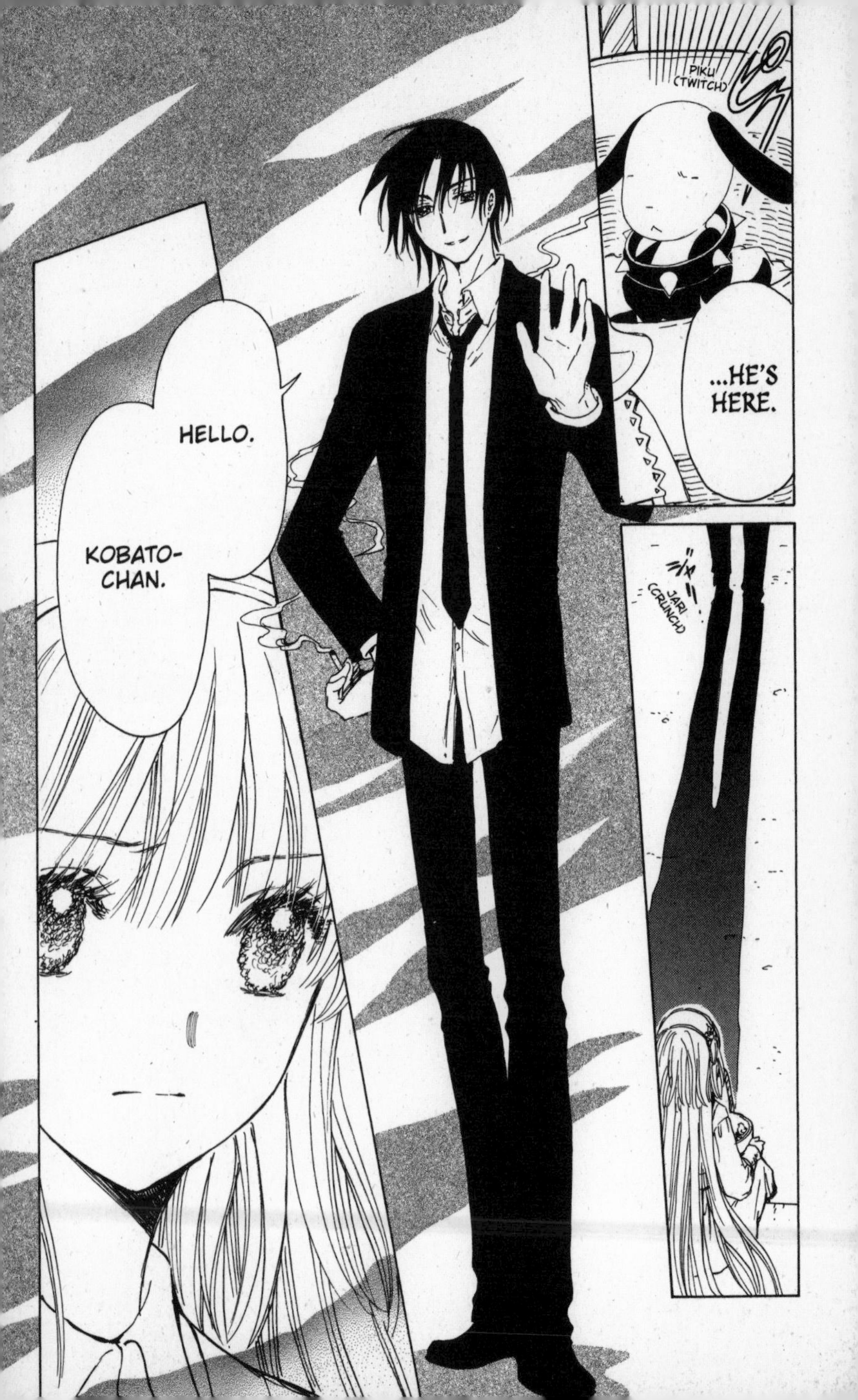
PIKU (TWITCH)
...HE'S HERE.
JARI (CRUNCH)
HELLO. KOBATO-CHAN.

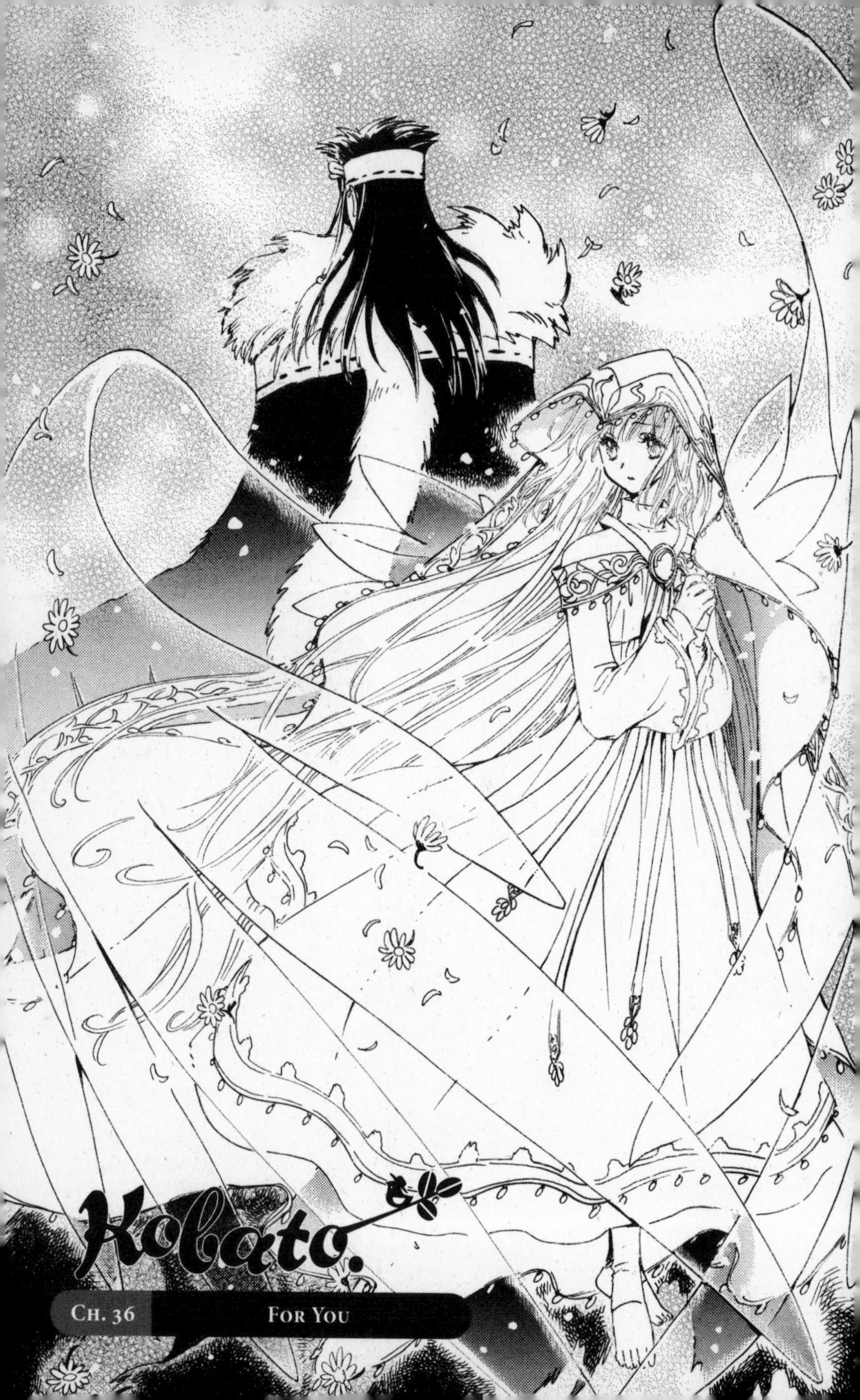
Kobato.
Ch. 36
For You

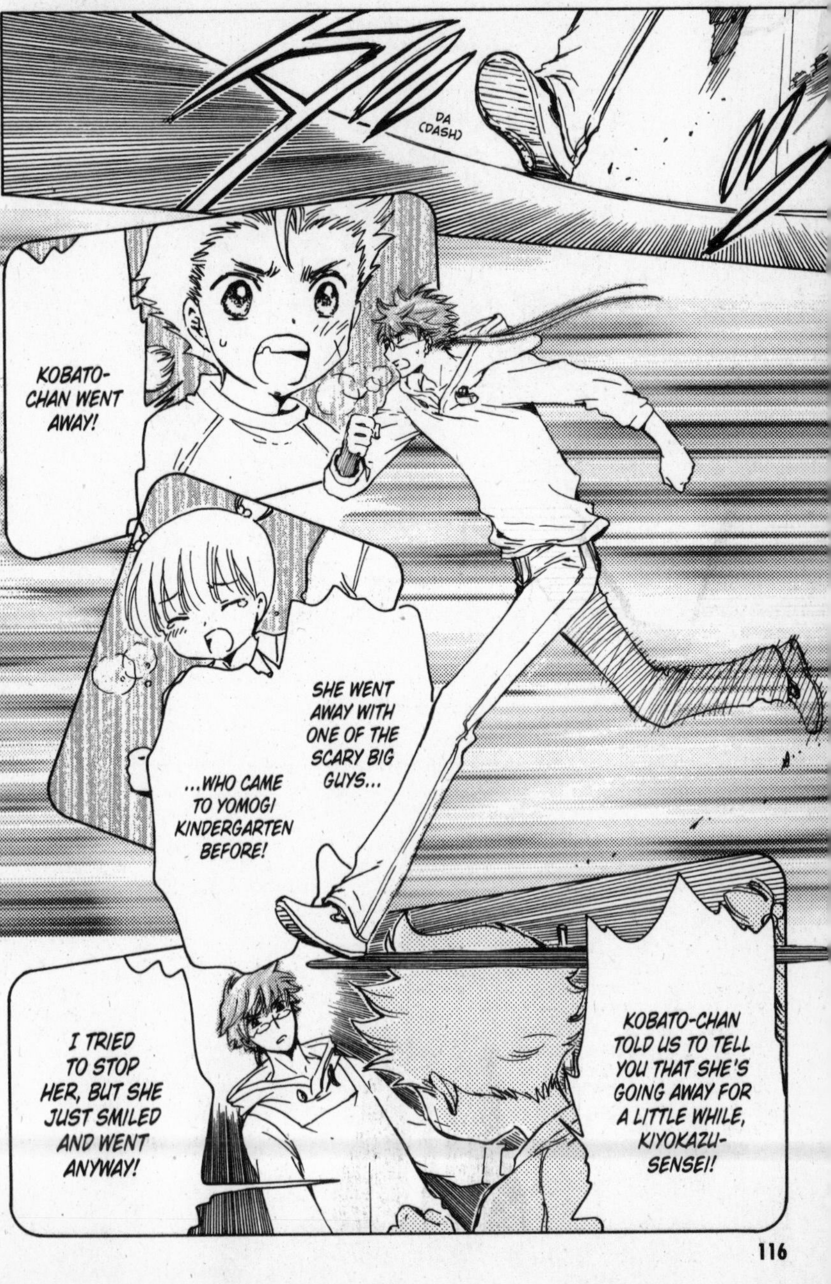
DA
(DASH)
KOBATO-CHAN WENT AWAY!
SHE WENT AWAY WITH ONE OF THE SCARY BIG GUYS...
...WHO CAME TO YOMOGI KINDERGARTEN BEFORE!
KOBATO-CHAN TOLD US TO TELL YOU THAT SHE'S GOING AWAY FOR A LITTLE WHILE, KIYOKAZU-SENSEI!
I TRIED TO STOP HER, BUT SHE JUST SMILED AND WENT ANYWAY!

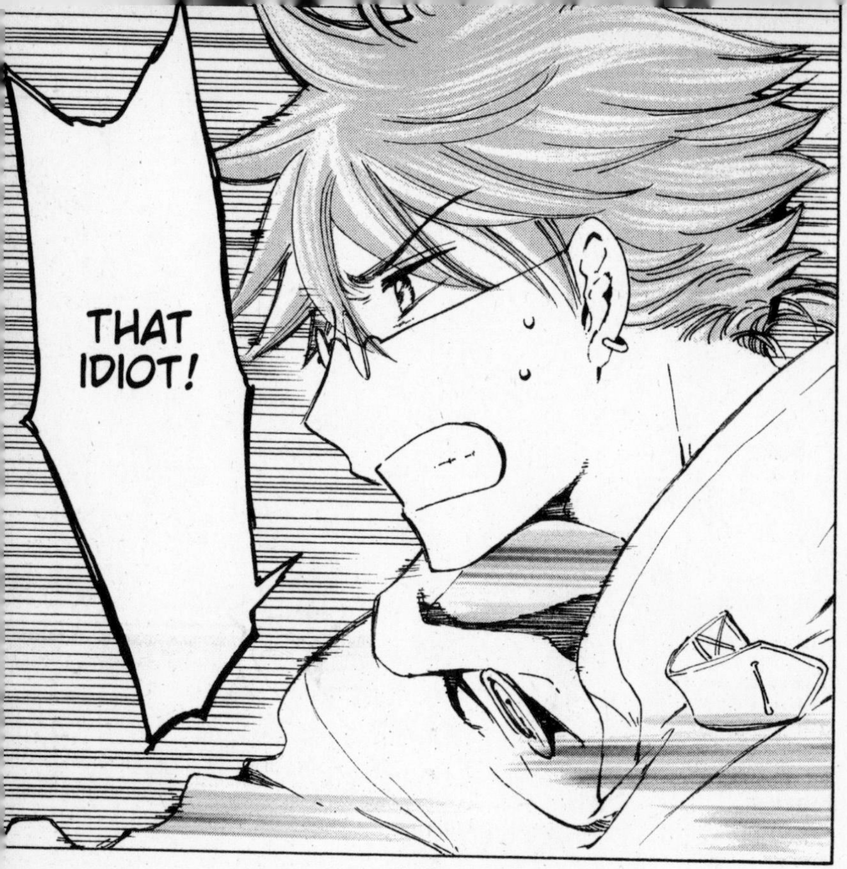
THAT IDIOT!

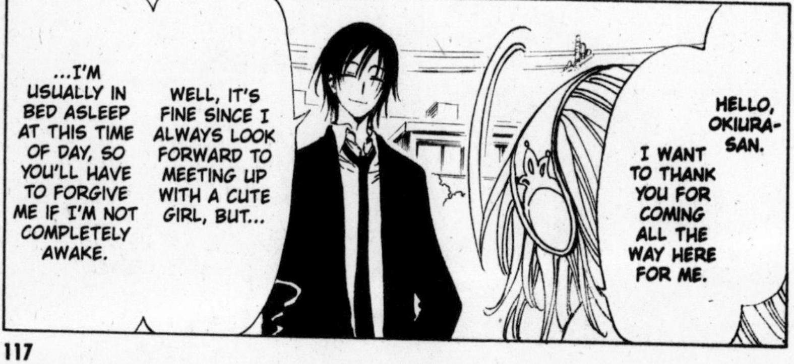
HELLO, OKIURA-SAN.
I WANT TO THANK YOU FOR COMING ALL THE WAY HERE FOR ME.
WELL, IT'S FINE SINCE I ALWAYS LOOK FORWARD TO MEETING UP WITH A CUTE GIRL, BUT...
...I'M USUALLY IN BED ASLEEP AT THIS TIME OF DAY, SO YOU'LL HAVE TO FORGIVE ME IF I'M NOT COMPLETELY AWAKE.

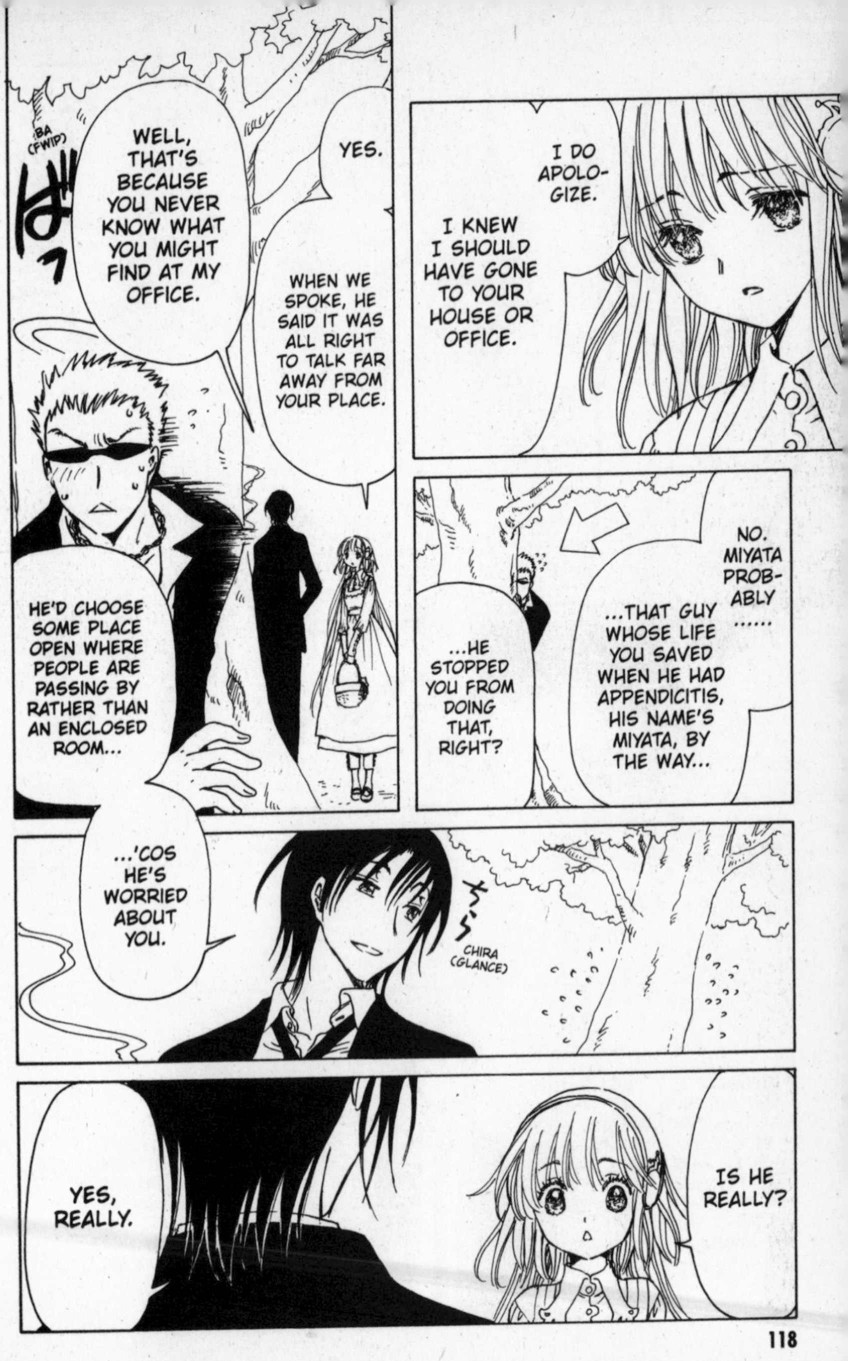
I DO APOLOGIZE.
I KNEW I SHOULD HAVE GONE TO YOUR HOUSE OR OFFICE.
NO. MIYATA PROBABLY......
...THAT GUY WHOSE LIFE YOU SAVED WHEN HE HAD APPENDICITIS, HIS NAME'S MIYATA, BY THE WAY...
...HE STOPPED YOU FROM DOING THAT, RIGHT?
YES.
WHEN WE SPOKE, HE SAID IT WAS ALL RIGHT TO TALK FAR AWAY FROM YOUR PLACE.
WELL, THAT'S BECAUSE YOU NEVER KNOW WHAT YOU MIGHT FIND AT MY OFFICE.
ば
BA (FWIP)
HE'D CHOOSE SOME PLACE OPEN WHERE PEOPLE ARE PASSING BY RATHER THAN AN ENCLOSED ROOM...
ちら
CHIRA (GLANCE)
...'COS HE'S WORRIED ABOUT YOU.
IS HE REALLY?
YES, REALLY.

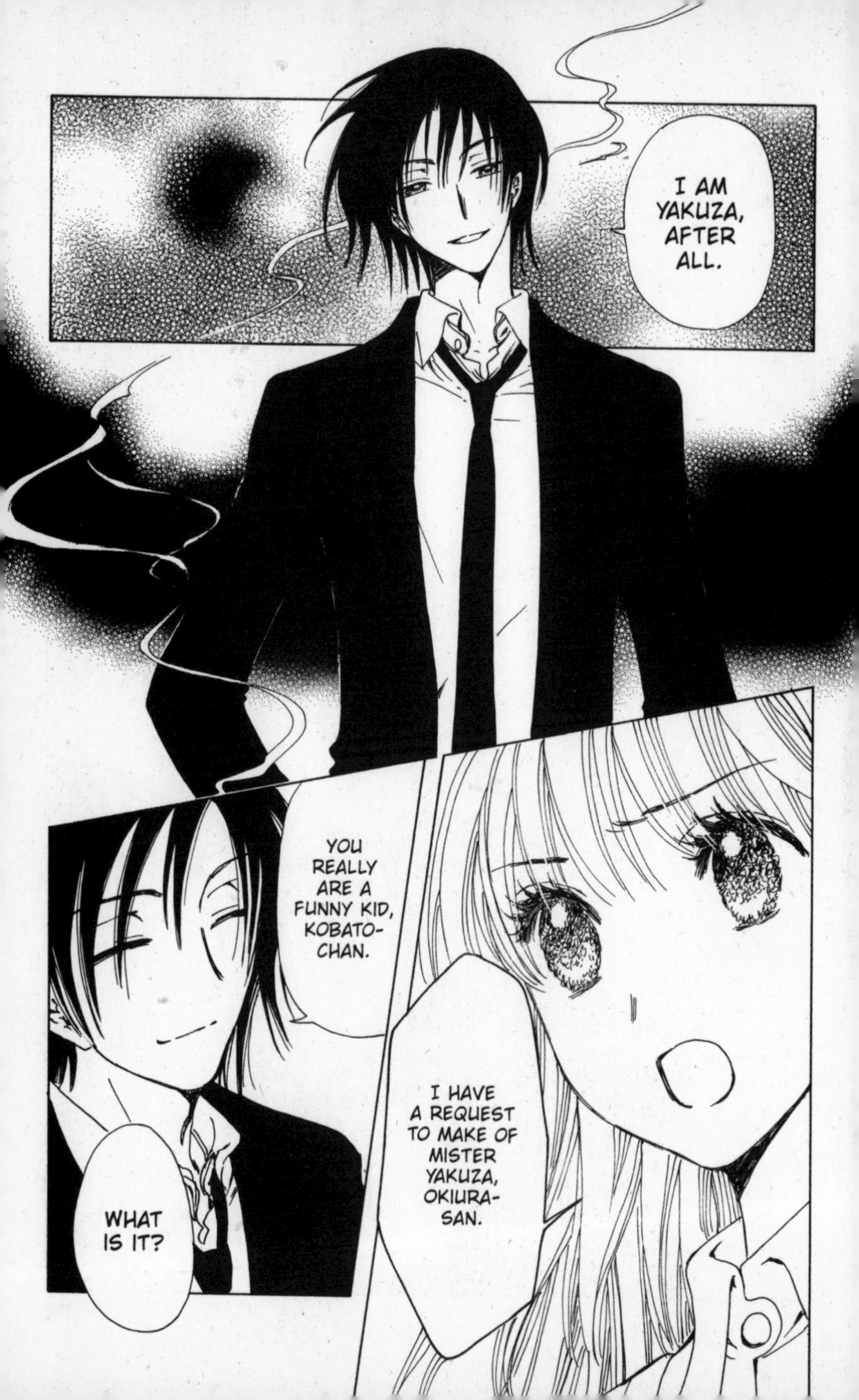
I AM YAKUZA, AFTER ALL.
YOU REALLY ARE A FUNNY KID, KOBATO-CHAN.
I HAVE A REQUEST TO MAKE OF MISTER YAKUZA, OKIURA-SAN.
WHAT IS IT?

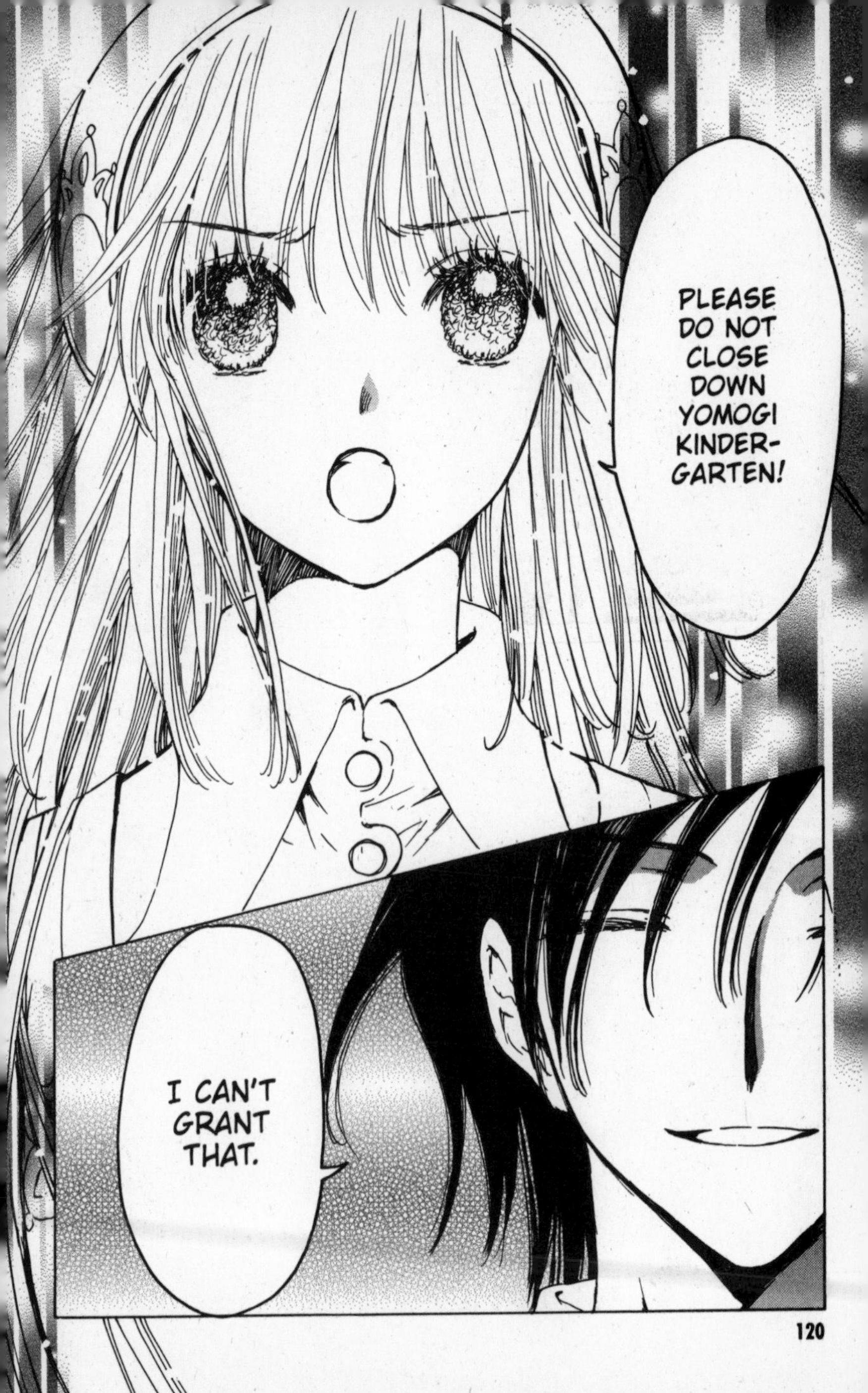
PLEASE DO NOT CLOSE DOWN YOMOGI KINDER-GARTEN!
I CAN'T GRANT THAT.

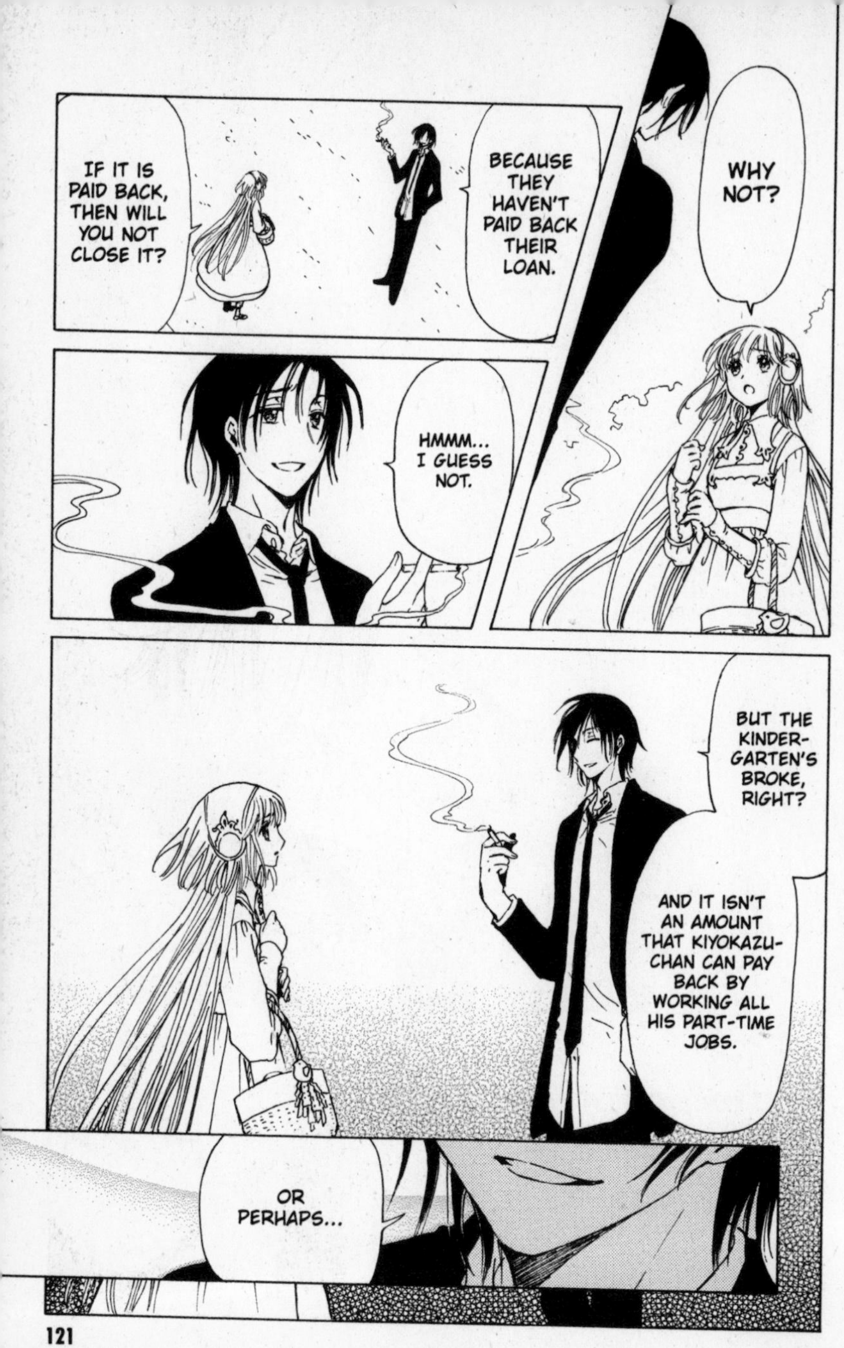
WHY NOT?
BECAUSE THEY HAVEN'T PAID BACK THEIR LOAN.
IF IT IS PAID BACK, THEN WILL YOU NOT CLOSE IT?
HMMM... I GUESS NOT.
BUT THE KINDER-GARTEN'S BROKE, RIGHT?
AND IT ISN'T AN AMOUNT THAT KIYOKAZU-CHAN CAN PAY BACK BY WORKING ALL HIS PART-TIME JOBS.
OR PERHAPS...

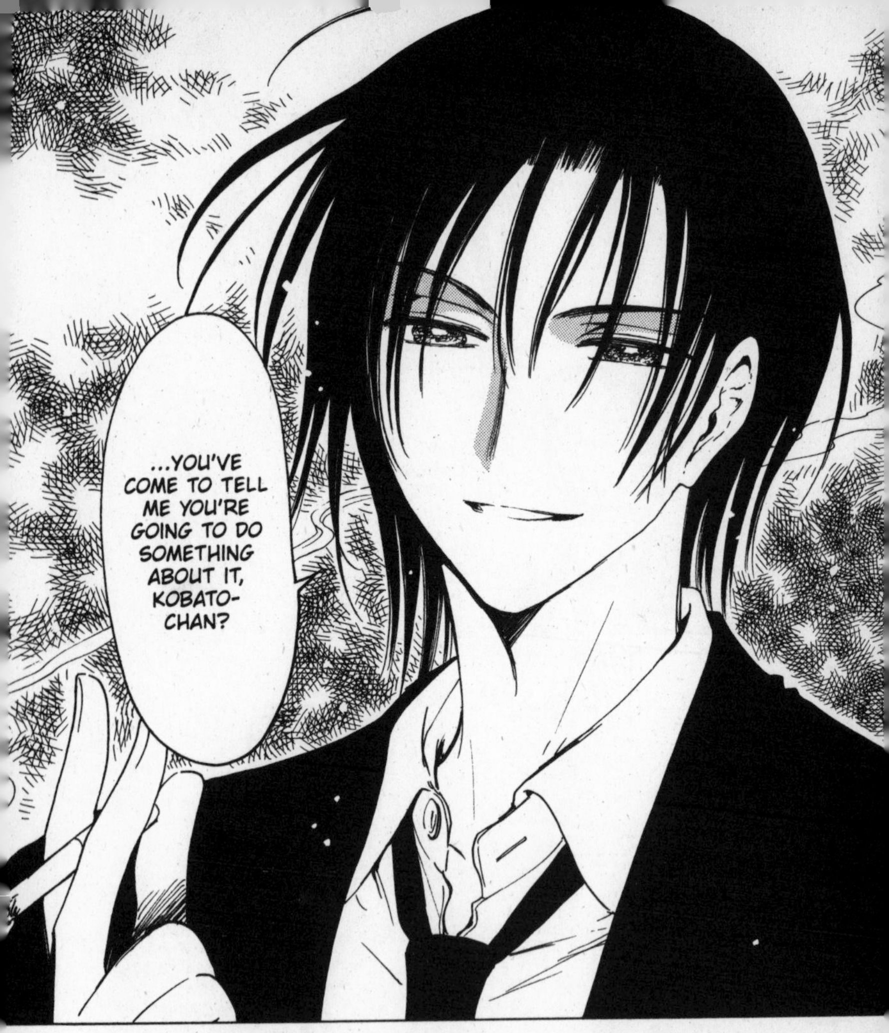
...YOU'VE COME TO TELL ME YOU'RE GOING TO DO SOMETHING ABOUT IT, KOBATO-CHAN?

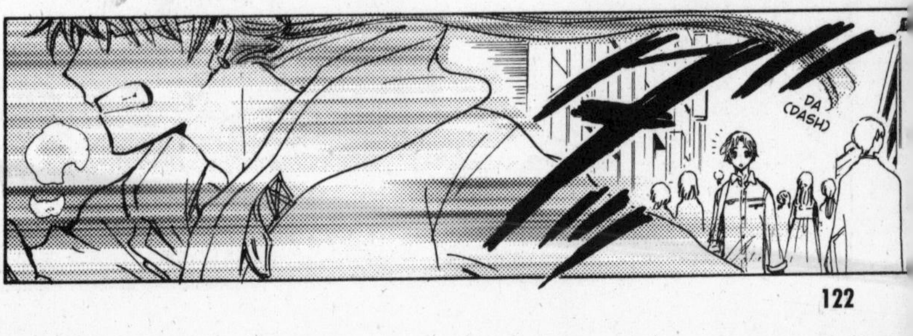
DA (DASH)

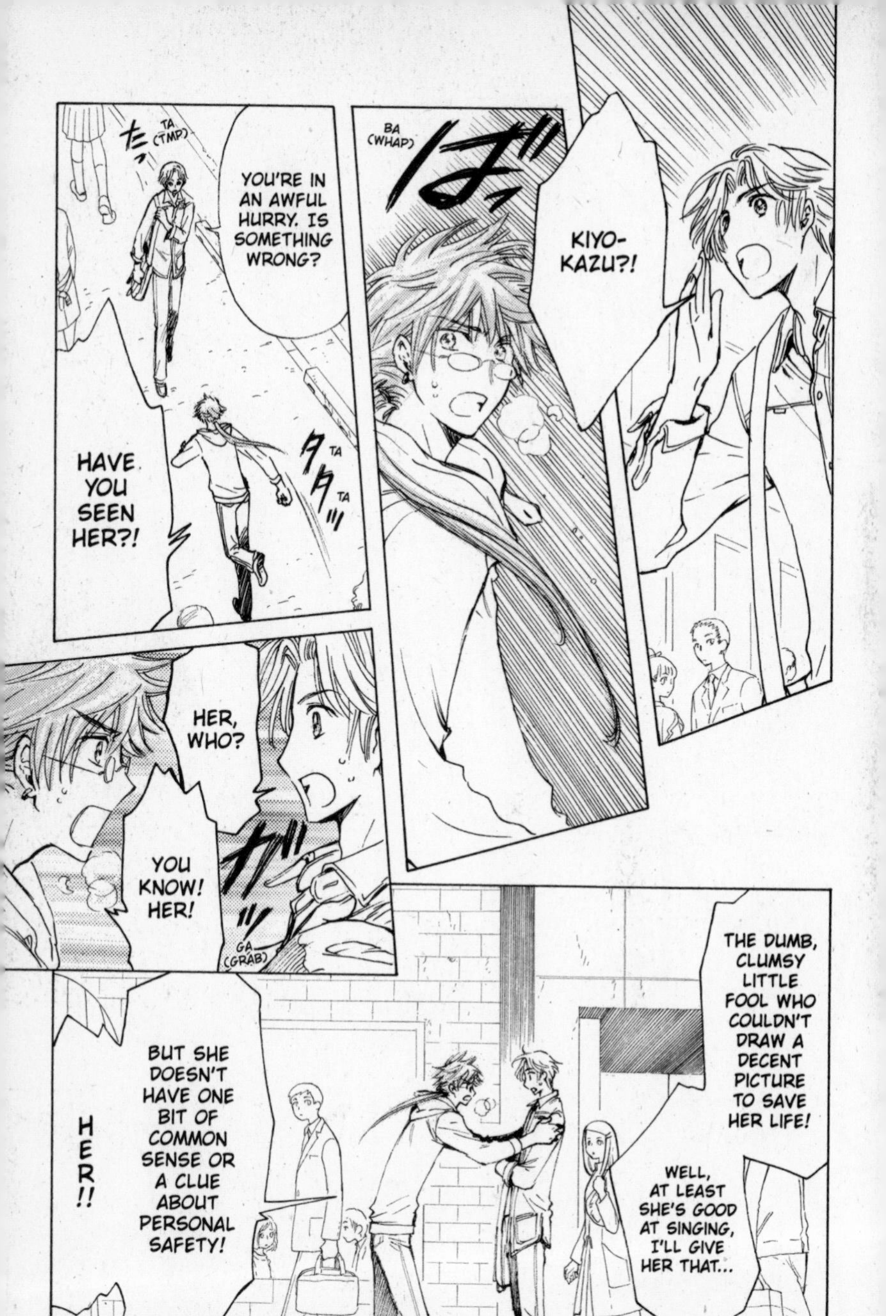
KIYO-KAZU?!
BA (WHAP)
YOU'RE IN AN AWFUL HURRY. IS SOMETHING WRONG?
TA (TMP)
TA
TA
HAVE YOU SEEN HER?!
HER, WHO?
YOU KNOW! HER!
GA (GRAB)
THE DUMB, CLUMSY LITTLE FOOL WHO COULDN'T DRAW A DECENT PICTURE TO SAVE HER LIFE!
BUT SHE DOESN'T HAVE ONE BIT OF COMMON SENSE OR A CLUE ABOUT PERSONAL SAFETY!
HER!!
WELL, AT LEAST SHE'S GOOD AT SINGING, I'LL GIVE HER THAT...

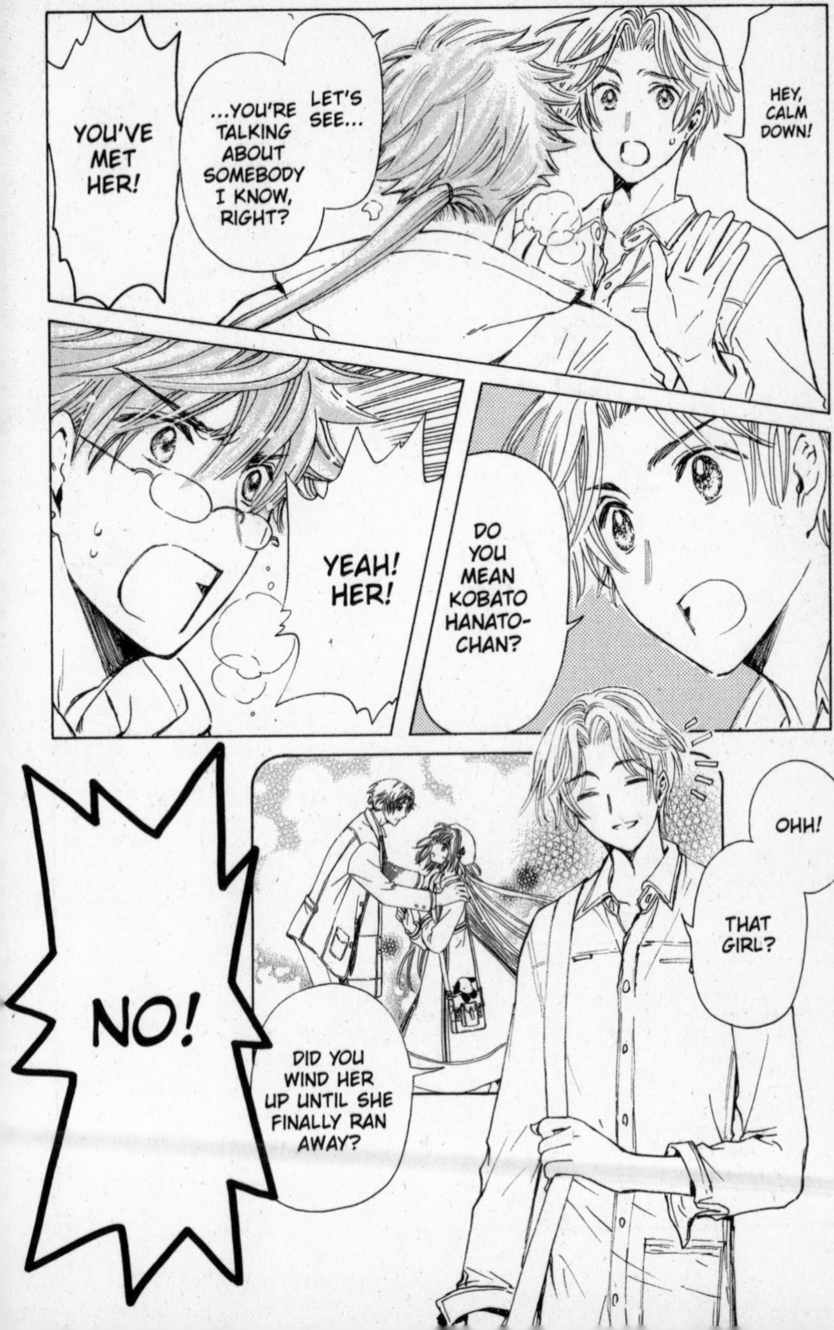
HEY, CALM DOWN!
LET'S SEE...
...YOU'RE TALKING ABOUT SOMEBODY I KNOW, RIGHT?
YOU'VE MET HER!
DO YOU MEAN KOBATO HANATO-CHAN?
YEAH! HER!
OHH!
THAT GIRL?
DID YOU WIND HER UP UNTIL SHE FINALLY RAN AWAY?
NO!

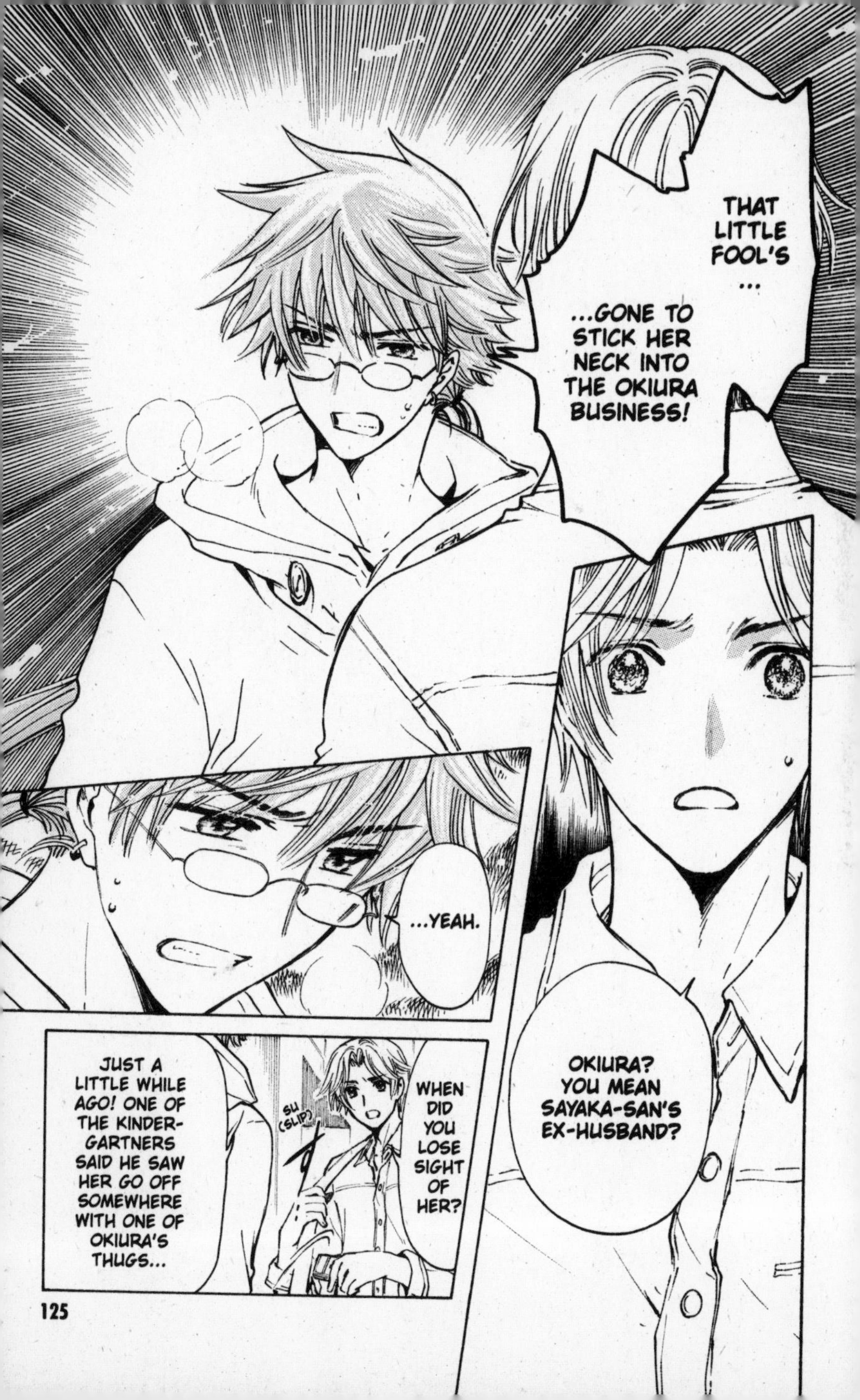
THAT LITTLE FOOL'S ...
...GONE TO STICK HER NECK INTO THE OKIURA BUSINESS!
OKIURA? YOU MEAN SAYAKA-SAN'S EX-HUSBAND?
...YEAH.
WHEN DID YOU LOSE SIGHT OF HER?
SU (SLIP)
JUST A LITTLE WHILE AGO! ONE OF THE KINDER-GARTNERS SAID HE SAW HER GO OFF SOMEWHERE WITH ONE OF OKIURA'S THUGS...

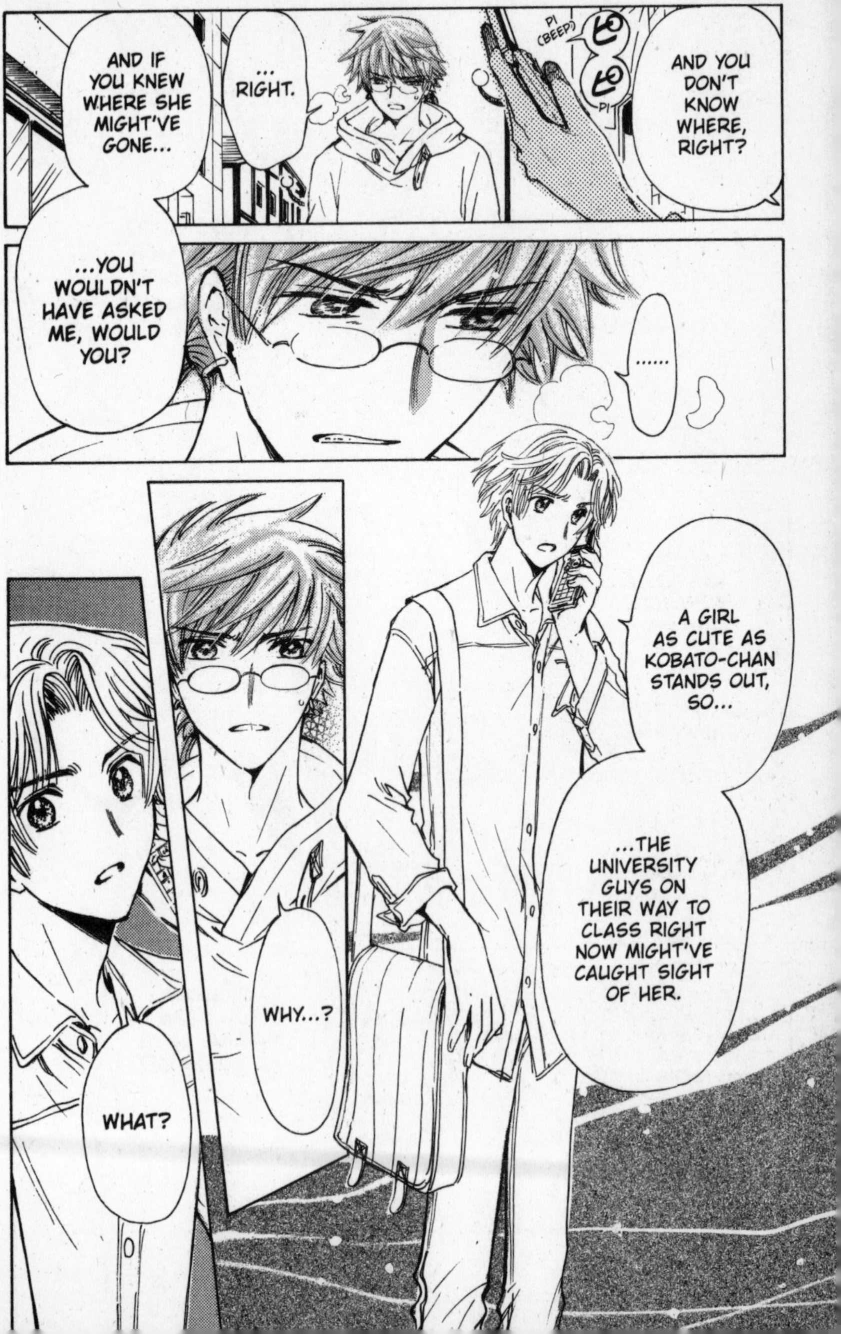
PI (BEEP)
PI
AND YOU DON'T KNOW WHERE, RIGHT?
... RIGHT.
AND IF YOU KNEW WHERE SHE MIGHT'VE GONE...
...YOU WOULDN'T HAVE ASKED ME, WOULD YOU?
......
A GIRL AS CUTE AS KOBATO-CHAN STANDS OUT, SO...
...THE UNIVERSITY GUYS ON THEIR WAY TO CLASS RIGHT NOW MIGHT'VE CAUGHT SIGHT OF HER.
WHY...?
WHAT?

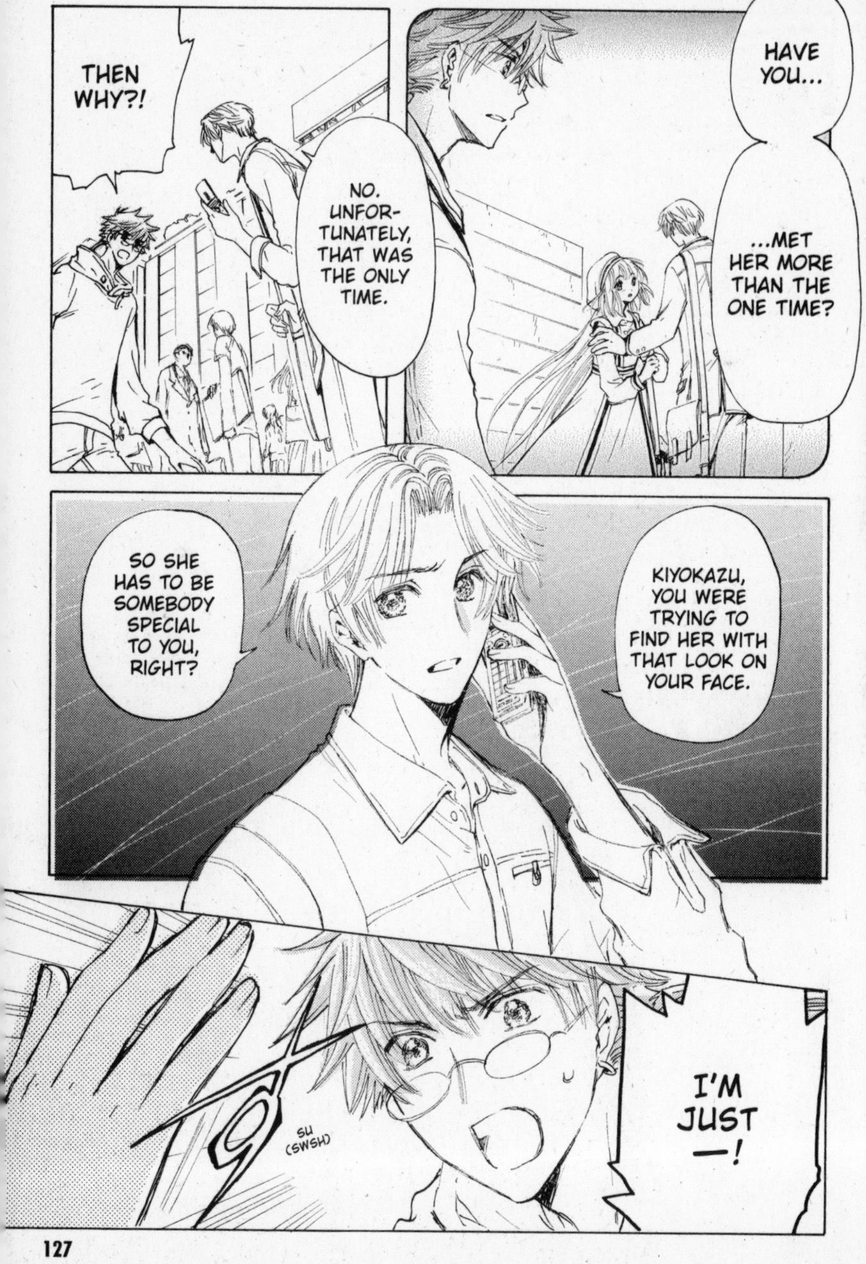
HAVE YOU...
...MET HER MORE THAN THE ONE TIME?
NO. UNFORTUNATELY, THAT WAS THE ONLY TIME.
THEN WHY?!
KIYOKAZU, YOU WERE TRYING TO FIND HER WITH THAT LOOK ON YOUR FACE.
SO SHE HAS TO BE SOMEBODY SPECIAL TO YOU, RIGHT?
I'M JUST —!
SU (SWSH)

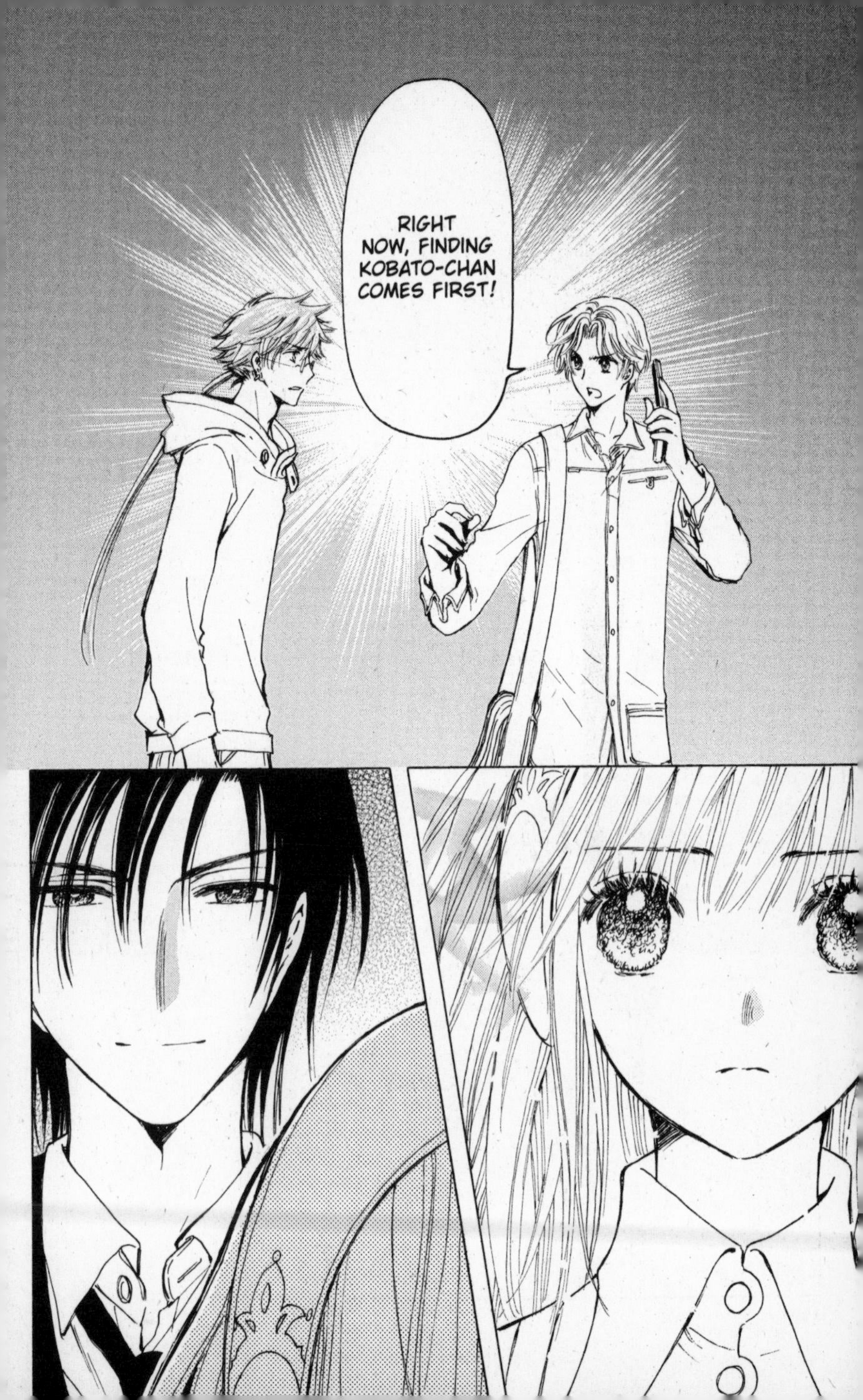
RIGHT NOW, FINDING KOBATO-CHAN COMES FIRST!

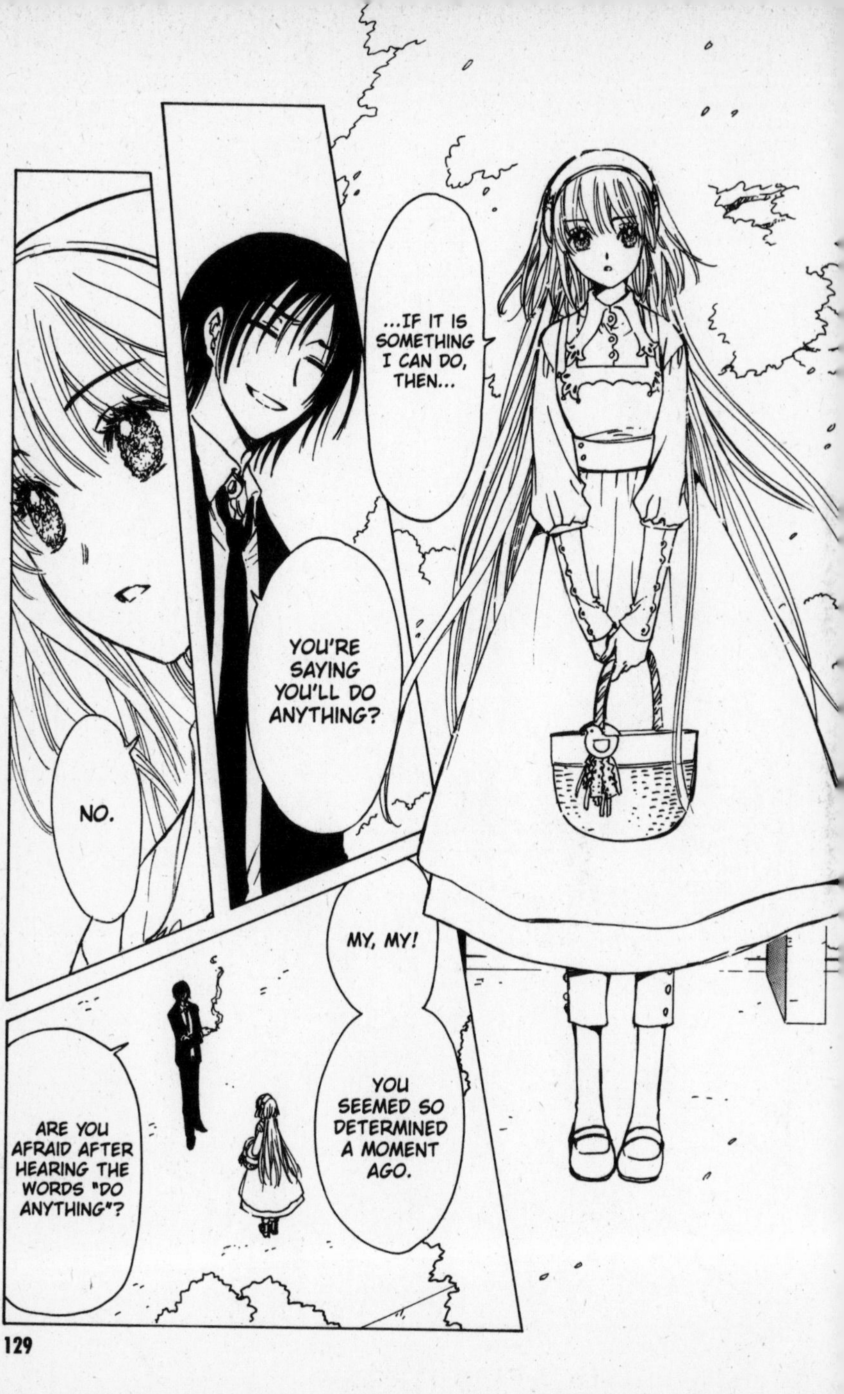
...IF IT IS SOMETHING I CAN DO, THEN...
YOU'RE SAYING YOU'LL DO ANYTHING?
NO.
MY, MY!
YOU SEEMED SO DETERMINED A MOMENT AGO.
ARE YOU AFRAID AFTER HEARING THE WORDS "DO ANYTHING"?

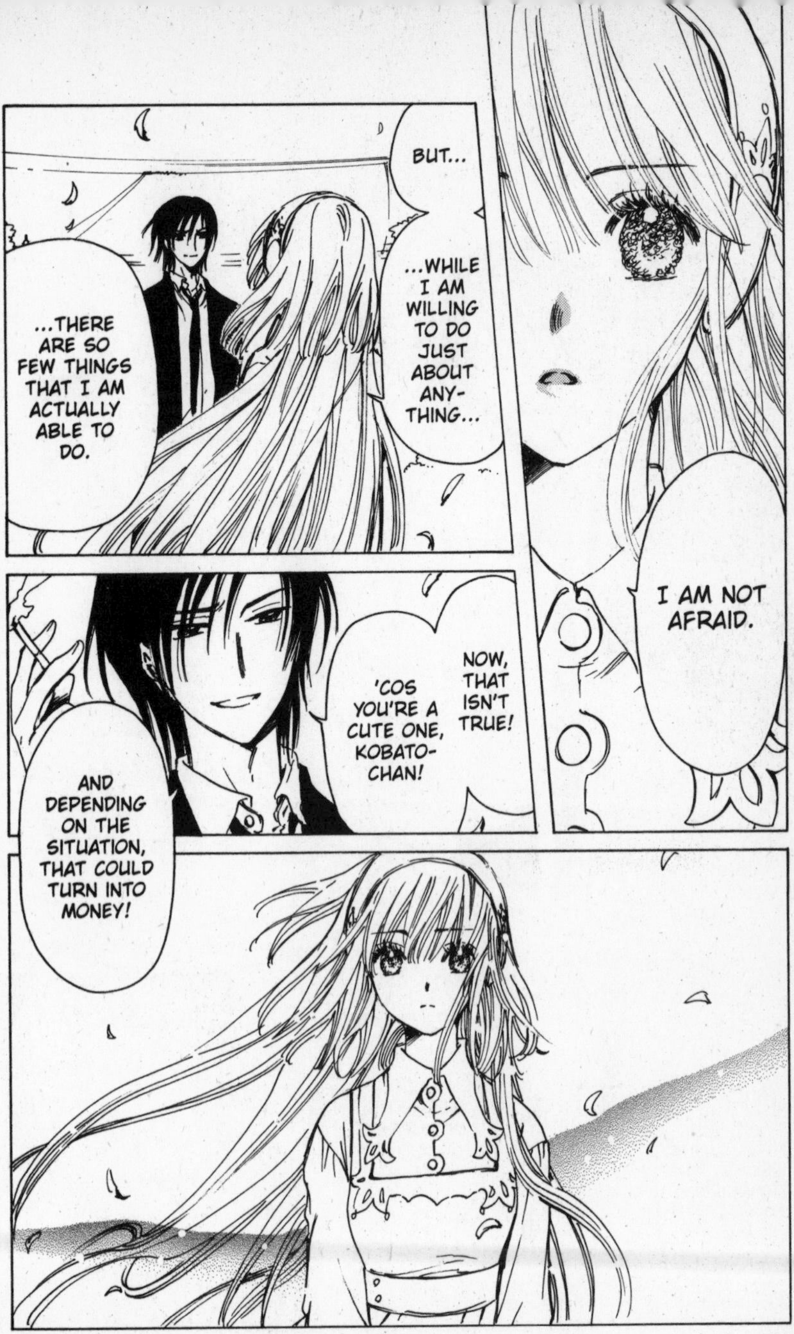
I AM NOT AFRAID.
BUT...
...WHILE I AM WILLING TO DO JUST ABOUT ANY-THING...
...THERE ARE SO FEW THINGS THAT I AM ACTUALLY ABLE TO DO.
NOW, THAT ISN'T TRUE!
'COS YOU'RE A CUTE ONE, KOBATO-CHAN!
AND DEPENDING ON THE SITUATION, THAT COULD TURN INTO MONEY!

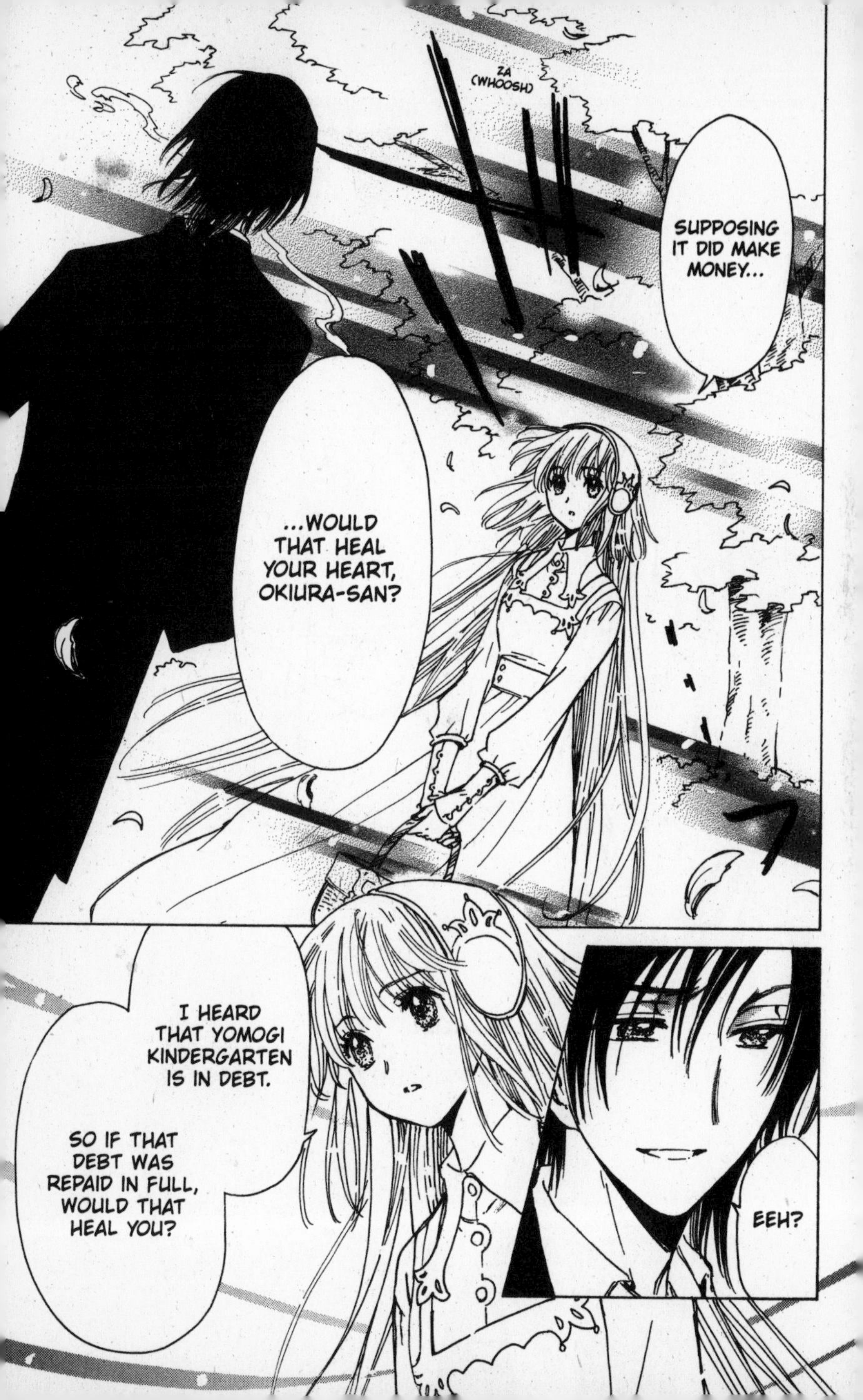
SUPPOSING IT DID MAKE MONEY...
ZA (WHOOSH)
...WOULD THAT HEAL YOUR HEART, OKIURA-SAN?
EEH?
I HEARD THAT YOMOGI KINDERGARTEN IS IN DEBT.
SO IF THAT DEBT WAS REPAID IN FULL, WOULD THAT HEAL YOU?

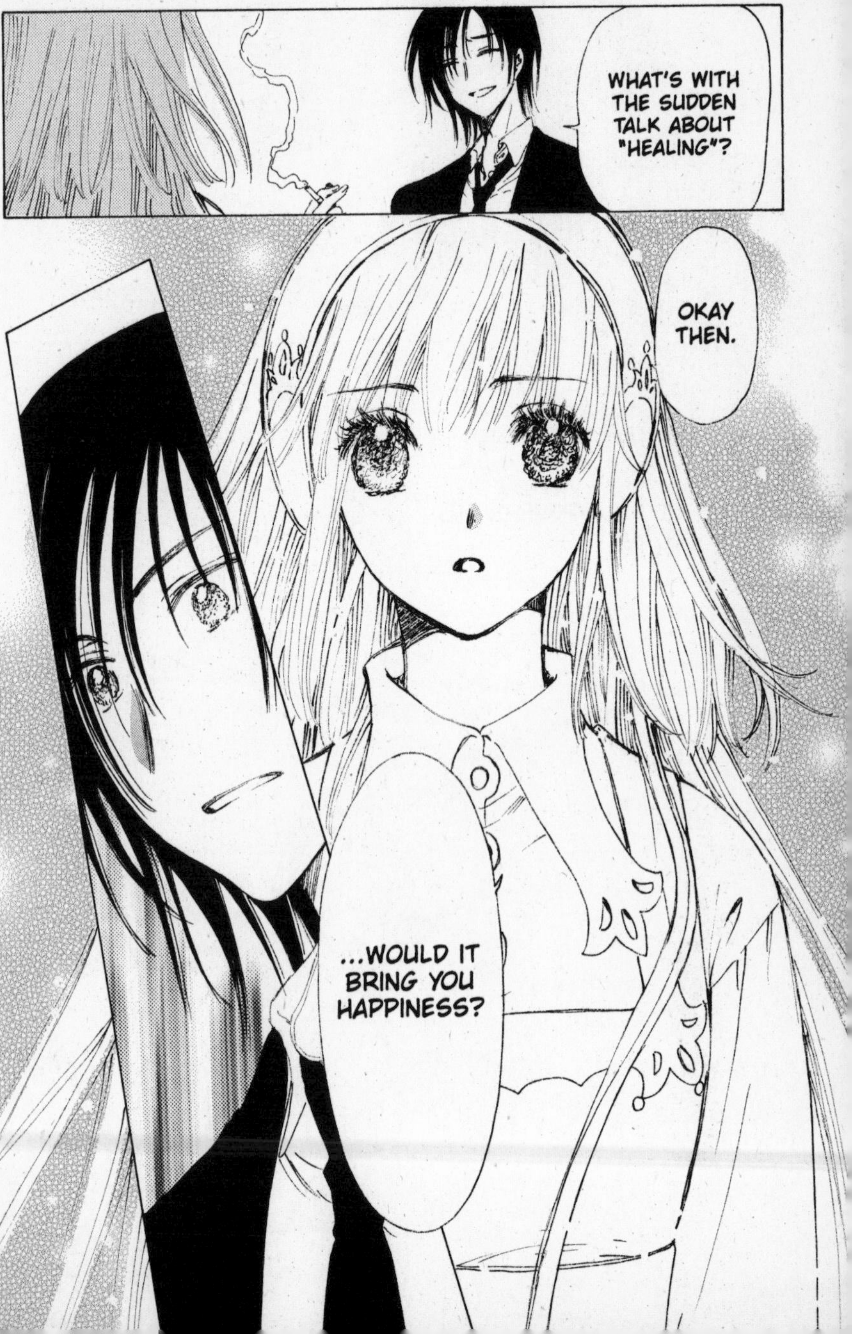
WHAT'S WITH THE SUDDEN TALK ABOUT "HEALING"?
OKAY THEN.
...WOULD IT BRING YOU HAPPINESS?

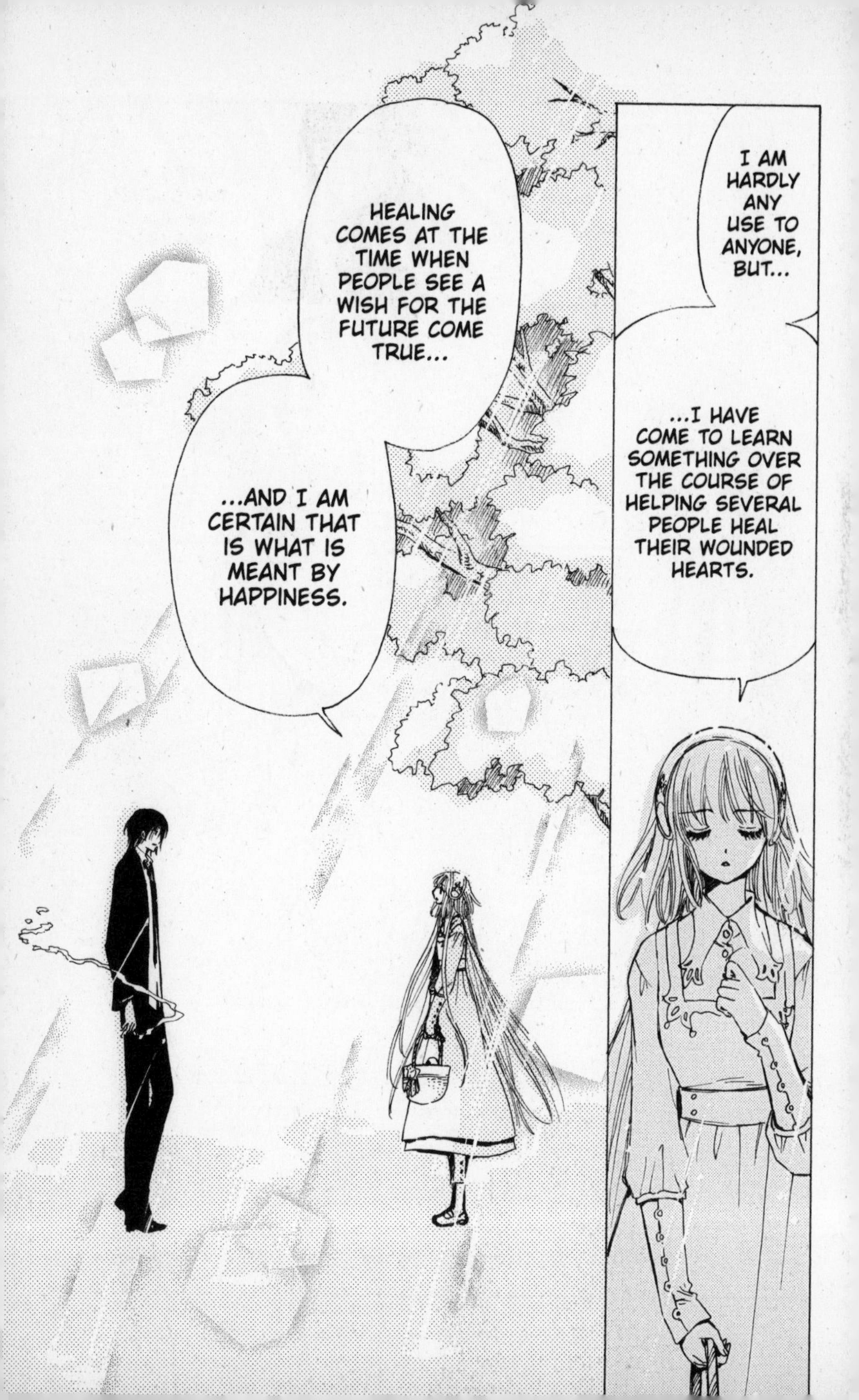
I AM HARDLY ANY USE TO ANYONE, BUT...
...I HAVE COME TO LEARN SOMETHING OVER THE COURSE OF HELPING SEVERAL PEOPLE HEAL THEIR WOUNDED HEARTS.
HEALING COMES AT THE TIME WHEN PEOPLE SEE A WISH FOR THE FUTURE COME TRUE...
...AND I AM CERTAIN THAT IS WHAT IS MEANT BY HAPPINESS.

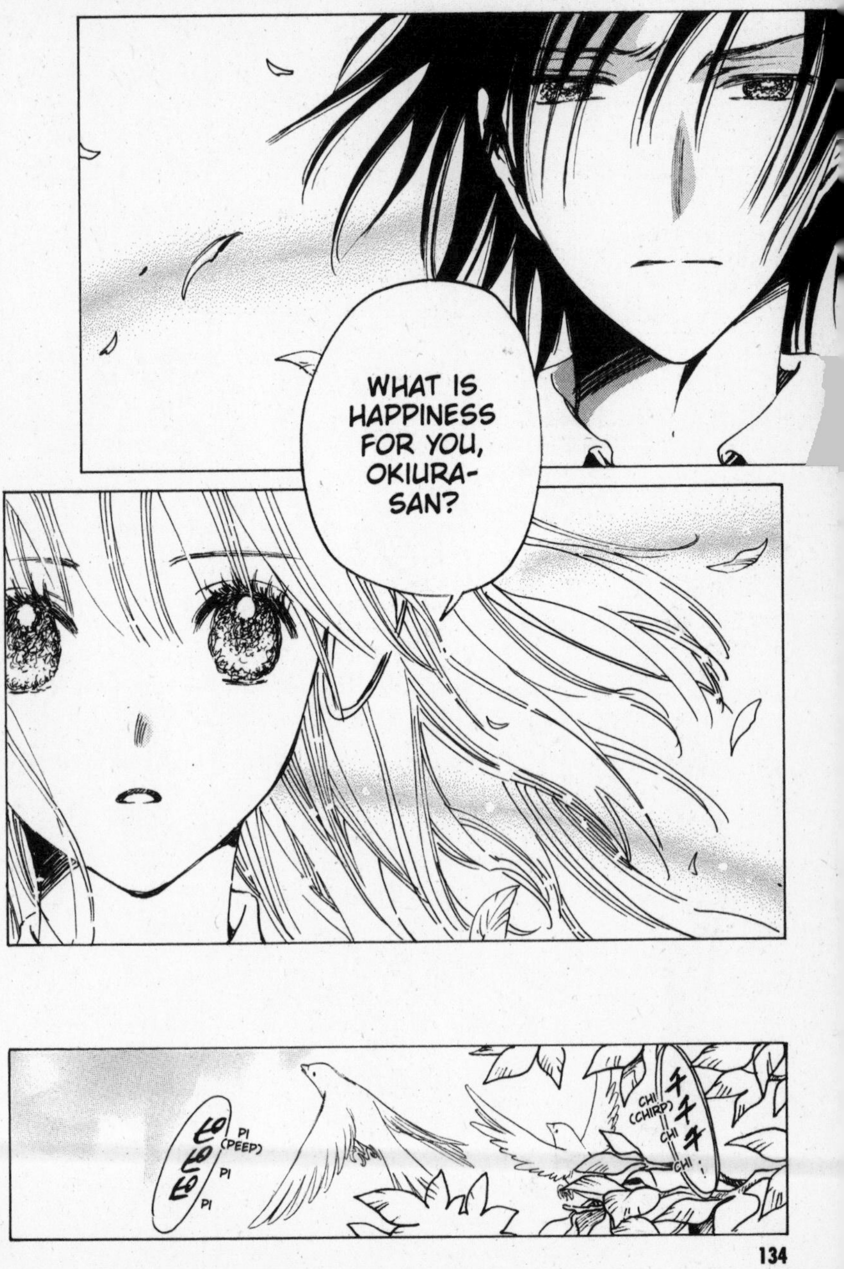
WHAT IS HAPPINESS FOR YOU, OKIURA-SAN?
チチチ
CHI (CHIRP) CHI CHI
ぴぴぴ
PI (PEEP) PI PI

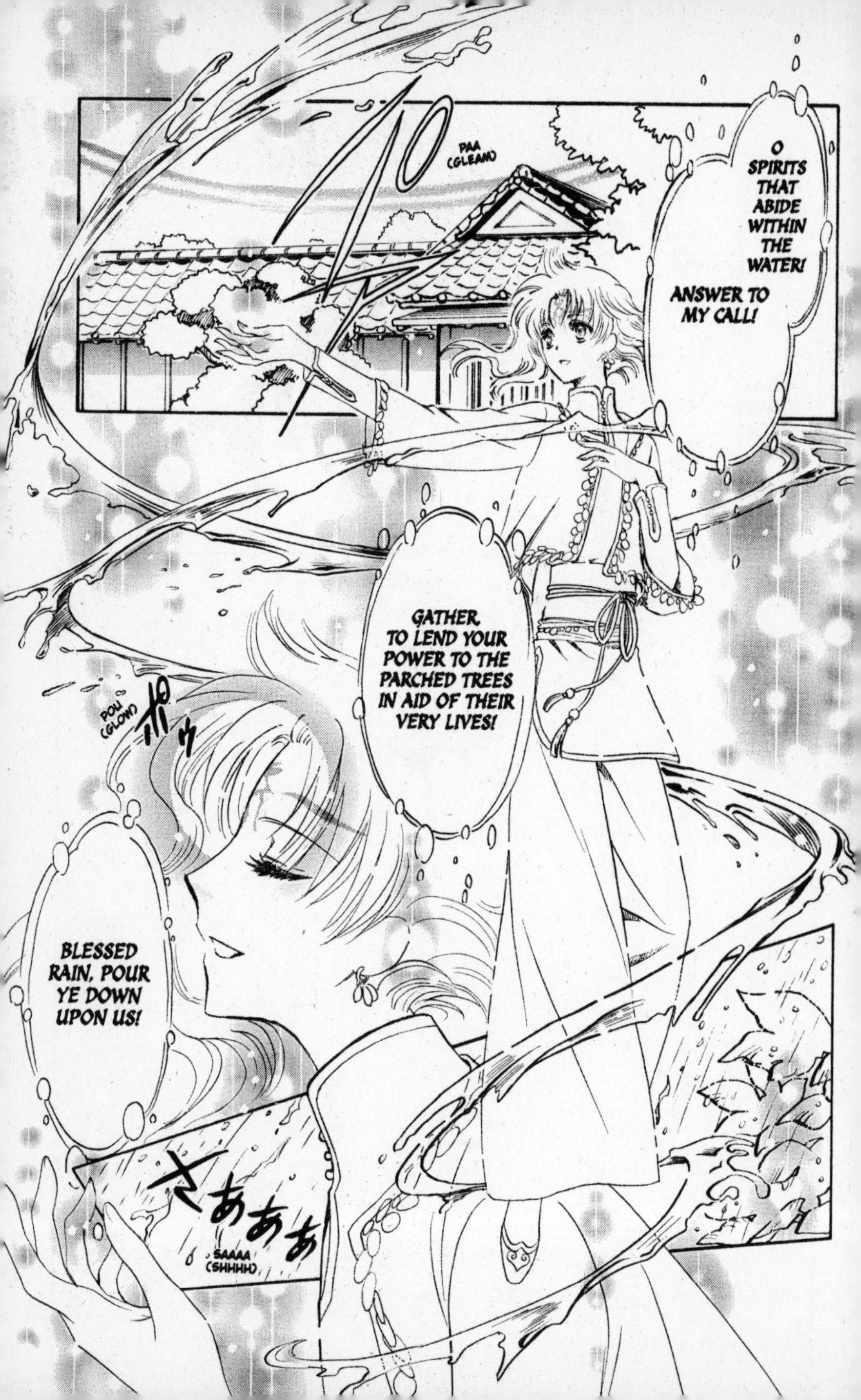
O SPIRITS THAT ABIDE WITHIN THE WATER!
ANSWER TO MY CALL!
PAA (GLEAM)
GATHER TO LEND YOUR POWER TO THE PARCHED TREES IN AID OF THEIR VERY LIVES!
POU (GLOW)
BLESSED RAIN, POUR YE DOWN UPON US!
さあああ
SAAAA (SHHHH)

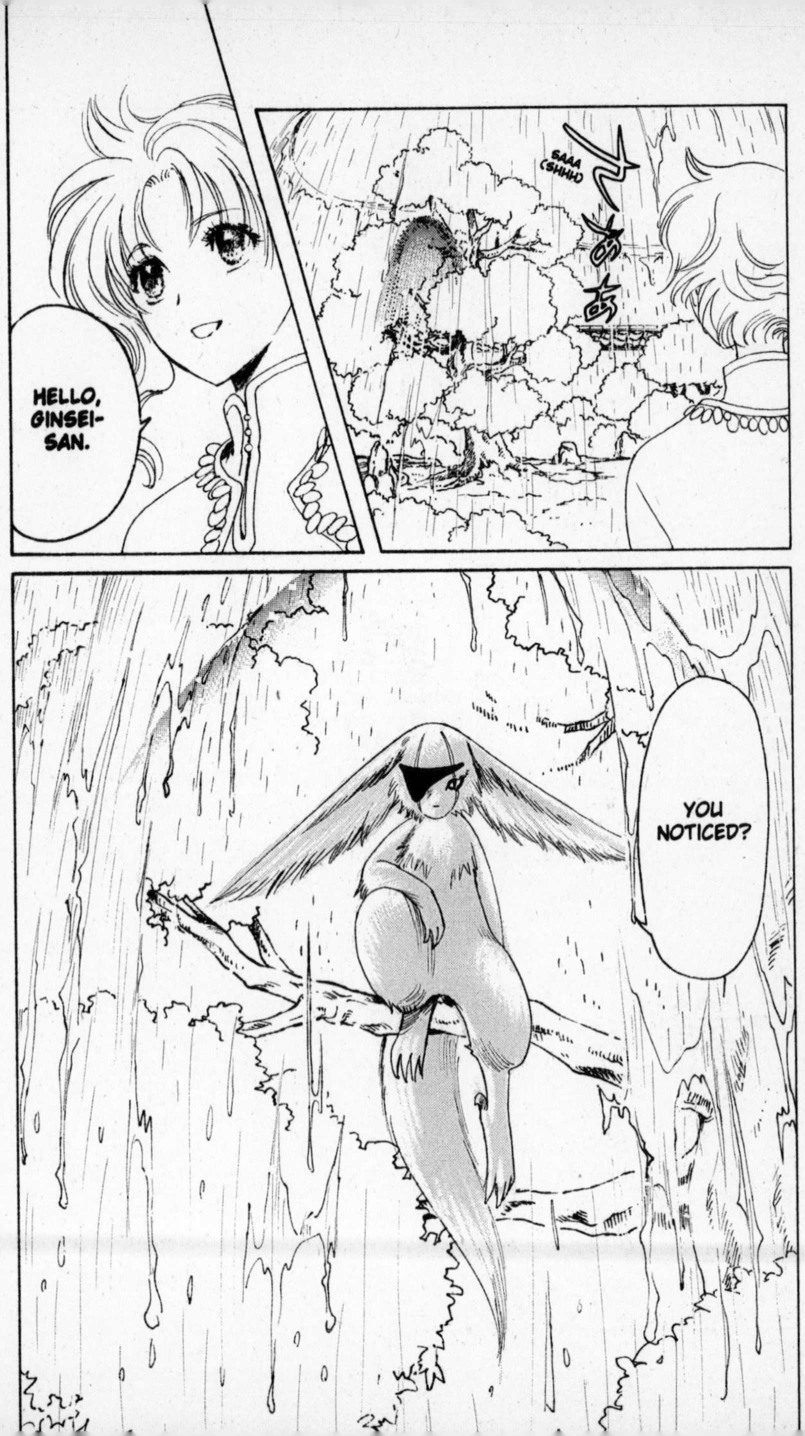
SAAA (SHHH)
HELLO, GINSEI-SAN.
YOU NOTICED?

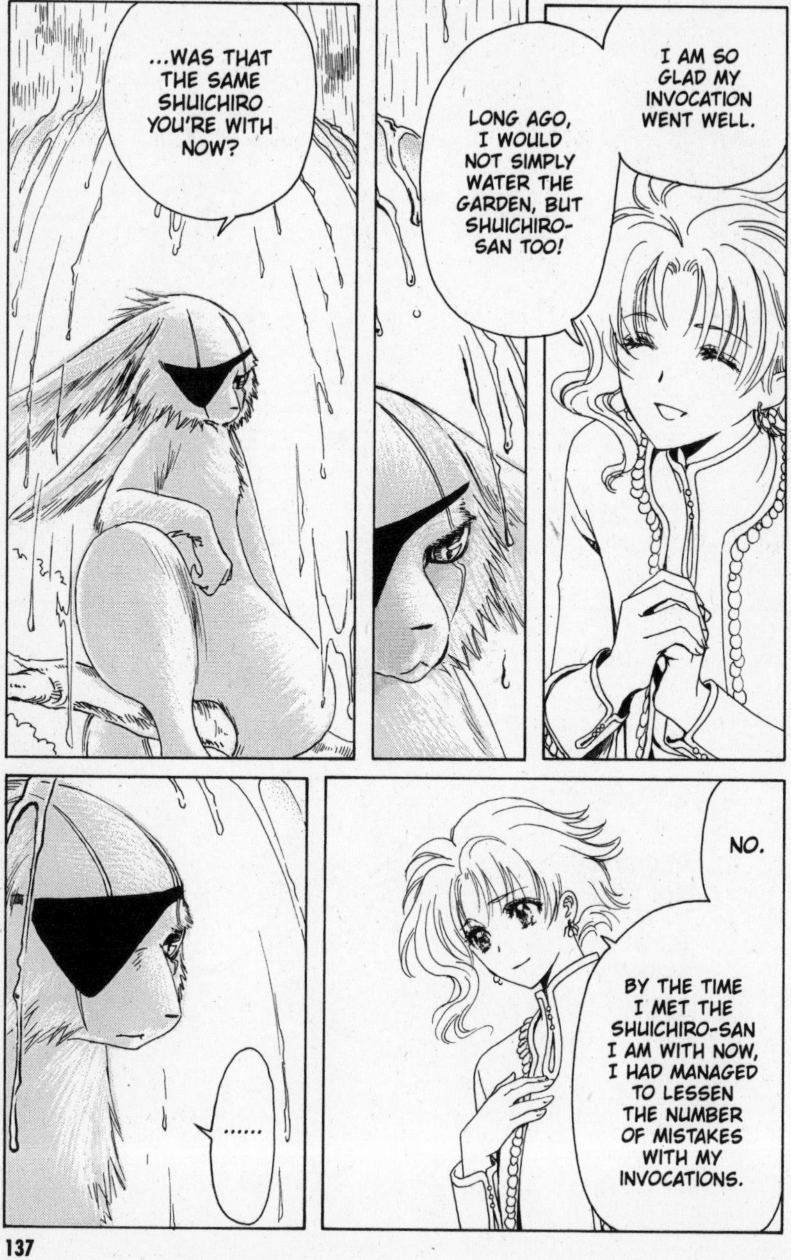
I AM SO GLAD MY INVOCATION WENT WELL.
LONG AGO, I WOULD NOT SIMPLY WATER THE GARDEN, BUT SHUICHIRO-SAN TOO!
...WAS THAT THE SAME SHUICHIRO YOU'RE WITH NOW?
NO.
BY THE TIME I MET THE SHUICHIRO-SAN I AM WITH NOW, I HAD MANAGED TO LESSEN THE NUMBER OF MISTAKES WITH MY INVOCATIONS.
......

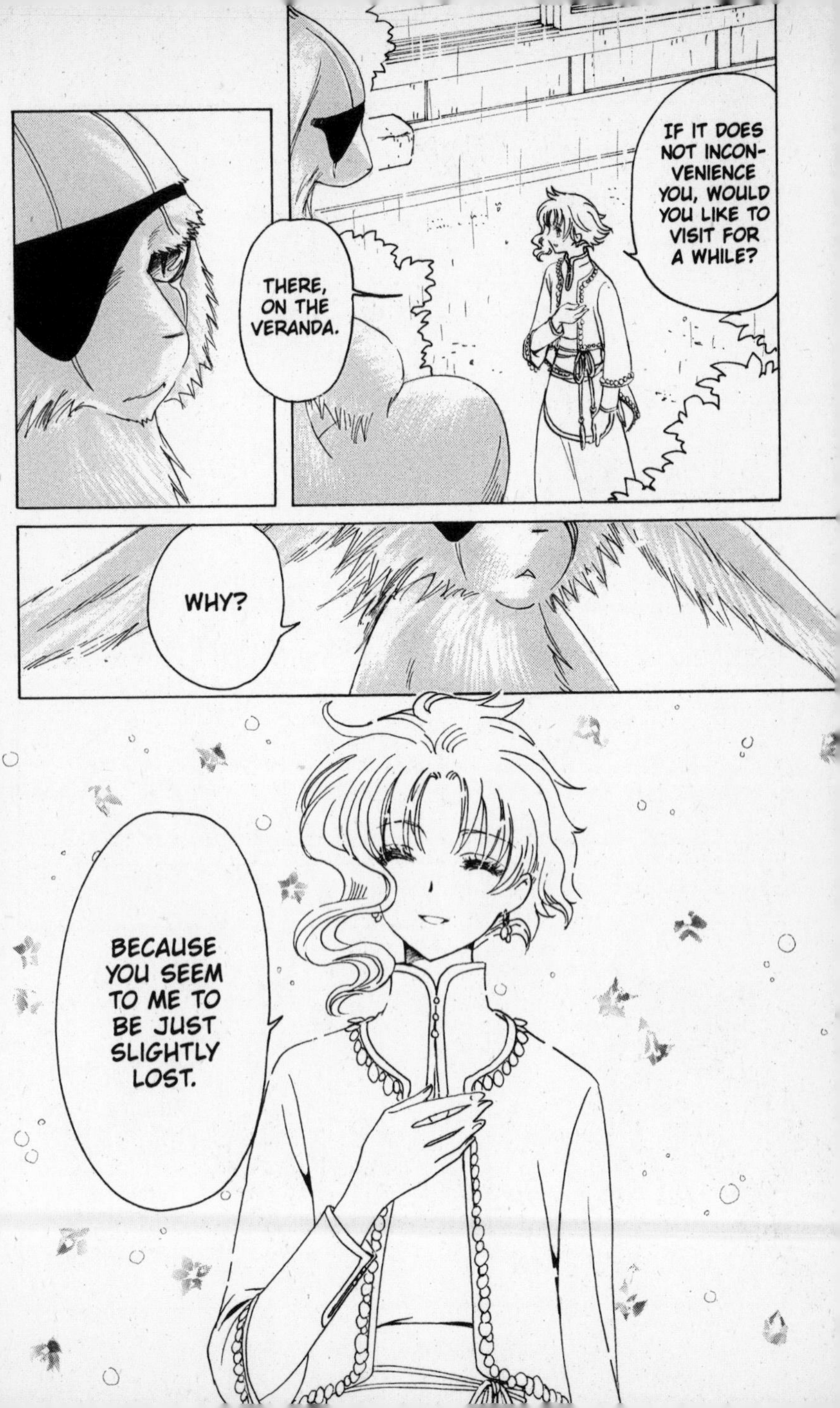
IF IT DOES NOT INCONVENIENCE YOU, WOULD YOU LIKE TO VISIT FOR A WHILE?
THERE, ON THE VERANDA.
WHY?
BECAUSE YOU SEEM TO ME TO BE JUST SLIGHTLY LOST.

......

DO.
(THOK)

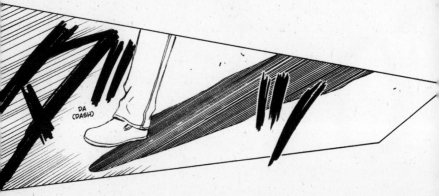

DA
(DASH)

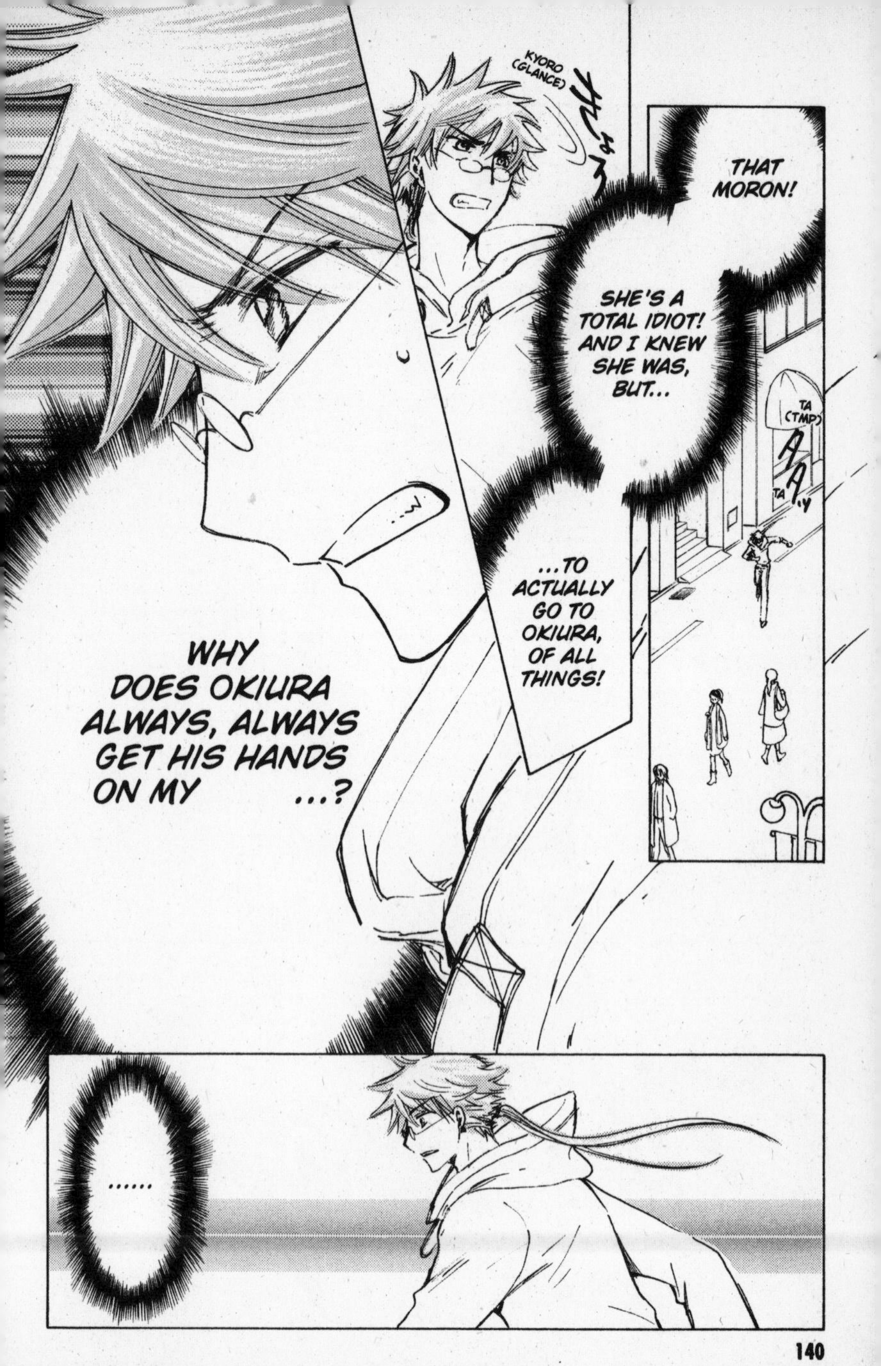
KYORO (GLANCE)
THAT MORON!
SHE'S A TOTAL IDIOT! AND I KNEW SHE WAS, BUT...
TA (TMP)
TA
...TO ACTUALLY GO TO OKIURA, OF ALL THINGS!
WHY DOES OKIURA ALWAYS, ALWAYS GET HIS HANDS ON MY ...?
......

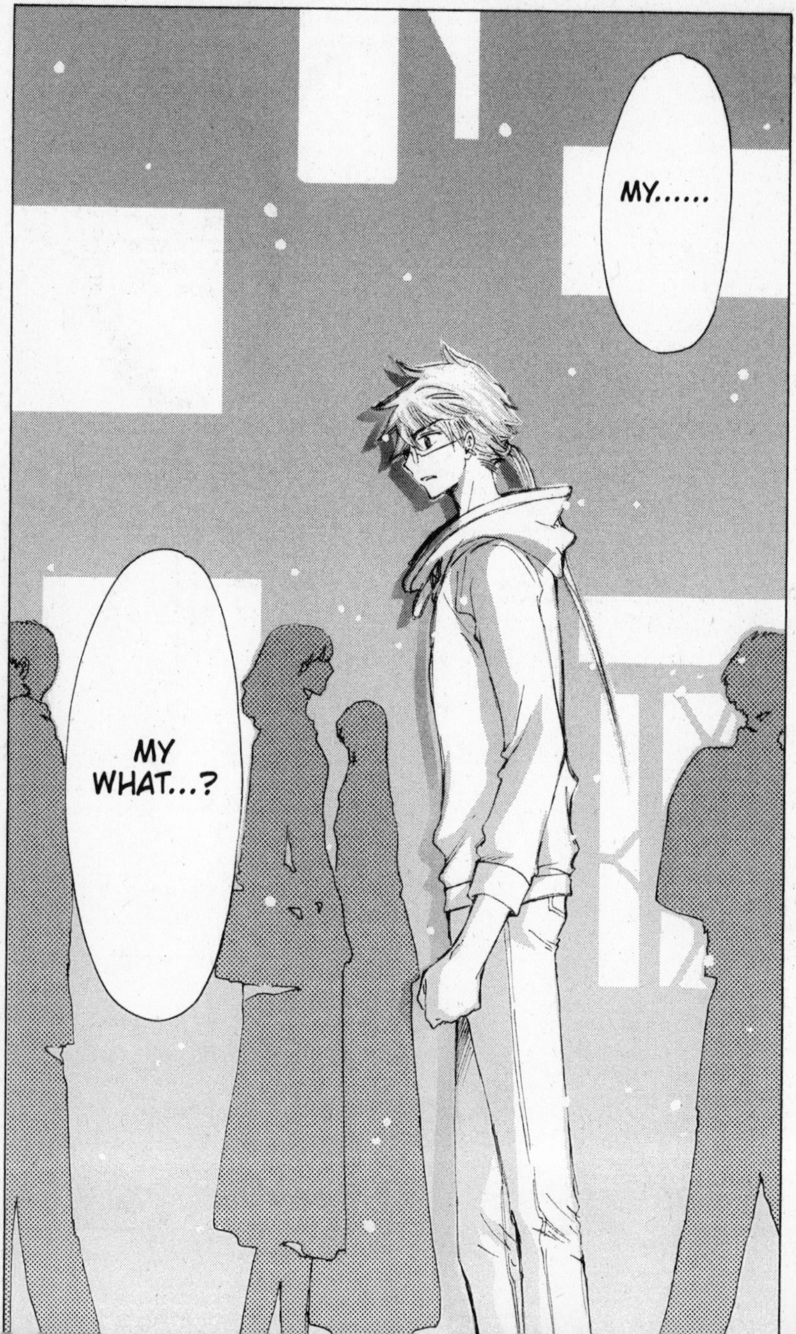
MY......
MY WHAT...?

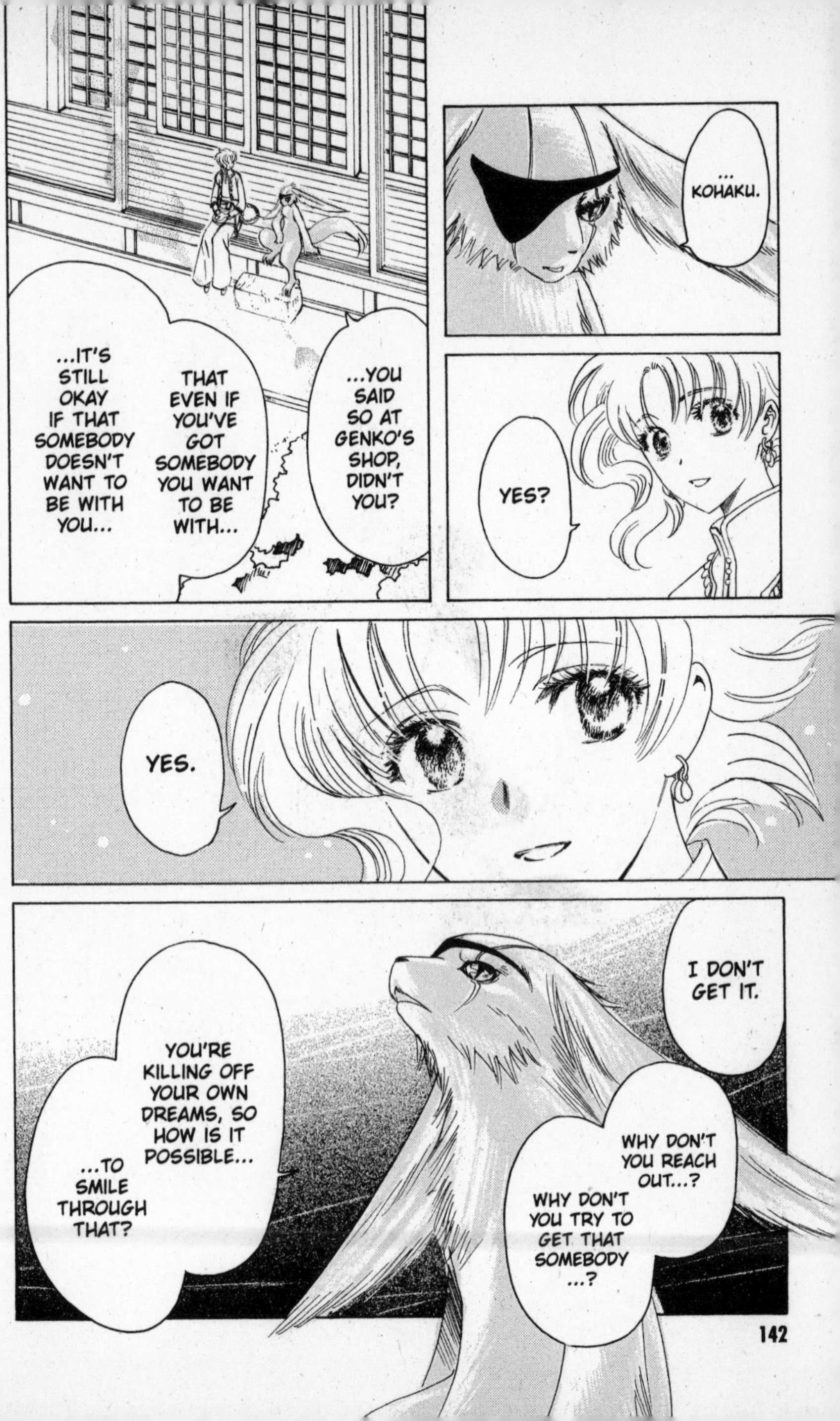
...KOHAKU.
YES?
...YOU SAID SO AT GENKO'S SHOP, DIDN'T YOU?
THAT EVEN IF YOU'VE GOT SOMEBODY YOU WANT TO BE WITH...
...IT'S STILL OKAY IF THAT SOMEBODY DOESN'T WANT TO BE WITH YOU...
YES.
I DON'T GET IT.
WHY DON'T YOU REACH OUT...?
WHY DON'T YOU TRY TO GET THAT SOMEBODY ...?
YOU'RE KILLING OFF YOUR OWN DREAMS, SO HOW IS IT POSSIBLE...
...TO SMILE THROUGH THAT?

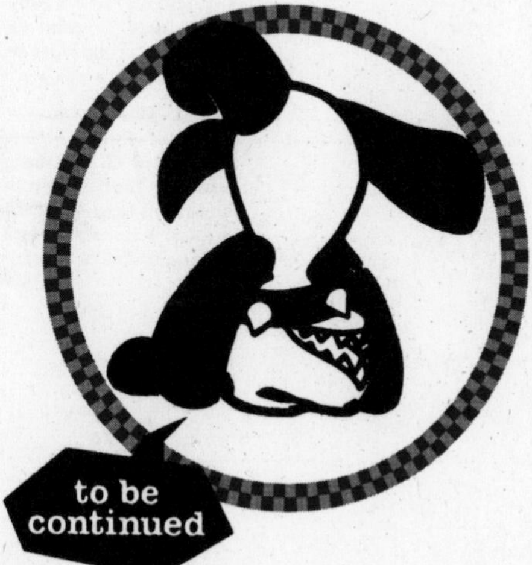
to be continued

TRANSLATION NOTES

COMMON HONORIFICS

no honorific: Indicates familiarity or closeness; if used without permission or reason, addressing someone in this manner would constitute an insult.

-san: The Japanese equivalent of Mr./Mrs./Miss. If a situation calls for politeness, this is the fail-safe honorific.

-sama: Conveys great respect; may also indicate that the social status of the speaker is lower than that of the addressee.

-kun: Used most often when referring to boys (though it can be applied to girls as well), this indicates affection or familiarity. Occasionally used by older men among their peers, but it may also be used by anyone referring to a person of lower standing.

-chan: An affectionate honorific indicating familiarity used mostly in reference to girls; also used in reference to cute persons or animals of either gender.

Page 88 - *Sharing a face*
Readers of other CLAMP series might recognize that in many CLAMP manga (most notably, *Tsubasa Reservoir Chronicle*), identical beings in different dimensions have identical souls. They may not have identical personalities since their environment is also a contributing factor, but they have the same soul.

Kobato.

INNISFIL PUBLIC LIBRARY
P.O. BOX 7049
INNISFIL, ON L9S 1A8

KOBATO. ⑤

CLAMP

Translation: William Flanagan • Lettering: Alexis Eckerman

KOBATO. Volume 5 © 2010 CLAMP. First published in Japan in 2010 by
KADOKAWA SHOTEN Co., Ltd., Tokyo. English translation rights arranged with
KADOKAWA SHOTEN Co., Ltd., Tokyo through TUTTLE-MORI AGENCY, INC.,
Tokyo.

Translation © 2011 by Hachette Book Group, Inc.

All rights reserved. Except as permitted under the U.S. Copyright Act of 1976, no
part of this publication may be reproduced, distributed, or transmitted in any form
or by any means, or stored in a database or retrieval system, without the prior written
permission of the publisher.

The characters and events in this book are fictitious. Any similarity to real persons,
living or dead, is coincidental and not intended by the author.

Yen Press
Hachette Book Group
237 Park Avenue, New York, NY 10017

www.HachetteBookGroup.com
www.YenPress.com

Yen Press is an imprint of Hachette Book Group, Inc. The Yen Press name and logo
are trademarks of Hachette Book Group, Inc.

First Yen Press Edition: December 2011

ISBN: 978-0-316-1

10 9 8 7 6 5

BVG

Printed in the Unit

YA CLAMP

Kobato. 5.

PRICE: $7.92 (3710/ya/ch)